THE ATLAS OF PAST WORLDS

JOHN MANLEY

THE ATLAS OF

A COMPARATIVE CHRONOLOGY O

PAST WORLDS

HUMAN HISTORY 2000 BC – AD 1500

CASSELL

Contents

TO MY FAMILY

Cassell Publishers Ltd
Villiers House
41/47 Strand
London WC2N 5JE

Text copyright © 1993 John Manley
Format copyright © 1993 Cassell

First published 1993
First paperback edition 1994

Distributed in the United States
by Sterling Publishing Co., Inc.
387 Park Avenue South, New York, NY 10016-8810

Distributed in Australia
by Capricorn Link (Australia) Pty Ltd
2/13 Carrington Road
Castle Hill
NSW 2154

British Library Cataloguing-in-Publication Data
A catalogue record for this book is available from the British Library

ISBN 0-304-34456-7

Typeset in Lasercomp Trump Medieval
by August Filmsetting, Haydock, St Helens
Printed and bound in Hong Kong by Dah Hua Printing Press Co. Ltd

PUEBLO BONITO

POVERTY POINT

MONTE ALBAN

EL PARAISO

CUZCO

EASTER ISLAND

19.95

FLAG FEN
STONEHENGE
LONDON
MOSCOW
PEKING
POMPEII
MEDINA AZAHARA
MEGIDDO
UR
SIRAF
CHANG'AN
PETRA
THEBES
MOHENJO-DARO
JENNE-JENO
MEROE
Equator
KALEMBA
GREAT ZIMBABWE
ROONKA FLAT

PROLOGUE

This book is designed to illustrate what human beings, through the societies they formed and the settlements they built and occupied, accomplished around the world at specific intervals in our history. It is intended to answer the kind of question that begins, 'When the pyramids of Egypt were being constructed, what was happening in South America, Asia, Europe or China?' As such, it works in a straightforward manner, providing factual information on ancient but contemporary sites. However, it also works on a more fundamental level.

By means of comparison between contemporary prehistoric or historic sites around the world, and by contrasts between different sites through time, a useful insight can be gained into the diversity of human experience and achievement. In particular this 'comparison and contrast' illustrates that the evolution of human groups from simple societies, such as the many small communities which live by hunting and gathering, to more complex societies, such as states and even empires, has not been even-paced, irreversible, inevitable or necessarily to the benefit of the individuals concerned. It is worth remembering that the capacity of our late twentieth-century brains is exactly the same as that of those hunters and gatherers who camped at some of the locations described in this book. Our technical expertise, of course, has increased exponentially from our first experiments with chipped stone tools, but our ability to think and act with intelligence has proved far less susceptible to improvement.

So much for the basic reasoning behind this book. It quickly became apparent that there is a very real danger of trying to put too much information before the reader. After all, human prehistory and history, covering a few million years, cannot safely be condensed into a few hundred pages. The process of description, therefore, has to be selective.

In order to understand each society or community and its associated settlements or structures, a reasonable number of pages has to be devoted to their description and analysis. The societies chosen have to represent all phases of human development, from those peoples who lived by hunting and gathering to those who organized sophisticated states and empires. There is also, in this book, a conscious attempt to mix some well-known sites, such as Roman Pompeii, with less-celebrated settlements, such as El Paraiso and Kalemba. Taking these criteria and space limitations together, it became apparent that no more than twenty-five sites and societies could be adequately explored. It is also essential that the completed text forms an integrated story, rather than an unrelated series of short stories. The all-important question then became – which twenty-five sites?

Given that one of our aims was to contrast different sites through time, another decision that had to be taken was *which* time periods would be most significant? Five specific years were chosen: 2000 BC, 1000 BC, AD 1, AD 1000 and AD 1500. It is easiest to make a case for the last one. After AD 1500 many indigenous societies were modified or disrupted by European voyages of discovery that exported a European way of life to much of the world. So comparing sites before the European veneer was added allows us a glimpse of native achievements before foreign contact and imported ideas began to change traditional practices. The first date, 2000 BC, marks a time when complex societies emerged in all five areas of the world, as defined in this book, but only in localized regions within these areas. For instance, in Africa the Nile valley had been home to a highly developed and already ancient state, yet the major part of the continent was still occupied by hunters and gatherers. Therefore, in 2000 BC there was still the widest variety of societies to choose from and, by taking regular time intervals to arrive at dates of 1000 BC, AD 1 and AD 1000, it is possible to chart – albeit crudely – the course of history.

The specific years that have been chosen must be considered to have some degree of elasticity. It is not possible to be precise about all aspects of any site in one particular year in the past; this applies as much to late medieval London as it does to Stonehenge. Yet it is possible, given intelligent assumptions, to paint a general picture of the society or site at a given time. Fastidious readers should perhaps add a 'plus or minus fifty years' to each of the five years in this book, to ensure a greater degree of historical accuracy.

Another of our aims is to make comparisons between sites in many parts of the world. Some geographical breakdown is required which serves to divide, at least initially, our selection of sites. Our dividing lines were eventually drawn to separate five areas: Europe, western Asia, Africa, eastern Asia and Oceania, and the Americas. Some of these divisions are less happy than others. While Africa and the Americas, and to an extent Europe, are

---

At Megiddo in Israel previous generations of settlers, stretching back over several millennia, have left building debris and refuse slowly forming the settlement mound or 'tell' that we see today.

easily definable geographic entities, eastern Asia and Oceania, ranging from central China to the South Sea islands and Australia, are more difficult to perceive as a distinct zone. Arbitrary and selective elements, however, are necessary for a book of this size and the essential artificiality of some aspects of selection must not be allowed to detract from the integrity of its conclusions.

The skeleton of this book, therefore, was arranged first. Five geographical areas (Europe, western Asia, Africa, eastern Asia and Oceania, and the Americas), five years (2000 BC, 1000 BC, AD 1, AD 1000 and AD 1500) and five sites and societies for each one of the years, one site from each geographical area, were the bones of the book. But that all-important question still remained – which sites?

Our selection process is determined, to an extent, by the need to pick sites that could illustrate a central theme for each chapter. Selection is also, of course, governed by more realistic factors, such as the ability to demonstrate that the site was occupied in or around the year in question, and that adequate information is readily accessible on the site itself. The theme of Chapter 1 is religion and the sites chosen are used to demonstrate the importance of religious beliefs to their users. Stonehenge is an obvious candidate for Europe, since it clearly reflects non-utilitarian architecture.

It is also important to select sites from three well-known civilizations of the (so-called) Old World – namely the Egyptian, Sumerian and Indus states. No book purporting, however briefly, to offer insight into human development can afford to overlook such societies. The choice from the Americas is not as difficult as it first appears. Despite the enormity of the area, few regions (coastal Peru being one of them) had produced evidence of complex societies by 2000 BC. El Paraiso was occupied at just the right time and has produced enough evidence of ritual and religion to suit our purpose.

The theme for Chapter 2 is 'Ways of Life', concentrating more on political, social and economic structures than on religious beliefs. For most of our time on this planet we have been hunters and gatherers, and it is appropriate that three such sites should be featured: Kalemba because it is a wholly typical and therefore.ordinary hunting camp; Roonka because it is probably the best-investigated archaeological site of its kind in Australia, and Poverty Point because it is quite exceptional in terms of our perceptions of the potential achievements of a hunting and gathering society. Flag Fen was selected simply because it is proving to be one of the most important sites for

later prehistoric Europe, and offers us a glimpse of a society probably ruled by a chief or chiefs. The city of Megiddo was included because it shows a highly developed urban way of life and also, for the sake of comparative chronology, links a part of our narrative to some Old Testament personalities.

The theme of 'Empires' runs through the third chapter. Here it is important to compare some of the world's most formidable ancient empires, as illustrated by the Roman and Han civilizations. By contrast, some of the smallest empires are also selected, as exemplified by the territories ruled from capitals at Meroe and Petra. Lastly, the civilizations of the Americas have produced some distinctive states, and Monte Alban provides us with an intriguing imperial capital in Mexico.

There is a sense almost of the exotic about the theme of 'New Directions' in Chapter 4. The chapter is so called because the societies that are described in it are either transplants into foreign environments or flourished in extraordinary ways in very unordinary locations. Thus Medina Azahara and Siraf were products of Islamic expansion into two very different regions, while the colonists who reached Easter Island found a small, volcanic and very isolated island. The town of Jenne-jeno on the inland Niger delta is a rare example of an indigenous African town, developed apparently in isolation from influential contact with Mediterranean civilizations. Meanwhile, Pueblo Bonito, in the seemingly inhospitable terrain of Chaco Canyon, is a magnificent example of the sophisticated masonry architecture achieved by the farming ancestors of the pueblo Indians.

In Chapter 5 we contrast some of the great cities of the world, which inevitably leads us to question the universality of the term 'city'. Clearly state symbols were of paramount importance in the planning of Inca Cuzco and Ming Peking, while a much less authoritarian process was responsible for the more organic and chaotic development of Moscow and London. A procedure of an entirely different dimension was behind the foundation and growth of the African city of Great Zimbabwe.

These are our reasons for choosing the twenty-five sites that form the core of this book. It can be argued that no two authors would make the same choice of sites, or years, or even geographical areas. But therein lies, hopefully, the strength of this book. It is almost certainly a unique combination of times and places, and as such may provoke some fresh and unexpected conclusions. Which only leaves us to touch upon that inconceivably long and complex period of prehistory before 2000 BC.

To begin at the beginning, however, we must consider the very origins of human beings before reaching the first chapter.

ORIGINS

We may not physically resemble the great apes of Africa, the gorilla and the chimpanzee, but genetically we are almost identical to them. This suggests that we all shared a common ancestor several million years ago. Our ancestor probably lived in open woodland in the tropics of Africa. It would have been a medium-sized primate, adapted to a mixture of tree-climbing and ground-living. On the ground it would have loped around on all fours, occasionally standing upright on two legs. By 4 million years ago, however, this occasional trait had developed into an essential habit. Rapid and fundamental changes in the anatomy of the feet and hips enabled these first hominids to stand upright and walk. At the same time brain size increased and the jawline was modified to a continuous curve with no projecting canines at the corners. The rest, as they say, is history.

Evidence that this adaptation had taken place in Africa at least 4 million years ago has been discovered at Laetoli in Tanzania. Preserved in volcanic dust, recording a precise moment in time, were the extraordinary line of footprints of two adults and a child. Forensic investigation shows that the adults were between 3 feet 9 inches and 4 feet 9 inches (1.1 and 1.4 m) tall and each weighed around 60 lb (27 kg). Another highly significant find was that of a partial skeleton of a single individual, nicknamed Lucy, at Hadar in the Afar region of Ethiopia. Lucy died some 3.4 million years ago and she clearly walked upright, although she retained many anatomical features similar to those of apes. The oldest known fossils referred to as *Homo* (Man) date from 2.5 million years before the present, and include the remains of a twelve-year-old boy from Nariokotome in Kenya who, although he died 1.7 million years ago, was physically little different from a modern boy.

During this long period of evolution in Africa small groups of hominids were obtaining their food by a mixture of hunting and gathering. The collecting of wild plants, nuts and berries probably contributed most to the diet, but the chance killing or scavenging of large mammals such as elephants provided protein, and also raw materials of bone, ivory and hide. Stone tools were manufactured and included heavy-duty choppers and sharp flakes which were used to dismember animals and cut meat from the carcass. Population numbers and life expectancy must have been exceedingly low, but there was obviously a steady if unspectacular increase in overall numbers, so that by 1.7 million years ago hominids had spread to western China and by 1.4 million years had reached Java.

Our knowledge of these remote episodes in our history is extremely fragmentary and liable to be substantially re-evaluated with each new discovery. However, it does appear that hominids were present in Europe some time before 700,000 and in Britain some time before 400,000 years ago. Skills and techniques handed down from generation to generation, and the challenge of varied environments during the Ice Ages, led to certain innovations, such as the use of fire, the ability to construct shelters and the organized killing of herds of large mammals by driving them over cliffs to their deaths.

The last distinctive group of hominids to emerge before the appearance of fully modern human beings are the so-called Neanderthals. They lived in diverse environments from the relatively arid Middle East to the cold forests and tundra of central and northern Europe. As well as using fire and building shelters, they were also the first group to demonstrate some care for the elderly and to possess a formal rite of burial for the dead.

Southern Africa seems the most likely candidate for the birthplace of modern humans (*Homo sapiens sapiens*), some 100,000 years ago. The species developed impressive new capabilities, including the ability to colonize some of the more inhospitable regions like the tropical rainforests. There is also evidence of a wider range of foodstuffs, including shellfish, the controlled employment of fire for drying meat and altering vegetation patterns, and the first appearance of art. Fully modern human beings were established in China and south-east Asia around 40,000 years ago. At about this time the first human groups reached Japan and, after a sea crossing of at least $37\frac{1}{2}$ miles (60 km), reached the continent formed by the linked landmass of New Guinea and Australia. When the peopling of the Americas took place is much more open to debate. The route has long been thought to be the dry bed of the Bering Strait, which would have emerged as vast quantities of sea water were frozen in the polar ice-caps at the heights of glaciations. Various suggestions have been put forward for the earliest migrations, ranging from as much as 40,000 to as recently as 15,000 years ago.

Around 10,000 years ago the last Ice Age came to an end and the world underwent a series of slow but dramatic changes which had far-reaching effects on human communities. Temperatures rose and the ice-sheets that had covered almost a quarter of the earth's land surface melted, allowing plants and animals to colonize latitudes which had previously been too cold to support them. Deserts, which had occupied half of the land between the tropics, shrank as water which had been previously frozen in the ice-sheets fell as rain. The hunter-gatherer communities expanded into these newly available environments, exploiting more varied and abundant animal and plant resources. More sophisticated hunting equipment, such as bows and arrows, traps and snares, led to smaller game being hunted. Greater knowledge of their surroundings allowed communities to manipulate wild plants and animals for their own advantage. Woodland was burnt to encourage grasses or berry-rich shrubs, while herds of animals could be followed from winter to summer pastures, culling superficial males for meat and skins but leaving the reproductive potential of the herd intact. Stone tools reflected the greater intensity and diversity of the food quest by becoming smaller in size. Hunters and gatherers living in such conditions are usually described as 'Advanced Hunters' and the communities at Roonka in Australia and Kalemba in Zambia around 1000 BC probably fell into this category. Some wild food sources were so abundant that large populations could be supported, and the complex of earthworks at Poverty Point in New Mexico hints at the social sophistication of such communities.

The most revolutionary impact on human societies in the last 10,000 years was caused by the development of agriculture. This reliance on domesticated animals and cultivated plants arose independently in widely distant parts of the world, yet at approximately the same time; in the Middle East by around 8000 BC, and in China and in Central America by around 6000 BC. In each of these areas a range of different plants was cultivated: wheat, barley and pulses in the Middle East, rice and millet in south-east Asia and maize, beans and potato in the Americas. Animal husbandry also developed to provide a secure source of high-quality protein, especially in Europe and the Middle East, where cattle, sheep, goats and pigs were reared. In South America, however, the domestication of the llama was designed to produce a reliable pack animal rather than a food source. There were no doubt many other local centres of domestication of plants and animals. From both major and minor centres either farmers themselves or the idea of farming spread inexorably, assimilating or destroying the life styles of hunters and gatherers which it encountered.

The reasons for the relatively sudden emergence of farming in different parts of the world were no doubt complex and dissimilar. What is certain is that the life of a farmer was considerably harder than that of a hunter-gatherer, so it cannot have been an invention which was taken up by communities simply because it represented an easy answer to the problem of getting food. The only

advantage primitive agriculture has over a way of life based on hunting and gathering was that it was capable of supporting more human beings per unit area. It seems reasonable, therefore, to suggest that population growth among the hunters in certain areas had resulted in a shortage of wild animals and perhaps plants, leading to attempts at conservation of the depleted stocks by ever-closer control. Such control might easily have led to the domestication of selected species of both plants and animals.

Whatever the reasons for the change, the consequences were far-reaching indeed. Some very generalized comparisons of the two life styles can help us to appreciate their underlying incompatibility. Hunters and gatherers needed a variety of vegetation, from open grasslands to woodlands, in which wild animals and plants could flourish. Farmers, on the other hand, usually sought to cut down the woodland to prepare fields for pasture or cultivation. Hunting families did not rear many children, since their mobile life precluded the carrying of large numbers of children from camp to camp. Farmers, however, since they were resident all the year round on the same plot of land, and since children could be usefully employed in a number of routine agricultural tasks, such as scaring birds from crops, tended to have larger families. The investment in the land that farmers made in terms of clearance and cultivation meant that they developed proprietorial rights over tracts of land in a much more formal way than the hunters and gatherers had. The farming economy, with its harvest at fixed times in the year, required elaborate storage facilities to hold grain for several months, whereas in a hunting economy the forest was regarded as a 'larder' and much of the catch from a successful hunting expedition was shared and consumed more or less immediately.

The hunters tended to focus their ritual practices on the fertility of plants and animals, whereas for farmers it was easier to make a connection between bountiful harvests and the power of the sun, which in turn fostered an interest in astronomy and prediction of the timing of equinoxes and solstices. Generations of farmers, keen to underline their rightful claims to parcels of land, often achieved this by emphasizing their descent from parents and grandparents who had farmed that land before them. Such circumstances encouraged the importance of lineage, remembered genealogies and the ancestors – none of which had been so significant in the world of hunter-gatherers. The small size of the hunting band and the absence of storage devices encouraged sharing of any food resources between band members. Such sharing, or reciprocity, existed between related members of early farming communities, but gradually lessened

Model figures of domesticated animals can still be seen in Jenne (Mali) in West Africa. When farming communities replaced hunters and gatherers, children began to play an important role looking after the grazing flocks and herds.

as kinship distance between the parties increased. One of the most fundamental distinctions, of course, between a farming way of life and one based on hunting and gathering was that the farmers constructed permanent villages and fortified towns, to protect themselves, their agricultural stores and the increased variety of exotic goods that they had acquired through trade. The farming village of Çatal Hüyük in central Anatolia, for example, flourished around 6000 BC, while the fortified town of Jericho in the Middle East existed 1,000 years earlier. In central China a fortified farming village was constructed at Banpo some time between 5000 and 4000 BC.

One hypothesis suggests that once the conditions for the storage of agricultural produce and the collection of prestige traded items by the exchange of agricultural surplus arose, then it became possible for influential individuals to manipulate reciprocal exchange for their own benefit. Pressure and persuasion could be put on each household in a village to produce a surplus which could then be redistributed by a central authority. Redistribution could come in the form of religious feasts for all the villagers; or it could be converted into religious or public architecture; or it could be used to feed specialists such as craftworkers who could produce artefacts for exchange, which were in turn distributed to households. The exchanges of food that took place between kinsmen in egalitarian villages were transformed into exchanges that took place between followers and leaders. The villagers could make demands on the leader's generosity since they might believe that the only justification for becoming 'rich' was to be able to redistribute to the less fortunate. The chiefly store was a public treasury, supplied by a few voluntarily and to which every individual had the right of free and equal access. Sometimes the flow of produce towards the chief was reinforced by the chief's position as a deity, or as an intermediary between the people and the gods. In these societies agricultural surplus was offered to the chief as a tribute to ensure a good relationship between the people and the supernatural. The balanced flow of gifts to the chief and their subsequent redistribution was a fragile process, however. A time could be reached when the chiefly demands for surplus exceeded the capabilities of the system to produce it. The chief may have been accumulating an increasing proportion of a decreasing surplus, and this could lead to unrest, rebellion and the replacement of one chief by someone more moderate. Of the societies described in this book, it is possible that those responsible for Stonehenge and El Paraiso in 2000 BC, the statues of Easter Island in AD 1000 and the buildings of

Great Zimbabwe in AD 1500 were ruled by chiefs.

The majority of the locations described here, however, were the product of societies which had reached a complex stage of development; they were organized states. They had managed to break out of the cyclical process of chiefly installation, rebellion and replacement by encouraging a growing secularization of authority and an emerging bureaucracy. The political centre was no longer upheld by its still-perceived relationship with the supernatural but in reality by control of armed forces. A principal theory of state formation thus revolves around a coercive set of circumstances. The argument relates that in some areas the growth of population eventually exceeds the carrying capacity of the land. When this occurs in a region where emigration is blocked because of the settled land of other communities, or where valuable agricultural resources are confined to a small area (as in river valleys like the Nile and Indus, or in Peruvian coastal valleys), the increased population fills all the available land, leading to agricultural intensification and irrigation. Eventually warfare arises out of a need to acquire more land, some villages lose their autonomy and a spiralling increase in the power and size of successful polities favours the emergence of an eventual state.

It is clear, however, that the 'average' state cannot be defined by reference to a single or even a series of diagnostic traits that are always present in states. Instead, each state may possess an amalgam of several features selected from a longer list of the principal attributes of states. We can identify some of the items on this longer list. One of the most frequently cited aspects of statehood is the controlled use of force by central government and the exclusion of personal force. An army or a particular class of warriors may be used to stifle any internal dissension and to indulge in territorial expansion. Fixed boundaries, therefore, are often a prerequisite of states. The personal exercise of force to settle disputes through such means as feuds and vendettas is no longer encouraged and is replaced by a formal system of law. The law is codified and is applied through established courts, administered by a judiciary. Justice is placed in the hands of the state.

Another key characteristic of states is the division of its citizens into a number of different categories. For instance, states are often associated with craft specialists, who are released from the task of food procurement by the surpluses of others, and who spend all their labour time in the production of prestige or utilitarian goods. Other divisions can be based on religious duties (the priesthood), political responsibilities (the ruling class) or differing degrees of access to the means of production (the economic classes). Yet another class of people within states comprises the bureaucrats, who are needed to count and control agricultural surpluses, to monitor the output of craft workers, to collect taxes and also to provide the organizational requirements of agricultural intensification and territorial expansion. As states grew in size and the citizen body increased in numbers, so both bureaucrats and law-makers needed a permanent form of communication to record such things as different taxes and laws. The solution was found in Mesopotamia during the fourth millennium BC, with the invention of a pictographic script which became the ancestor of all ancient Middle Eastern scripts.

Agricultural intensification has long been linked with ancient states. Such intensification could come about as a result of irrigation or of shortening the fallow period. Irrigation schemes could be undertaken only by societies in which there was a clearly recognized authority structure capable of ordering the construction of dams and channels over a widespread area. Often associated with irrigation is another attribute of states: an increasing density of population. The economy of states is often characterized by a tendency to shift from more traditional means of transferring goods, such as gift exchange of prestige items, towards the mass production of utilitarian goods and their trading according to market exchange. Land may also become an alienable commodity, capable of being sold, bought, amassed and rented for profit. The regular use of coinage may appear as a medium to facilitate transactions. States may also affect the settlement patterns within their territories. An evenly distributed arrangment of similar-sized settlements may be converted into an increasingly hierarchical pattern where densely populated urban sites dominate a number of rural satellites. Urban centres may appear for economic reasons, for defence (as in the case of walled towns), for status requirements as the loci of political and administrative centralization and as the places for monumental architecture.

There are, of course, different types of state. The earliest form of statehood is one in which the flow of goods is dominated by a ruling élite which, as in a chiefdom, maintains its monopoly over exchanges by its control of the supernatural and its consequent ability to guarantee the well-being of the community. For this role the élite is entitled to tribute and labour, and redistribution loses its former function. The Inca state, with its capital at Cuzco, was founded on these principles, where the mode of production was stimulated by the popularization of the cult of the Inca. The productive output of conquered peoples was intensified under the banner of a sacred Inca ideology which masked the real relations of oppression. The next stage in the evolution of states is when authority is no longer based on access to deities but on the monopoly of prestige goods. These latter are passed down the social hierarchy in return for tribute and labour. The subsequent devaluation of ritual control paves the way for the separation of sacred procedures from economic practices, mirrored by a division of the secular and religious functions of heads of state. A more developed form of statehood, and one which is exemplified by most of the state-level societies in this book, is based on city-states or territorial states. These states are typified by the emergence of a class of entrepreneurs working in a partly or fully commercialized economy which may include money, private property, large private estates, a growing class of landless labourers and central marketplaces. Territorial states develop from city-states through conquest, when attempts are made to convert trade relations between independent city-states into relations of tribute between a capital city and provincial towns.

The development of the first urban, literate state in southern Mesopotamia in about 3500 BC was to have profound consequences on subsequent human history. Within a few centuries a similar independent process of development had led to the emergence of states in Egypt (c.3200 BC), the Indus valley (c.2500 BC) and northern China (c.1800 BC). The remains of the cities, temples and tombs of these four primary states reflected new levels of cultural and economic achievement, while through the use of writing on clay tablets and inscriptions their citizens left us a legacy of the earliest historical records.

The formation of states, and often their disintegration, however, proved to be a highly irregular and uneven phenomenon. By the year 2000 BC, when the major part of this book commences, some states were already ancient history; others, like the Indus state, were on the point of collapse; while the majority, as in the Americas, had yet to emerge. In those areas of the Old World where the spread of farming had transformed both peoples and landscapes, however, there was a kaleidoscopic pattern of egalitarian communities, chiefdoms and states. In most, if not all, of these the first gods, of whatever form, were of paramount importance. It is to these gods that we now must turn. Meanwhile, in the greater part of Africa and much of the Americas small bands of hunters and gatherers pursued their quarries and followed a way of life that had existed for hundreds of thousands of years.

CHAPTER 1

THE FIRST

2000 BC

GODS

2000
BC

INTRODUCTION

The five sites that form the core of this chapter were chosen because they represent at least two different types of society in existence around 2000 BC, and because they have all produced ritual structures that shed light on our theme of 'the first gods'. Stonehenge and El Paraiso were the products of communities most probably ruled by chiefs, who perhaps wielded both sacred and secular power, while Ur, Thebes and Mohenjo-daro were representatives of the classic states of the so-called Old World. The importance of ritual or religious foci on each of the sites is quite clear. In the case of Stonehenge it is the entire stone circle, while at El Paraiso it is seemingly restricted to the room in that complex containing the four fire pits. At Ur the towering ziggurat signals an overwhelming religious presence, as does the pyramid-temple of Deir el-Bahri at Thebes. At Mohenjo-daro the carefully constructed baths on the citadel probably acted as a setting for sacred performances. At some of these sites we know the names of the first gods. The moon god Nanna lived on top of the ziggurat at Ur, while at Thebes the pharaoh himself was the son of a divinity. At Mohenjo-daro the presence of a large number of terracotta figurines argues for the presence of a female deity or deities. In pre-literate societies the nature of the divinities must be a matter of speculation. However, it may well be that the sun and moon, at least, were revered at Stonehenge, while at El Paraiso a god or power connected with fire seems to have been pre-eminent.

Religion was, therefore, an important feature, perhaps the most important, for many people in these early communities. Religion had attained such a dominating position because individuals perceived that their own welfare depended on a correct relationship with the supernatural. To that end religious officials or priests held positions of great authority, often assuming secular control as well as becoming priest-kings or chiefs, or even personifications of deities themselves. Such priest-kings ruled the living with the consent of the divine, a combination that could inspire great fear and loyalty among the population.

The widespread adoption or emergence of agriculture provided the conditions for the appearance of religious officials. Successful farming depended on the regular risings and settings of the sun, and its increasing warmth during the growing season. Without any knowledge of the physical laws of the universe, it was relatively simple for influential individuals to claim the ability to predict and regulate the movements of celestial bodies. For instance, among the Pawnee of North America, the deities were regarded as having withdrawn from earth during the winter. They would return again in spring as soon as the first thunder was heard. To honour this return, a ceremony known as the Thunder Ceremony was performed. This was followed by one called Paruxti, in which the deity of this name was supposed to be called to earth. Then came the ceremony known as the Planting of the Corn, which was followed in turn by a series of agricultural rites. All these ceremonies were performed in public, and the villagers planted their crops at the end of the rituals. It is in such agricultural contexts that the unknown gods at Stonehenge and El Paraiso may have moved.

With increasing social and economic complexity, a priesthood of some kind developed. Its purpose was always twofold: first, to elaborate and manipulate the religious beliefs so that they would strengthen the authority of the rulers; and second, to maintain and enhance the priests' economic security. Freed from the urgent requirements of having to spend a greater part of their lives in securing food, they strove to ensure that their role in guaranteeing the well-being of the population was reinforced by analysis and synthesis of religious phenomena. Where the economic order was such that the wealth and power of the community was actually concentrated in their hands, as at Ur, Thebes and probably Mohenjo-daro, they could develop into an aristocracy which at times expressed itself in abstract thinking of a high order. It is, of course, difficult to judge the commoners' perspective on the conjunction of sacred and secular power in the hands of a priest-king or in a college of priests who were seen to direct a ruler. It may be that some saw through the artifice of the ideology. It was more likely, however, that they saw nothing untoward in the closeness of the relationship between religious and civil power.

2000
BC

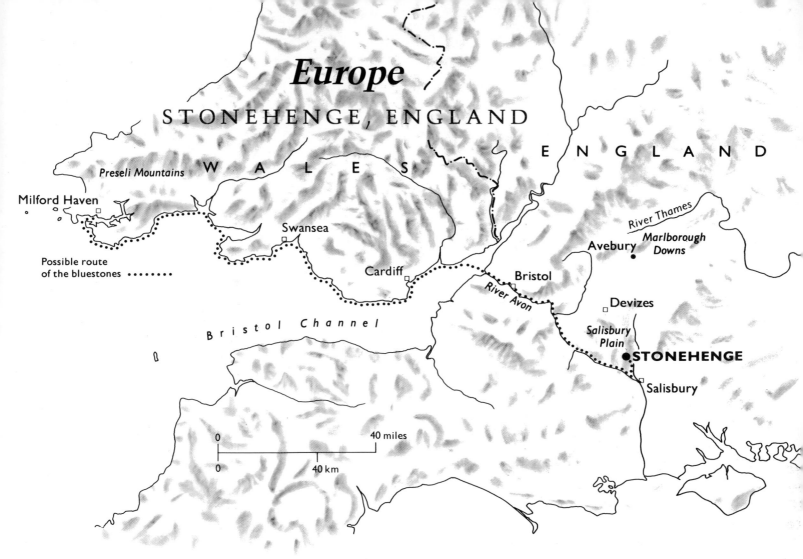

Preseli Mountains

Milford Haven

WALES

ENGLAND

River Thames

Marlborough Downs

Avebury

Swansea

Possible route
of the bluestones •••••••

Cardiff

Bristol

River Avon

Devizes

Bristol Channel

Salisbury Plain

●STONEHENGE

Salisbury

0   40 miles

0   40 km

This map of southern England and south Wales illustrates the possible route of the bluestones from the Preseli Mountains to Stonehenge, although some scholars argue that bluestones occurred naturally on Salisbury Plain. The larger sarsens were brought from the Marlborough Downs to the north of Stonehenge.

By the year 2000 BC Stonehenge, on Salisbury Plain, had been in existence for at least several centuries. It began life as one of a group of large henge monuments that was constructed in southern England. Around 2000 BC, however, Stonehenge was transformed from an important monument into a unique one. Thousands of people were persuaded or forced to leave their fields and animals and erect a remarkable setting of huge sarsen stones in the centre of the henge. Nothing in the world like it had been built before or would be built again. Details of exactly how it functioned are still being argued about. What is obvious, though, is that Stonehenge still exercises a powerful hold on the public imagination, just as those who were responsible for its transformation must have had power over those who worshipped there 4,000 years ago.

Stonehenge had always been slightly different. As a henge it was distinctive since the encircling chalk bank was inside its accompanying ditch, unlike most other henges, which were delimited by external banks and internal ditches. The site itself was apparently chosen with some care. Four standing stones, the so-called Station Stones, demarcate an approximate rectangle within the henge, whose short axis is aligned on the midsummer sunrise and whose long axis is reasonably directed at the northerly setting of the midwinter moon. If this right-angled crossing of celestial events was the reason for its siting, however, then the preliminary astronomical observations had not been quite accurate. A few miles to the south would have been a better position for Stonehenge. There is a further problem in that the Station Stones may not have been part of the first phase of the monument.

Some precision was also needed in arranging the huge sarsen blocks, as well as an extraordinary amount of muscle power. The sarsens, the heaviest

2000
BC

Left: A ditch, with an internal bank, surrounds the stone circle of Stonehenge. A slight depression marks the line of the ditch, although much of the inner bank has long since disappeared. These perimeter earthworks were probably built to separate onlookers from the priests officiating at the sacred stones.

Below far left: A stone from the inner horseshoe-shaped setting. The tenon on top was designed to slot into a mortise hole carved on the underside of a stone lintel. The lintel joined it to another upright and thus comprised a trilithon. The mortise-and-tenon was probably a common technique used in contemporary carpentry.

Below left: A continuous circle of lintels was manoeuvred on to those uprights forming the outer circle of stones. Despite the fact that the ground slopes slightly, the height of the uprights was carefully gauged, and the circle designed so that the lintel stones would all be horizontal. These lintels were carved with slightly concaved inner edges, so that from inside the monument they emphasize the circularity of the settings. Some early bluestones – the much smaller stones, inside the uprights – remained from an earlier stage, or else were re-erected on the site.

of which weighed some 51 tons, were brought a distance of around 20 miles (30 km) from the Marlborough Downs, probably dragged on wooden rollers or sledges by a mixture of human strength and animal traction. Considerable time and energy were expended on squaring and dressing the stones, and on the fashioning of mortise and tenon joints which would secure the lintels to the uprights. It is these lintels that are perhaps the most spectacular feature of Stonehenge. They were fixed in place by a technique that clearly had its origin in carpentry. The stones were finally arranged into two settings. The inner one consisted of the tallest sarsens, which formed five separate trilithons (two uprights joined by a lintel) laid out in a rough U-shape or horseshoe, with the open end facing the north-eastern entrance to the henge. Surrounding this configuration was a complete circle of lower sarsens joined by a contiguous circle of lintels. The raising of these uprights and the elevation of the lintels must have been a difficult and laborious process. Only crude estimates of the time taken and number of people needed can be made, but given a workforce of 500 people, the sarsen monument would have taken thirty-four years to build.

2000 BC

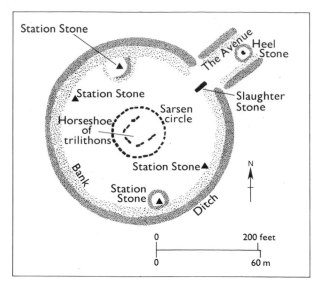

Stonehenge around the year 2000 BC. The taller sarsens were positioned in a U-shaped setting, facing the entrance and the start of the Avenue.

Detailed examination of Stonehenge reveals just how skilled its architects and builders were. Considerable technical problems were tackled with the confidence that only generations of experience can provide. Once the herculean task of transporting the sarsens to the site was completed, groups of workers used rounded sarsen mauls, or hammer stones, of different sizes to dress and polish the stones. Then the knowledge of carpentry was translated, through the skill of stonemasons, into a number of impressive masonry joints. Stone pegs or tenons were fashioned on the top of the uprights to fit into the deep mortise holes pounded out of the undersides of the lintels. The ends of these delicately curved lintels were carved in such a way that the protruding V-shaped end of one lintel sat snugly into the V-shaped groove of its partner. The earth-fast megaliths, weighed down by their own immovable bulk, thus gripped each other in an unbreakable embrace, casting a spell on contemporary and future observers. There were mistakes, of course. One fallen lintel stone, lying across the prostrate Altar Stone, exhibits two deep mortise holes on its underside but also the tell-tale depressions of two erroneously placed holes on its upper side. Even these builders, divinely inspired as they were, could still make a simple human error.

No less accomplished were the surveyors who assessed the potential problems of the chosen location. They realized that the site was not flat but fell some 6 inches (15 cm) from south to north, and 15 inches (37 cm) from west to east. The natural slope was exaggerated in the setting of the

2000
BC

five trilithons, in that they rose in height towards the south-west, so that the tallest faced the approach from the Avenue, a processional way flanked by a bank and ditch which ran in a straight line away from the entrance of the henge for a distance of some 1,750 feet (530 m). But in the layout of the sarsen circle the opposite effect was achieved by nullifying the gradient. The thirty lintel stones, each weighing some 6 to 7 tons, were to be exactly horizontal, so that some uprights on the northern side of the site had to be over 12 inches (30 cm) taller than their counterparts on the far side of the circle. All such surveys and calculations must have been carried out and checked before moving the stones since the sarsens were of such a size and so difficult to move. Not only were the lintel stones level; they were also slightly curved in order to follow the line of the almost-perfect circle.

The massive uprights were probably raised by a potent combination of ropes and levers, muscle and will-power. A stone was levered forward until its end hung over the edge of its square stone hole. This hole had one sloping side, down which the base of the stone slid, before jarring to a halt at its bottom. Then hundreds of people, straining on ropes and forcing down levers, slowly hauled the dead weight into an upright position. Getting the

An aerial view of Stonehenge illustrates the circular setting of stones surrounded by an encircling bank and ditch. The linear banks and ditches defining the Avenue can be observed approaching the site from the top of the picture, with the Heel Stone in the Avenue and next to the modern road.

lintels on to the megalithic pillars would have been even more exhausting. In all probability the stones were levered upwards on top of a platform or scaffold of squared timbers. As each lintel was prized upwards, a new log was jammed underneath it. The process was repeated alternately at either end until, at last, the lintel cleared the tops of the stone tenons on the uprights. Once the lintel had been pushed sideways and secured in place, the platform could be dismantled and re-erected around the next stone. Thirty lintels meant thirty time-consuming lifting operations, testing the determination of men and the divine inspiration of the gods to the limits. And then, of course, there remained the five lintels waiting to be manoeuvred higher than before, to bridge the towering trilithons.

Whoever officiated or participated at the ceremonies in the shadows of those trilithons probably approached and left the sacred site by means of the Avenue. As they left the monument they passed by several standing stones at its start, including the famous Heel Stone, which may have played a part in sightings of the midsummer sunrise from within the sarsen circle. Perhaps this long entrance and exit helped preserve the aura of sanctity of the participants by keeping them apart from the crowds, who may have been looking on from a distance.

The most remarkable feature of the landscape surrounding Stonehenge, however, is the large concentration of round mounds or barrows, around 400 in all, that were built within a 3-mile (5-km) radius of the monument. These usually covered

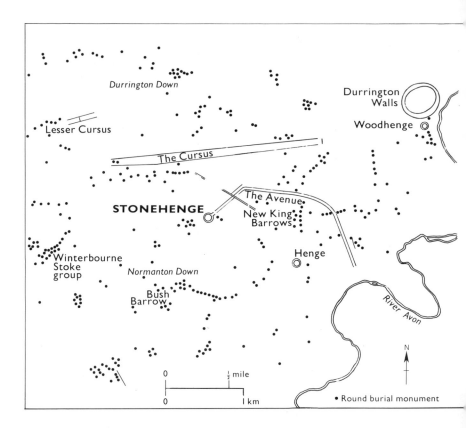

Stonehenge attracted a huge number of burials, with groups of burial mounds or barrows spread in a haphazard circle around the monument.

single graves and were often grouped in cemeteries, either in loose aggregates or in a linear pattern. Many of these burials were interred between 2000 and 1500 BC and there can be no doubt that the power of Stonehenge persuaded communities to bring their dead to be laid to rest within sight of those great, grey sarsens. Only the privileged few were afforded the rite of barrow burial, as the prestigious grave goods buried with the dead around Stonehenge demonstrate. Hundreds of chalk-white mounds, bright against a green landscape, thus surrounded and protected the lintelled stone circle at its centre.

We will never know the name of the influential individual who organized the incredible feat of civil engineering that resulted in Stonehenge, never hear the words with which he decreed the sanctity of this landscape, and never visit the location of his home, where his crops grew and animals grazed. It is only in death that he may be visible. For the individual buried underneath the Bush Barrow, a little way south of Stonehenge, lay with ornate weapons and such symbols of authority that his identification as the chief architect behind this unique site is not implausible.

2000 BC

The man's skeleton was discovered underneath its chalk mound, lying on its back with the head to the south and the feet to the north. The remains of a wooden-framed helmet were found near the head. A bronze axe lay near the right shoulder, while two fearsome daggers lay adjacent to the right forearm. At least one of these had a wooden pommel decorated with thousands of minute gold rivets arranged in a zigzag pattern. Near the daggers lay a gold belt-hook, while on the man's chest, and probably originally attached to a woollen tunic, was a thin lozenge of sheet gold. A smaller gold lozenge and the remains of a third dagger were found by his right hand. In life the fingers of that hand had certainly gripped the wooden shaft of a polished pebble macehead which in death still accompanied the deceased. In death too he could look to the north and see the eternal result of his earthly authority, the sacred ring of Stonehenge.

We know so much about the deaths yet so little of the lives of these people, for their hearths, homes and villages have not survived. Because of this imbalance in the evidence, there have been rival theories to account for their dominance. The daggers in the graves strongly suggest a warlike tendency, and the possibility that these peoples were invaders from across the Channel cannot be discounted. Another possibility is that they lived as pastoralists, moving around and across Salisbury Plain, driving sheep and cattle before them and living in temporary, easily erected (and therefore easily destroyed) shelters. Raiding is frequently endemic in pastoralist societies as different groups seek to maximize herd size by fair means or foul, and often come into conflict over diminishing grazing. In such situations they tend to seek to dominate the more sedentary farmers with whom they exchange meat and milk for grain. Whatever

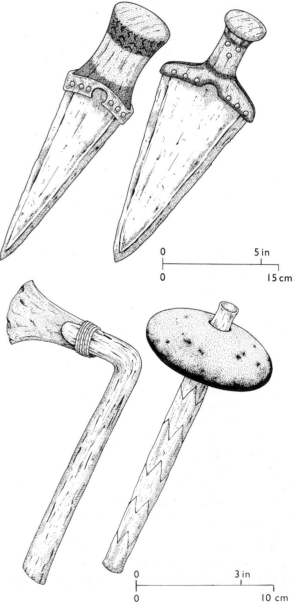

Above: A detailed illustration of the three ornate gold items buried in the grave beneath Bush Barrow. Controversy still surrounds the question of whether the largest piece was originally flat or slightly domed.

Above right: The similarity between daggers with bronze blades and wooden hilts decorated with gold pins from Bush Barrow and the Finistère site at Kernonen in Britanny, suggests that the international language of status was elaborate and expensive metalwork.

Right: Among other artefacts buried under Bush Barrow were this ceremonial bronze axe and a mace with bone inlays and pebble head, probably a symbol of authority.

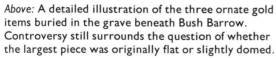

2000
BC

Fact or Fiction? How the last part of the great journey from the Preseli Mountains of south-west Wales might have looked. Here the bluestones are rafted up the River Avon prior to being dragged overland the short distance to Stonehenge. However, recent research suggests the bluestones were actually carried to the plain by a glacier.

the origin of their sudden pre-eminence around 2000 BC, even these powerful individuals could not afford to ignore the influence of Stonehenge, which had existed already for several centuries. They could not destroy it, so they had to transform it. The bluestones that may have been brought by earlier generations on an epic journey from the Preseli Mountains in south-west Wales were unceremoniously dug up and removed. In their place was erected the horseshoe of trilithons surrounded by the awesome sarsen circle. And as the ultimate status symbol, thirty lintel stones made a horizontal circle of stone.

Who were the powerful gods that inspired such effort? During all the periods of Stonehenge there was an entrance in the north-east aligned on the midsummer sunrise and it seems credible that at least one of the gods must have been the sun itself. The other major orientation lies at a right angle to that of the sun and points to the setting of the midwinter moon in the north-west. The sun and moon may well have ruled over a pantheon of deities personified by a number of other celestial bodies.

The chiefs and priests who worshipped among the sacred stones derived their authority from their ability to communicate with these gods, to control their movements and to predict their turning-points. Through such knowledge they could establish the dates for important festivals and ceremonies, decide on the days for planting and harvesting, and become masters of time itself. For the common people it was all a matter of faith. Belief that the chiefs and priests spoke to the gods, that without such communication the sun would fail to rise or the moon refuse to set, and that in the absence of these regular rituals the framework of society would collapse.

And those beliefs had spread among many different societies in 2000 BC. From the north of Scotland to the south of Ireland, from the west of France to Spain, hundreds of stone circles were erected. Some were monstrous undertakings, representing the toil of thousands over decades; others, using small slabs of slate, were the work of a few families counted in days. Great numbers of chiefs and priests, speaking countless languages and dialects, officiated within these temples of stone. They preached and enlightened a population that must have run into millions, and they led them in the worship of the sun and the moon. Stonehenge may have been the most sacred centre of a widespread cult, perhaps a place of pilgrimage, a megalithic Mecca on Salisbury Plain.

2000 BC

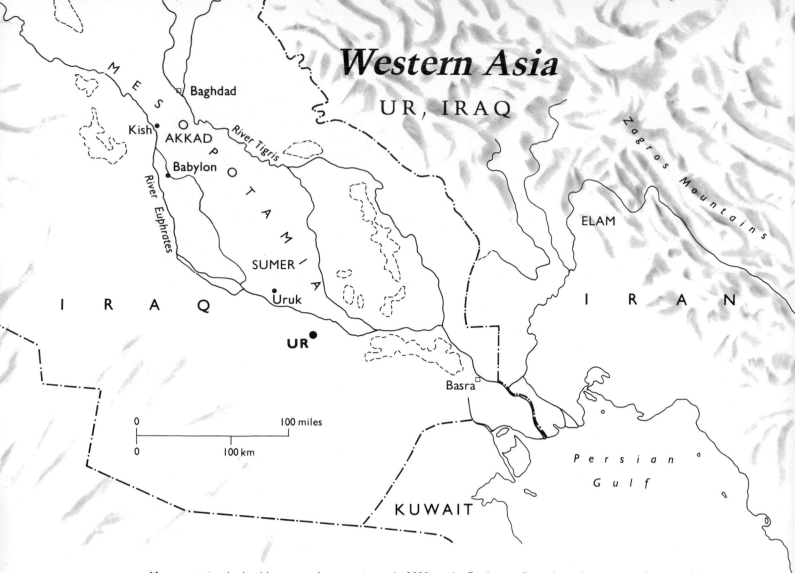

Western Asia
UR, IRAQ

Mesopotamia, the land between the two rivers. In 2000 BC the Euphrates flowed much nearer to the city of Ur, and the coastline at the head of the Persian Gulf then was closer to the ancient cities.

2000 BC

Mesopotamia, meaning literally the land between the two rivers, was one of the earliest centres of civilization. The Tigris and the Euphrates, draining the Anatolian highlands in the north and the Zagros Mountains to the east, carried silt-laden waters across the marshy plains to empty them in the Persian Gulf. Whoever managed to control these rivers, by canals and irrigation channels, and divert their fertile alluvium on to agricultural land would thrive and prosper. Such control was the platform which supported the development of Sumeria, a civilization of fortified cities, ruled by kings and regulated by priests and bureaucrats, a civilization in which the gods could both protect and punish any or every citizen.

The development of Sumerian unity had been a lengthy and uneven process. After 2500 BC the authority of the Sumerians was undermined and eventually a Semitic-speaking ruler, Sargon of Akkad, established political control over a large part of Mesopotamia. This dynasty was eventually destroyed by a wave of immigrant nomadic peoples from Iran. In the ensuing power vacuum the Sumerians regained the initiative, and the chance to reforge political unity was seized by Ur-Nammu, the governor of Ur, a city situated on the east bank of the Euphrates close to the head of the Gulf. Around 2113 BC he rebelled against his superior, the king of Uruk, and proclaimed himself 'King of Ur, King of Sumer and Akkad'.

Rapid consolidation of the empire followed, along with a burst of building activity at Ur itself. However, this so-called third dynasty spanned just five kings. By 2000 BC a catastrophe had occurred. The Sumerian empire had collapsed and just a few years previously the city had fallen to a people known as the Elamites. The last king of Sumer was taken prisoner to Iran, where he died. The gods had forsaken the land of Sumer although Ur itself would prosper anew in the succeeding centuries.

The view across the sacred precinct towards the ziggurat of Ur. Although the ziggurat was restored, the walls in the foreground were conserved as found. During Ur's excavation by Sir Leonard Woolley thousands of tons of rubble were lifted in small baskets and carried down to a custom-built light railway to be removed.

The city of Ur in 2000 BC. Two protected harbours within the city walls were linked by canals to the Euphrates, while the sacred walled precinct at the centre of Ur was dominated by the massive height of the ziggurat.

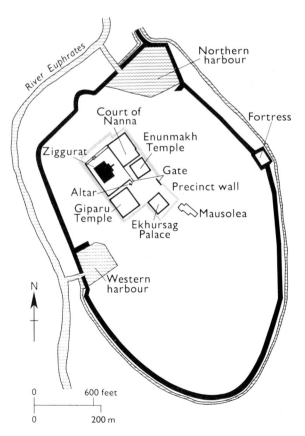

The importance of the gods to the inhabitants of Ur is reflected in the architecture of the city. The heart of the city was taken up with a walled, sacred precinct, containing a variety of temples and dominated by the towering ziggurat, dedicated to the patron deity of the city, the moon god Nanna, and his wife, Ningal.

The city itself was defended by massive mud-brick defences, which enclosed a roughly oval area of some 150 acres (60 ha). Inside lived around 20,000 inhabitants. The lower, steeply sloping half of the defensive wall was constructed of sun-dried mud bricks and lay against the side of a mound formed by earlier phases of the city. The upper courses of the wall were built of fired mud bricks, which were more durable. Two harbours within the city walls were linked by canals to the Euphrates, while another canal led water around the eastern and southern sides of the defences, effectively ringing the city with water.

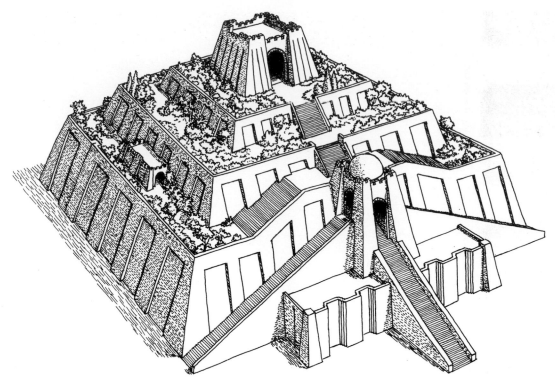

Within the north-west corner of the sacred precinct stood the ziggurat, a stepped pyramid of solid mud brick. Its core was faced with a thick skin of fired bricks set in bitumen. It had at least three storeys and its rectangular base measured some 200 by 132 feet (60 by 40 m). The monument was oriented so that its four corners marked the cardinal points. Against the north-east side three long flights of steps converged to give access to the mound mid-way between the first and second terraces. From that point further flights of steps led to the second and third terraces, and finally to the house of Nanna, which stood on the summit. Several architectural tricks were employed by the designers of the ziggurat to improve the appearance of the mud-brick mountain. The walls of the storeys were inclined so as to lead the eye upwards, while their exteriors were enlivened by the addition of flat buttresses. The storeys decreased in height towards the summit, while the main flights of steps interrupted the horizontal lines of the terraces. But most intriguing of all, it is possible that the terraces of the ziggurat were covered with soil in which were planted trees, shrubs and flowers: the house of Nanna on top of an artificial mountain masked by vegetation. This was the cosmic mountain of Sumerian mythology which symbolized life-giving forces, and it was the ideal setting in which men and gods could meet. Like all mountains, it was impressive and visible from afar. The only other building on the ziggurat was a small, rectangular structure of unknown purpose situated on the first terrace.

A reconstruction of the ziggurat at Ur. The side walls of the ziggurat are studded with hundreds of drainage holes, which suggest that the flat tops of the three terraces of the ziggurat could well have been covered with soil, and planted with date palms, olive trees, fig trees and vines.

2000
BC

The central monumental stairway was probably used as the prinicpal processional way. Its sharp and regular inclination is designed to lead the eye up to the holy of holies on the ziggurat's summit – the house of Nanna.

The ziggurat's front face was approached by three brick stairways, each of exactly 100 steps. The central stair projects straight out from the huge building, while the other two stairs flank the façade on each side. All three stairways converge on a great gateway between the first and second terrace.

2000 BC

The remaining area of the precinct was occupied by temples and ancillary buildings. A kitchen, where food was prepared for Nanna's priests, and a shrine to Nanna lay to the north of the ziggurat. This structure may have been the earthly residence of the moon god, who descended from on high down the steps of the ziggurat. An altar may have stood in front of the towering monument, while at a lower level was the brick-paved court of Nanna, surrounded by storehouses. To the south of the ziggurat lay a building known as Giparu, the temple of Ningal and official residence of her priestess, while the area to the south of the court of Nanna was occupied by the temple of Enunmakh, dedicated to both Nanna and Ningal. These temples were reached by means of a gateway in the east corner of the ziggurat terrace, through which steps led down into the lower precinct. Beyond these structures was the royal palace and shrine known as Ekhursag, which was associated with the cult of the ruling king. Further away, and just outside the precinct wall, a series of tombs may have housed the bodies of the royal family, or of high-ranking priests and priestesses.

The mausolea, probably of the royal family – but perhaps of priests and priestesses – consisted of two distinct elements: subterranean brick-built burial vaults with ridged roofs for the bodies and superstructures, also of brick, constructed directly above them. Stairways linked the buildings above with the burial vaults below.

Most of the remaining area within the city walls was used for housing, and the standard of private housing for the comfortable classes was remarkably good. The basic house plan was a two-storey unit built around a central courtyard which was open to the skies. The walls were built of mud brick, which was then plastered and whitewashed. There were probably no windows in the exterior walls, the light coming instead from the central courtyard. A staircase led from the court to a wooden gallery which ran around the inside of the upper storey, and gave access to the living rooms of the family. Downstairs were the guest rooms, the kitchen, the servants' quarters, the lavatory with a drain in its paved floor, and a private shrine for the household gods. The normal dwelling, therefore, might contain over a dozen rooms.

Our knowledge of the workings of Sumerian society has been largely derived from one of its greatest achievements: the art of writing. Major commercial transactions were recorded on clay tablets using the split end of a reed, the wedge-shaped marks making up the script known as cuneiform. Like our own writing, cuneiform ran from left to right, and the temple scribes perfected their craft to such an extent that several hundred signs could be impressed on a clay tablet no bigger than a hand. Once a tablet was completed it was sun-dried or baked and then stored. Important contracts were placed inside a clay envelope, which then had a copy of the document written on its exterior, and was often sealed with a cylinder-seal impression. Document and cover were then placed in the kiln together for baking. Most of the cuneiform records were stored in temples, which, in a society where there was little formal distinction between the sacred and the secular, performed a variety of religious and civil functions.

For the citizens of Ur, the moon god Nanna was the real ruler of their lives, while the king and his ministers were mere mortal representatives, on earth to ensure that the god's wishes were carried out. The temples, therefore, acted as sacred storehouses, for as a landowner the god received regular tithes or rents. As there was no coinage, these was paid in kind. From the countryside came huge quantities of agricultural produce, and the towns provided jars full of scrap copper, gold and silver.

These enormous reserves were used to support the temple staff and also to feed the populace in times of war. Detailed accounts were made of all incoming materials and their subsequent allocation to specific individuals. Some of the temples were also factories where women, girls and slaves worked at particular tasks, including the production of woven cloth. The output of

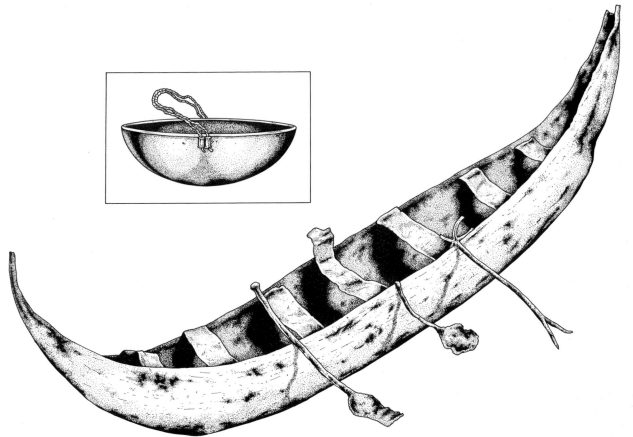

Ur was a phenomenally wealthy imperial city in the centuries prior to 2000 BC. From the royal tombs of earlier centuries archaeologists have recovered such elaborate treasures as this 2-foot long (60 cm) model boat of beaten silver (strikingly similar to the present-day boats of the Marsh Arabs of southern Iraq) and a golden libation bowl.

individuals was meticulously recorded, and rations from the temple reserves were given according to the quantity of cloth produced. There were even special rates for the sick. The god was also deemed to have other earthly needs and one of these was satisfied by the practice of religious prostitution. Every temple possessed a body of women who formed part of the god's household – his wife, concubines and servants. Various grades existed, from the wife of Nanna, who was a high priestess, to the ordinary prostitutes, who served the male citizens of Ur.

The Sumerians believed in many gods and these were honoured throughout the empire, although every city had its own patron deity. In one respect this principal god was so far removed from the ordinary citizen that each person had his own personal god, who acted as mediator between him and the city god, and who may have been worshipped in household shrines. On the other hand, the main divinity, personified by the king, was distinctly worldly: he had a temple for a house; he required his faithful to provide him with food, clothing and concubines; his ceremonies ensured the recurrence of the seasons and the success of the harvests; and he led his people into battle. The religion of the Sumerians was very much bound up with material considerations. They feared the wrath of the gods in their daily lives and therefore made placatory offerings of food and wine in the temples, where meals were shared by the temple officials. The influence of the supernatural was felt in many spheres of life. Although medicine was a well-practised science and appropriate drugs were prescribed, it was also believed that malignant spirits caused illnesses, and these demons had to be exorcised by magicians whose job it was to conjure away evil and restore the afflicted to health.

2000 BC

The economic prosperity of Sumer depended upon its agriculture and commerce. The carefully irrigated fields produced prodigious quantities of barley, spelt, onions and other vegetables. Several varieties of date were cultivated, dates providing one of the staple foods of the population. Since irrigation channels ran through the fields of many different owners, and because they needed regular maintenance if they were not to clog up with weeds, an efficient and communal administration was needed to supervise tasks such as cleaning channels and distributing water to certain properties. Grain was used for bread, porridge and beer, while wine was produced from dates as well as grapes. Cattle and goats provided milk and cheese, and fish were abundant in the rivers and canals. The diet for the majority was probably vegetarian, with meat as an occasional luxury. The clothing needs of the population were met by wool produced in abundance from the scattered flocks, while flax for linen was grown in the northern part of Mesopotamia. Maritime trade brought great prosperity and Ur and its neighbours at the head of the Persian Gulf were well placed to reap the rewards. It was certainly a profitable business, as records of the contents of a ship that docked at Ur in about 2048 BC show. In its hold were gold, copper ore, ivory, precious woods and fine stone for making statues and vases. These raw materials were worked upon by the craftsmen of the city before the finished articles were re-exported to the north and west via the land routes. Although transactions were carried out through barter, there was a complex financial system which involved credit, interest rates and central-government price-fixing.

For all its complexity the Sumerian empire came to an abrupt end. In 2006 BC the city of Ur was besieged and overrun by the Elamites, a subject people who dwelt in the Zagros Mountains to the east. That date marks the end of the Sumerian people as an independent nation, although the city of Ur would rise again under different rulers, and Sumerian language, ideas and literature would be preserved and studied until the disappearance of cuneiform script in the first century BC. A limestone monolith on which were carved scenes showing the moon god Nanna giving instructions to the king, and the latter constructing the ziggurat, was smashed by the intruders. In 2000 BC Ur probably lay partly in ruins, with an Elamite garrison imposing martial law on a subject population. The ziggurat still stood, but for the time being the gods had departed.

A distant view of the ziggurat with, in the foreground, the excavated remains of the royal tombs of Ur (2600 BC–2460 BC). There were sixteen 'royal' graves in this one cemetery.

Africa

THEBES, EGYPT

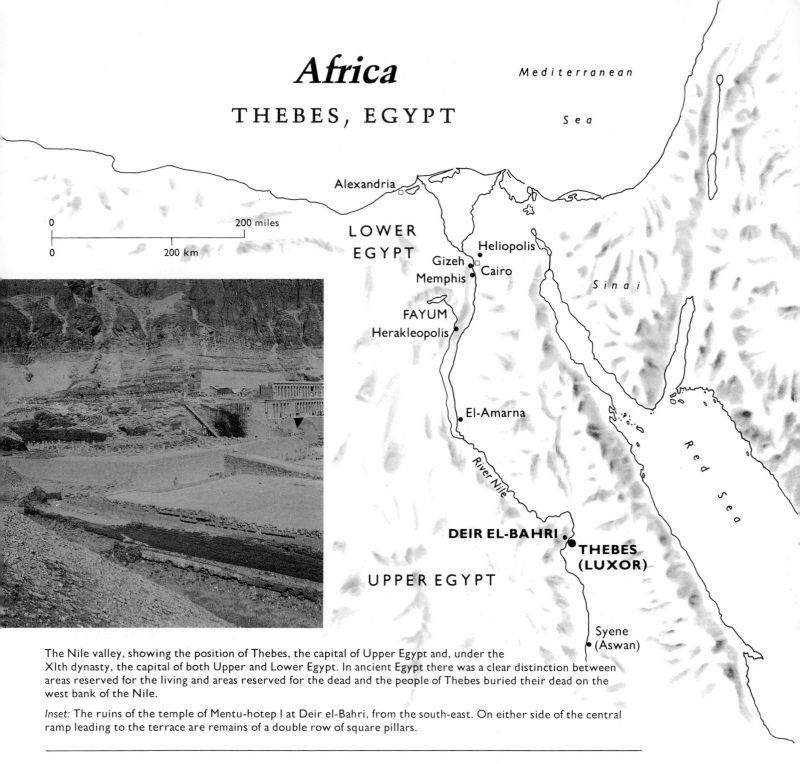

Mediterranean Sea

Alexandria

LOWER EGYPT

Heliopolis
Gizeh
Memphis
Cairo

Sinai

FAYUM
Herakleopolis

El-Amarna

River Nile

Red Sea

DEIR EL-BAHRI
THEBES (LUXOR)

UPPER EGYPT

Syene (Aswan)

The Nile valley, showing the position of Thebes, the capital of Upper Egypt and, under the XIth dynasty, the capital of both Upper and Lower Egypt. In ancient Egypt there was a clear distinction between areas reserved for the living and areas reserved for the dead and the people of Thebes buried their dead on the west bank of the Nile.

Inset: The ruins of the temple of Mentu-hotep I at Deir el-Bahri, from the south-east. On either side of the central ramp leading to the terrace are remains of a double row of square pillars.

During the month of July the Blue Nile, rising in the Ethiopian highlands, becomes swollen with the heavy rains and changes into a raging mountain torrent. It flows to the north, down and across the deserts of Sudan, before it is joined by the waters of the White Nile at Khartoum, and further north by those of the Atbara. The river then follows a huge curve, sweeping around to the west, before resuming its northwards course and crossing the southern frontier of modern Egypt. Sometimes its path is impeded by reefs of hard, igneous stone which create the rapids or cataracts.

The waters tumble over the first cataract at Aswan and some 156 miles (250 km) later, glide past the modern town of Luxor. This was ancient Thebes, the capital of Upper and Lower Egypt under the pharaohs of the XIth dynasty. There are still hundreds of miles for the Nile to flow before it divides to fan out over the delta of Lower Egypt and empty into the Mediterranean. In the age of the pharaohs, the annual flooding of the Nile, when the river deposited its fertile layers of silt and alluvium, lent a timeless and cyclical quality to Egyptian civilization.

2000 BC

The funerary temple of Mentu-hotep I, seen from the north-east. The temple lies beyond the colonnaded terraces of the temple of Queen Hatshepsut of the XVIII dynasty. Behind towers a mountain known in ancient times as Meretseger – she who loves silence.

The plan of Deir el-Bahri, constructed by Mentu-hotep I across the river from the living city of Thebes. The nearby Valley of the Kings is largely from later dynasties.

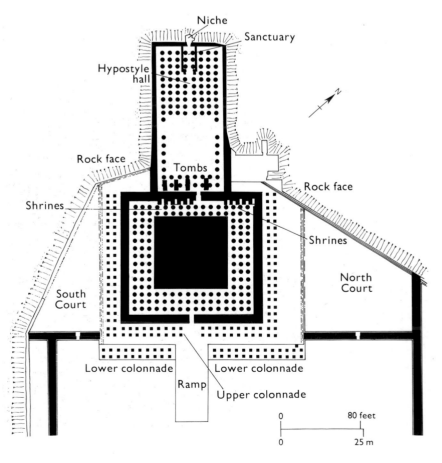

Once this ordered cycle of life on the Nile was disrupted, then the kingdom of the pharaohs began to disintegrate. Such conditions prevailed around 2180 BC, at the collapse of the VIth dynasty. In a surviving papyrus an official named as Ipuwer castigates an unnamed king for letting the country fall into ruin, describing the calamitous conditions that prevailed: 'Squalor is throughout the land; no clothes are white these days . . . the Nile is in flood yet no one has the heart to plough . . . Corn has perished everywhere . . . The dead are thrown in the river . . . Laughter has perished. Grief walks the land.' For more than a century the country was divided, with Lower and Middle Egypt under the control of kings based in Herakleopolis, south of Memphis, while Upper Egypt remained independent under the rulers of Thebes. The situation was resolved around 2055 BC, when a Theban prince, Mentu-hotep I Nebhepet-re, triumphed over his countrymen in the north and reunited Egypt under the rule of one pharaoh from his capital at Thebes. The new king firmly established the XIth dynasty and ruled for fifty-one years, time enough to restore order to the towns and countryside. When he died, shortly before 2000 BC, he was able to bequeath to his successor Mentu-hotep II, a population for whom civil war was a distant legend rather than a painful memory. During his lifetime, Mentu-hotep I constructed an elaborate burial place and temple for his afterlife at Deir el-Bahri, on the west bank of the Nile. It is this monument, more than any other, which allows us an insight into the ancient Egypt of 2000 BC, and also a glimpse of the gods of the citizens of Thebes.

Built on a terrace and framed by the massive backdrop of sandstone cliffs to the west, the funerary temple of Mentu-hotep I grew steadily more impressive as mourners approached it along the 3,300-foot-long (1-km) causeway. The causeway led from the valley building at the edge of the cultivated strip, where some of the preliminary funerary rituals were performed, westwards across the desert to a large forecourt, surrounded on all sides but the west by high walls. Sandstone statues of the king holding in his hands a crook and flail, the traditional emblems of the god Osiris, flanked each side of the causeway. Those on the south side probably portrayed him wearing the crown of Upper Egypt, while those on the north carried that of Lower Egypt. These powerful symbols stressed both the unity of the two halves of Egypt and the eternal afterlife of the king as he was transformed into Osiris, the king of the dead.

The causeway ended in a ramp which led up to the front terrace, supported by a double row of square pillars. The rigid horizontal appearance of the front terrace must have been softened by the planting of rows of sycamore and tamarisk trees, which partially hid the lower part of the temple. The terrace itself was formed by two distinct sections: a massive, almost square platform was attached to a much narrower building platform or stem that was cut back into the cliff face. On the platform, a central structure about 73 feet (22 m) square sat within a building which was itself surrounded on all sides but the west by colonnades. The central structure possessed neither internal chambers nor corridors, being composed of solid rubble encased by limestone walls. Much controversy has surrounded the function of this structure. Some have reconstructed it as a pyramid, perhaps intended to mark the false burial chambers for the king which lay directly underneath its centre. Others argue that it originally resembled a mound, the primordial mound which had long been regarded as a powerful magical symbol. Whatever its shape, between it and the walls of the building in which it stood was an ambulatory, the flat roof of which was carried on rows of polygonal columns. Further west on the narrow 'stem' and under the shadow of the cliff were a cloistered court and a columned hall. Right at the end of the hall was a small sanctuary which contained an altar and, in a niche hewn out of the very cliff, a statue of the dead king.

There are also problems of interpretation with regard to the burial chamber of Mentu-hotep I, for the temple enclosure contains two tombs. The first was entered from a large pit in the forecourt from where a passage was tunnelled some 460 feet (140 m) to a point directly beneath the mound. There two chambers were discovered, one on top of the other, connected by a vertical shaft. The upper chamber contained a seated statue of the king and an empty wooden coffin; the lower produced only a few pots and three crudely made wooden boats. Some Egyptologists have suggested that these chambers were used in a mock burial ceremony by the king when he was celebrating the Heb-Sed festival, held in honour of his earthly rule during the thirty-ninth year of his reign. Others prefer to see these chambers as the tomb of the king in his personification as the god Osiris. The real tomb lay at the end of an even longer tunnel that was entered from the columned hall, from where it descended westwards for a considerable distance under the cliff face. The chamber at the end of the passage was lined with granite and contained a shrine made of alabaster and granite. The chamber had been robbed in antiquity. It is presumed that the shrine held a painted wooden coffin containing the mummy of the pharaoh, but no trace of either coffin or mummy has ever been found.

Part of the double row of square pillars along the front of the temple. All of the columns would have carried hieroglyphic inscriptions but some are now too badly damaged to read and many columns are completely missing.

The ambulatory, showing the remains of some polygonal columns. The columns were arranged in rows of three and formed a deep colonnade on the north, south and east sides of the central square building.

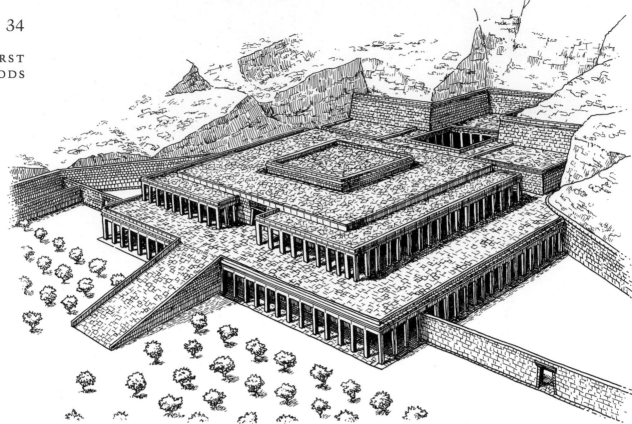

A reconstruction of Deir el-Bahri. The exact form of the monument in the centre is not known. It could have been a pyramid, but it may well have been a flat-topped stone mound, or even a mound of earth supporting trees.

2000
BC

The king was not the only one to be buried at Deir el-Bahri. Between the square platform and the 'stem' of the monument was a row of six shrines of limestone. Behind each shrine was a vertical shaft that led down to a tomb chamber. The tombs and shrines belonged to six queens or princesses of the royal family. The limestone sarcophagi of two queens, Kawit and Ashayet, were discovered, both decorated on their exteriors with exquisitely carved reliefs, depicting scenes from daily life. It may be that the funerary temple of Mentu-hotep I was originally planned as just the square element, since the construction of the court and hall that comprised the 'stem' meant that these tomb entrances were covered with the paving, walls or columns of the extension.

An important distinction must be drawn between the pyramids of the Old Kingdom and the novel and unique structure that was Deir el-Bahri. In the pyramids at Gizeh the intention of the builders was to perpetuate the dominant position of the pharaoh in the afterlife. At Deir el-Bahri, on the other hand, the pharaoh was to enjoy his afterlife in the company of the gods whose worship was conducted in his temple. Inscriptions on the foundation deposit tablets show that the temple was dedicated to Mentu-Re, a god who was the

Upper Egyptian equivalent of the sun god of Lower Egypt. In addition, the primordial mound, although originating in Lower Egypt as a symbol of creation, may have been adopted by the cult of Osiris as a symbol both for creation and for renewal of life.

Little is known of the layout of the city of Thebes, on the east bank of the Nile, around 2000 BC. Mentu-hotep I and the kings of the XIth dynasty were the first to establish it as the capital of all Egypt and it remained the capital for centuries under the succeeding dynasties which constituted the New Kingdom, being continually modified and redeveloped. It does appear, however, that shortly after 2000 BC any visitor to Thebes would have wandered along the straight, intersecting streets of a regularly planned city. The city stretched for over 3,300 feet (1 km) from north to south and was centred on the area later occupied in the New Kingdom by the temple of Karnak. Five excavations in and around the Karnak temple complex have shown glimpses of a grid-iron street pattern on a different alignment to the New Kingdom architecture, as well as houses, circular grain silos, storerooms and a section of the city wall.

Mentu-hotep I was not content with simply establishing Thebes, however. He was also a

Left: A granite statue, now damaged and headless, with the cartouche of Senusret II or III carved on his belt-buckle. It now stands in front of the temple.

Right: This inscription from a square column reads: 'Wadjet, goddess of Lower Egypt, grants eternal rule to the Horus Semitaui, the beautiful god, son of Re, Mentu-hotep. The beloved, living like Re, and living for ever.' Mentu-hotep was obviously reinforcing his legitimate claim over both Lower and Upper Egypt.

Below: A delightful carved wooden model from XIth dynasty Thebes, which illustrates the everyday process of bread-making. Such wooden models were often placed with the wealthy deceased in their tombs.

2000 BC

Drawing of a model room, found in another tomb of an XIth dynasty noble. The wooden model shows in more detail the everyday processes of brewing and baking. Representations of anything that nobles might need in the afterlife were often buried in the tomb. These models were roughly the size of a modern doll's house.

2000
BC

campaigning monarch and he led Egyptian armies against the Libyans, the Asiatic forces and the Nubians to the south. By the time of the succeeding XIIth dynasty, the first of the Middle Kingdom, a series of forts was being constructed in Nubia. The fort at Buhen, situated on a gently shelving plateau on the banks of the Nile, was in existence by 1967 BC. Its mud-brick fortifications were clearly designed to withstand a siege, enclosing an inner citadel and an outer area. The interior had a rigid orthogonal layout similar to that of the capital at Thebes.

The first gods of the Egyptians were many and varied, ranging from household deities to local and state gods. There was always, however, an intimate connection between religion and the state, since Egypt remained a country governed for most of the

time by a supreme ruler who was considered to be the son of a divinity. In the Old Kingdom the first god to receive royal approval and acceptance by the populace was the sun god Re. The king took the name of Son of Re, and on his death was assumed to have joined his father in the heavens. The centre of worship for Re was the town of Heliopolis, now an exclusive suburb of modern Cairo. After the collapse of the Old Kingdom and during the lifetimes of the pharaohs of the XIth dynasty, the religion of royalty became the religion of the people in the form of the god Osiris, the king of the dead. Now every Egyptian, not just the king, could become an Osiris at death and enjoy the benefits of the afterlife. Regional gods, of course, continued to draw the faithful. Often they were animal gods, like Bastet, the cat goddess, whose centre was at Bubastis, where hundreds of bronze cats were dedicated to her. Local deities, too humble to merit temples, included the ugly and deformed dwarf Bes, god of marriage and joy, and protector from evil. A pregnant hippopotamus symbolized the goddess Tauert, bringer of fertility, and was frequently represented on amulets worn by women of all classes.

Just as there was a strong link between religion and the state, so too there were connections between religion and the economy. The great temples were not congregational houses where the masses could pray but were, in reality, administrative offices and storehouses managed by a hereditary priesthood on behalf of the pharaoh.

Those storehouses were filled with the agricultural fruits of the Nile. The annual inundations and a sophisticated system of irrigation meant that bountiful harvests of barley and emmer wheat could be reaped from the soft and muddy ground. Sheep or pigs were used to trample the seed into the ground, while sheep, oxen or donkeys played another role by treading the grain. The diet of the nobles consisted of various cuts of meat from animals kept principally for slaughter, supplemented by vegetables, cheese, butter, duck and goose eggs, honey, poultry and fish. The diet of the poor was a good deal less varied, being based on the staples of beer and bread. The two activities of brewing and baking were depicted on a model building from a noble's tomb of the XIth dynasty. Both were organized with efficiency and had much in common, starting with the making of dough, the yeasty froth from the beer supplying yeast for the leavened bread.

Papyrus documents throw light on the two halves of the Egyptian economy. On the state side there were the bulging storehouses of the temples and of the royal palaces. Produce collected from the people in the form of taxes was redistributed back to them as regular wages and rations, or as hand-outs to cover any periods of famine or agricultural interruption brought about by civil strife or invasion. On the individual side the letters of an XIth-dynasty farmer called Hekanakht are illuminating. He lived and farmed to the south of Thebes, writing letters back to his family on trips away from home. In a barter economy, his attitude to fellow farmers and the world at large was one of shrewd economic calculation. He urges one of his household to retain one bull from among some animals about to be sent out, since he has a good chance of making a 50 per cent profit on the sale of the animal at a future date.

A little before 2000 BC Mentu-hotep I was laid to rest at Deir el-Bahri, having ruled for fifty-one years. The mourners accompanying the coffin on its journey westwards along the causeway had good reason to grieve. The man whose body they shouldered had reunited all of Egypt, established Thebes as its capital, expanded the frontiers of the state and once again sent Egyptian ships down the Red Sea to the 'Land of Punt' (probably in the region of the Horn of Africa) in search of frankincense and myrrh. The citizens of Thebes felt safe in the enduring and cyclical progression of their civilization. The Egyptian state was based not on continuing development or improvement but on the regular inundations of the Nile, which provided a rhythmical and regular agricultural return. The aim of society was to preserve its traditional beliefs and practices, formulated in pre-dynastic times and handed down from generation to generation. Even the art of the ancient Egyptians did not evolve, but instead tried to copy the art forms of the original perfect state. In the land of the pharaohs political and religious ideology were one and the same thing. The ideal human society for the Egyptians was a divine creation. It was based on continuity with the past and the well-being and peaceful succession of a line of kings, who were themselves divinities. So the mourners at Deir el-Bahri grieved, but they also derived comfort from the accession of Mentu-hotep II. And even when the XIth dynasty was overthrown and power was usurped by a new dynastic line, the kings of the XIIth dynasty showed a pious regard for their predecessors, thus ensuring religious and political continuity and the lasting support of the people.

Eastern Asia and Oceania

MOHENJO-DARO, PAKISTAN

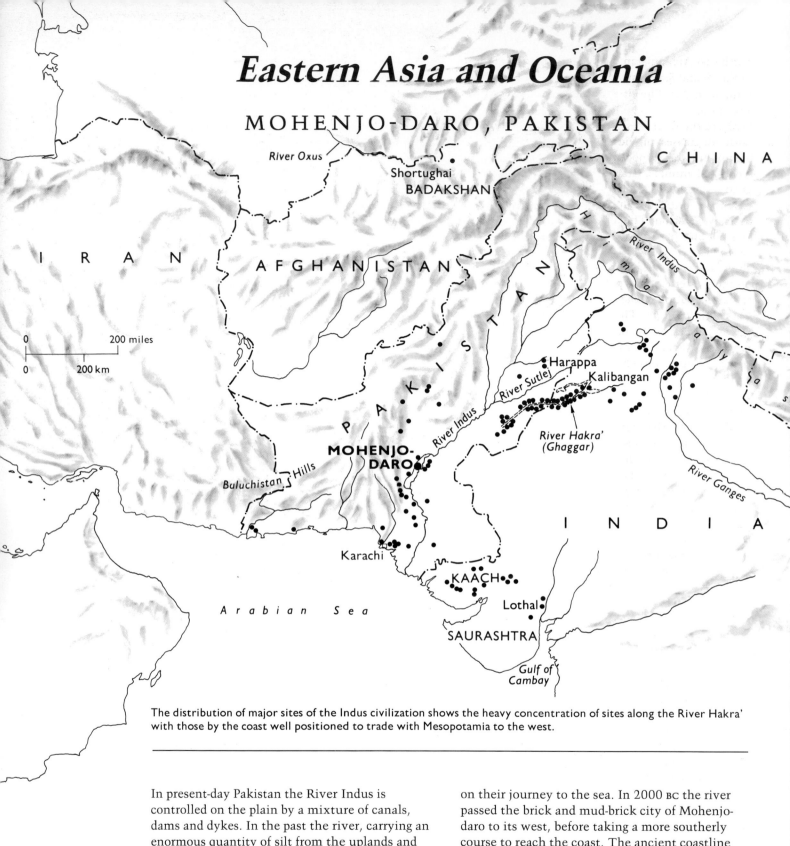

The distribution of major sites of the Indus civilization shows the heavy concentration of sites along the River Hakra' with those by the coast well positioned to trade with Mesopotamia to the west.

2000 BC

In present-day Pakistan the River Indus is controlled on the plain by a mixture of canals, dams and dykes. In the past the river, carrying an enormous quantity of silt from the uplands and swollen by the meltwaters of the Himalayas, would flood annually, inundating large areas of the plain and depositing a life-giving sediment of fertile alluvium. Occasionally, the volume of water was so great that the flooding and deposition would remodel the landscape, and as the waters receded, they would take a new course

on their journey to the sea. In 2000 BC the river passed the brick and mud-brick city of Mohenjo-daro to its west, before taking a more southerly course to reach the coast. The ancient coastline was also probably nearer to Mohenjo-daro than at present.

The river has given its name to a number of ancient sites which have been collectively described as the Indus civilization. Most of these settlements flourished on the plain of the Indus, although there were some far-flung outposts in north-east Afghanistan, in the Punjab, to the south in Kacch and Saurashtra and to the west near the Iranian border. The cities of the plain prospered as a result of the fertile gifts of the Indus. On both banks of the river there were trees interspersed with tall grasses, providing a suitable habitat for elephant, tiger, rhinoceros, buffalo and other woodland animals. Gradually, as distance from the great river increased, the grasslands became more extensive, until the alluvial plain gave way to desert vegetation. The mature Indus civilization was not an isolated phenomenon. A settled agrarian society, based on wheat and barley, cattle, sheep and goats, began to appear around 7000 BC on the western fringes of the Indus valley, spreading out on to the Indus plains during the fourth millennium. The period from *c*.3000–2500 BC can be seen as one of incipient urbanism, providing the basis for the emergence of full urbanism in *c*.2500 BC. The cities of the Indus civilization developed from about 2500 to 1800 BC, and they formed the most significant settlements in one of the earliest urbanized cultures of the Old World. Some cities seem to have been more successful and perhaps more influential than any others – Harappa in the north and Mohenjo-daro in the south. Several other major cities have been identified, but are as yet either not excavated or only in the early stages of excavation. One of the most remarkable is Dholaviva in Kacch, which seems to rival Mohenjo-daro and Harappa in size. In 2000 BC the former covered at least 247 acres (100 ha) and probably had a population close to 40,000, and recent studies have discovered structural remains more than ½ mile (1 km) to the east of the present area of the site. A word of warning is necessary, however, before describing Mohenjo-daro. The Indus civilization is still a shadowy entity, unclear even in broad outline and lacking the kind of detail that we possess for Mesopotamian states such as Sumer.

The cultural uniformity of the Indus cities appears to have been quite remarkable. Not only are similarly styled artefacts found from settlements that were separated by thousands of miles, but the uniformity extended to activities such as town-planning. At Harappa and Mohenjo-daro, and at a third impressive settlement east of the Indus called Kalibangan, the basic form of the ideal Indus city was achieved. This consisted of two distinct elements: on the west a citadel mound built on a high podium of mud brick, with a long axis running N–S, and to the east, dominated by the citadel, a lower city, consisting of the principal residential districts. Although the scribes living in these cities were literate, texts were largely confined to seals, and repeated attempts to

A general view of the buildings on the citadel looking towards the Great Bath, the most famous building in Mohenjo-daro. Buildings were constructed on top of a series of huge mud platforms, laid down to ensure that the foundations were raised above the level of the surrounding plain.

decipher them have failed. We are thus left with only the sites and the artefacts that have been recovered from them as the primary evidence from which to reconstruct a complex civilization. So, unlike the contemporary states of Sumer and Middle Egypt, the Indus valley civilization has left no lists of dates or of kings, and no names of famous battles or of all-powerful gods to flesh out their story. The first gods of the Indus people must therefore be resurrected from their discarded seals and broken figurines.

The citadel at Mohenjo-daro was built of burnt brick, mud brick and mud – its base consisting of a series of great mud platforms. It now rises to a height of about 43 feet (13 m) above the level of the plain, but it has suffered badly from spring floods, which have from time to time enveloped the site, transforming the single mass of the citadel into a number of seemingly unrelated mounds. The nearest branch of the Indus is presently about 3 miles (5 km) away to the east, but it may have flowed closer in antiquity. The architects of the citadel platform were also troubled by the prospects of flooding and to counter this danger they protected the citadel by a mud-brick embankment

2000 BC

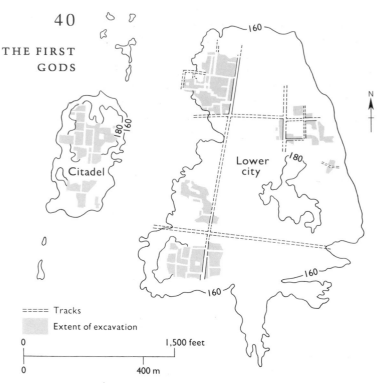

The general layout of Mohenjo-daro, with the 'citadel' to the west and the 'lower city' to the east. The shaded areas indicate the extent of the excavations. The map shows how the city is built on high ground, above the 160-feet (49-m) contour line.

The Great Bath was approached by flights of brick steps, finished with timber treads set in bitumen or asphalt, brought from deposits in the Baluchistan foothills.

or bund some 43 feet (13 m) wide. On top of the citadel, excavations have revealed various buildings, but the evidence for their function is rarely unequivocal and many are capable of more than one interpretation.

Easiest to understand are the solid, baked-brick, rectangular towers constructed at the south-eastern corner of the citadel. Two of these towers flanked a postern gate, and the discovery of about 100 baked-clay, oval sling pellets in their vicinity implies that these towers formed part of the fortifications that probably enclosed the whole of the citadel. Less obvious in function is the complex known as the Great Bath, which occupied a central area in the citadel. Its principal element comprised a rectangular sunken pool, 40 feet (12 m) in length from north to south, 23 feet (7 m) wide and about 8 feet (2.5 m) in depth. Flights of brick steps, formerly furnished with timber treads set in bitumen or asphalt, led down into the pool from the north and south. To ensure that the bath was watertight, the floor was laid with bricks set on edge in gypsum mortar. The sides of the pool were similarly mortared, and behind the walls a thick damp-proof course of bitumen was inserted. Near the south-west corner of the pool an outlet led to a high-arched drain which took excess waters down the western side of the citadel mound. A range of small rooms stood to the east of the pool, and in one of these was a large double-lined well which no doubt was the source of water for the pool. To the north, across a lane, was a building block which contained eight small bathrooms arranged in two rows on each side of a passage. The Great Bath may have been part of a religious and ceremonial centre, offering ritual immersion and perhaps the services of a resident priesthood. Such ablutions are significant features of modern Hinduism and other religious systems and the location of these baths at Mohenjo-daro in a central position seems to imply an official cult, sanctioned by the rulers of the city.

Immediately to the west of the Great Bath a remarkable group of twenty-seven blocks of brickwork was uncovered, criss-crossed by narrow ventilation channels. Earlier interpretations of this structure focused on its use as a granary, with the channels allowing under-floor circulation, so preventing the grain from coming into contact with the damp floor. It was also suggested that the structure was associated with brick loading-bays below the granary from which corn was raised into the citadel. Such interpretations cannot be proved, however, and although this was clearly a building of some civic importance, its true significance cannot yet be gauged. To the north and east of the Great Bath were other large and prestigious buildings, which may have been the offices or

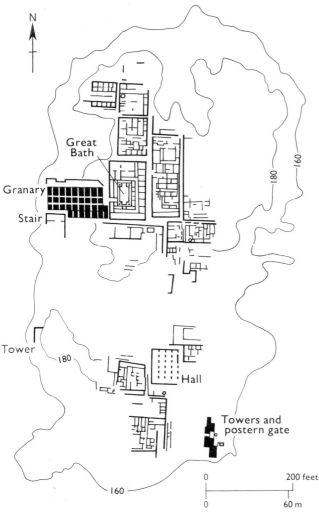

houses of the well-to-do at Mohenjo-daro were enclosed from sight and sun and were built around a central, internal courtyard. A well-preserved house in the southern part of the city enclosed a square courtyard measuring 43 feet (13 m) on each side. Rooms were arranged around the yard and, as befitted a population for which the height of the water table was of paramount importance, careful consideration was given to drainage. Earthenware drains led from underneath some of the rooms into the street outside, while other drains were incorporated vertically into the walls, probably serving an upper storey. Bathing, water supply and waste disposal were highly desirable domestic facilities for the average citizen of Mohenjo-daro and nearly all the larger houses were equipped with wells, indoor bathing-platforms and seated latrines connected to sewers underneath the streets. One of the great achievements of the city engineers was the sinking of an enormous number of vertical wells, lined with wedge-shaped bricks. Rough calculations suggest that the city was served by at least 700 wells, with an average frequency of one in every third house.

Not all were so affluent at Mohenjo-daro, however. There were groups of single-roomed tenements where the poorer classes lived. In

A detailed plan of the 'citadel' showing the central position of the Great Bath and the extent of the sites excavated.

Eight small bathrooms were constructed on both sides of the Bath's central passage and to provide privacy were arranged so that no two opened facing each other.

quarters of administrators, or possibly the priests who controlled the city and also perhaps the surrounding territory which it dominated. The southern part of the citadel has furnished the clearest evidence for the gods of the Indus. Here an oblong hall was unearthed, with four rows of brick plinths supporting wooden columns. The floor between these plinths was made of finely laid bricks, recalling the floor of the Great Bath. In a suite of rooms inside the hall a stone statue of a seated male was discovered and nearby there were a number of large worked stone rings of uncertain use. They resemble the finds from what is possibly a temple in the lower city.

To the east of the high citadel mound at Mohenjo-daro lay the lower city, which was also constructed on a vast mud and mud-brick platform. Divided into rectangular blocks by the street pattern, the individual buildings of the lower city differed considerably in size and function. The addition to residential areas, there were many shops and workshops, producing wares for local consumption and for export: for example, potteries, dyers' vats and metalworkers', shell-ornament makers' and beadmakers' shops have been discovered. Religious structures were also located in the lower city as well as on the citadel. One such building consisted of a high, oblong platform, approached from the south by two symmetrically arranged stairways and through a monumental double gateway. In the courtyard inside the building was a ring of brickwork, over 3 feet 3 inches (1 m) in internal diameter, akin to the stone rings on the citadel. But most suggestive of the structure's function was the discovery of a small stone statue, representing a seated or squatting man with his hands resting on his knees. The face is bearded and the hair is in a bun at the back; the eyes were originally inlaid with shell or faience. This was likely to have been one of the first gods of the Indus people.

Mohenjo-daro was undoubtedly a key site in a group of over seventy Indus settlements that are known from a huge area, larger than modern Pakistan. The majority lie on the plains of the Indus and its tributaries, or by the side of the now-dry course of the Hakra' or Ghaggar River, which flowed to the south of the Sutlej River. Trading ports were established as far away as the Iranian border and south to the Gulf of Cambay, where the most impressive entrepot is the site at Lothal. In north-east Afghanistan, on the southern plain of the Oxus, lies the furthest outpost at Shortughai. This appears to be an isolated colony, probably established to exploit the trade in lapis lazuli and copper from the neighbouring mines of Badakshan.

Without the advantage of a decipherable script we have to reconstruct the Indus society of 2000 BC from the excavated evidence. It is clear that the success of the state was founded on a productive agricultural base. From the Indus sites plentiful animal bones, together with the depiction of certain animals on seals, indicate that humped cattle, sheep, goats and fowl were the commonest domesticated species, with some suggestion of pig, buffalo, elephant and camel. Wheat and barley

---

A view of a lower city side street with a typical covered drain. Waste was discharged from the homes into the drains through earthenware pipes and carefully built chutes. Although unpaved and dusty, the streets at Mohenjo-daro were nevertheless supplied with a remarkable network of drains.

were two staple crops, along with some rice cultivation. A fragment of woven cotton from Mohenjo-daro probably means that the craft of weaving textiles was already well developed by the time of the Indus settlements. The sowing of wheat and barley would take place in those lands inundated by the river floods and newly revealed as the waters receded. Such planting required little or no ploughing or manuring and a minimum of labour and implements. It did, however, make maximum use of the rich alluvial silts.

The agricultural surplus made it possible to support a number of crafts and specialists, who produced the material goods for the people of the Indus state, including stone implements, copper and bronze tools, pottery and occasional gold and silver ornaments. The lapidary's trade was extensively practised, as the vast numbers of beads, weights, ornaments and steatite seals suggest. The seals probably carried names or ranks and possibly qualities, and were used to mark clay tablets

Below: A number of decorated ceramic beads from Mohenjo-daro and Harappa, used for jewellery.

Below right: The masonry that survives at Mohenjo-daro is almost entirely of the most durable fired or burnt brick. The vast size of the 'citadel' and the many excavated buildings present a considerable challenge to the specialists involved in conserving Mohenjo-daro's visible remains.

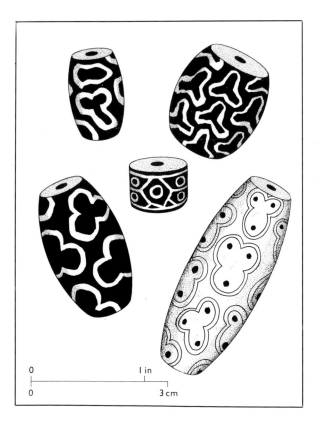

attached to traded commodities. Yet our knowledge of the wealth of the material goods must be tempered by the recognition that many perishable goods, such as textiles, have not survived.

Trade within and outside the Indus empire must have been considerable. Just a few tantalizing hints of the commercial connections between the contemporary cities of Mesopotamia and the Indus have been uncovered. A handful of beads and seals of Indus type found in Mesopotamia argue that the trade between the two was probably in less durable materials such as timber, cotton and spices. But the Mesopotamian evidence is reinforced by deciphered inscriptions, which show that merchants from Ur carried on a trade with various countries, including 'Dilmun', 'Magan' and 'Meluhha'. The first has been convincingly identified as Bahrain, and the last probably refers to the Indus plain or to Mohenjo-daro itself; the whereabouts of Magan remains unknown.

The gods of the Indus are almost as elusive as the traders. Buildings which may have been temples and stone sculptures, probably cult icons, have been located at Mohenjo-daro. In addition there are a great number of female terracotta figurines which seem to be representations of a

great mother goddess. Some people have claimed a
tenuous link between the deities of the Indus
civilization and those of later Hinduism, although
the cultural process which would have allowed
such a connection has never been explicitly
documented. One of the most characteristic
depictions of an Indus god is to be found on a series
of seals from the Indus cities. The seals show a
seated figure in Yogic position with an erect penis,
flanked by wild goats and wearing a buffalo-horned
headdress. The stone seals also illustrate a variety
of composite or half-human animals, which again
seem to be distant ancestors of the figures from
later Indian religion. Furthermore, it may be that
water played a special role in the consciousness of
the people. Did the water in the Great Bath
symbolize the sacred Indus, much as the Ganges
became a material representation of the goddess
Ganga in later Hinduism? At Kalibangan a further
religious element was uncovered when a well and
ritual pits containing ashes or animal bones were
taken to be evidence for religious practices
involving animal sacrifice, ritual ablution and fire
worship.

In the centuries before 2000 BC, therefore, an
extensive and elaborate society had emerged on the
plains of the Indus. Certainly it appears that a
strong central government, sacral in character, was
the most significant unifying force in the Indus
civilization. We cannot rule out the possibility of a
state-wide religion which dominated regional
religious traditions but allowed them to continue.
Such a strong, central government could not
prevent the decline of the Indus civilization,
however. The agricultural base of Indus society
was founded on the fertility of the river. While the
Nile, the Euphrates and the Tigris were more
successfully constrained, the Indus and its
tributaries could become wandering and
malevolent spirits over a broad, flat plain. Some
time after 2000 BC the Indus civilization collapsed.
Its cities were either abandoned, as at Mohenjo-
daro, or rapidly shrank in size. The reasons for such
a catastrophe are still unclear. Some have suggested
that tectonic upheavals down-river from Mohenjo-
daro resulted in extensive flooding of the site and
its territory; others have argued that the river, also
subject to periodic changes of its bed, chose a new
channel much further away from the site; and
others see the decline in terms of over-exploitation
of the environment through excessive felling of
trees. The debate as to why the cities of Egypt and
Mesopotamia endured, while those of the Indus
disappeared, will continue.

In the shadows and the
stillness of this lane in the
lower city it is not
difficult to imagine the
appearance of one of the
world's oldest and most
monumental cities some
4,000 years ago. The
regularity of the
brickwork course is still a
testimony to the skill of
the builders of Mohenjo-
daro.

2000
BC

The Americas

EL PARAISO, PERU

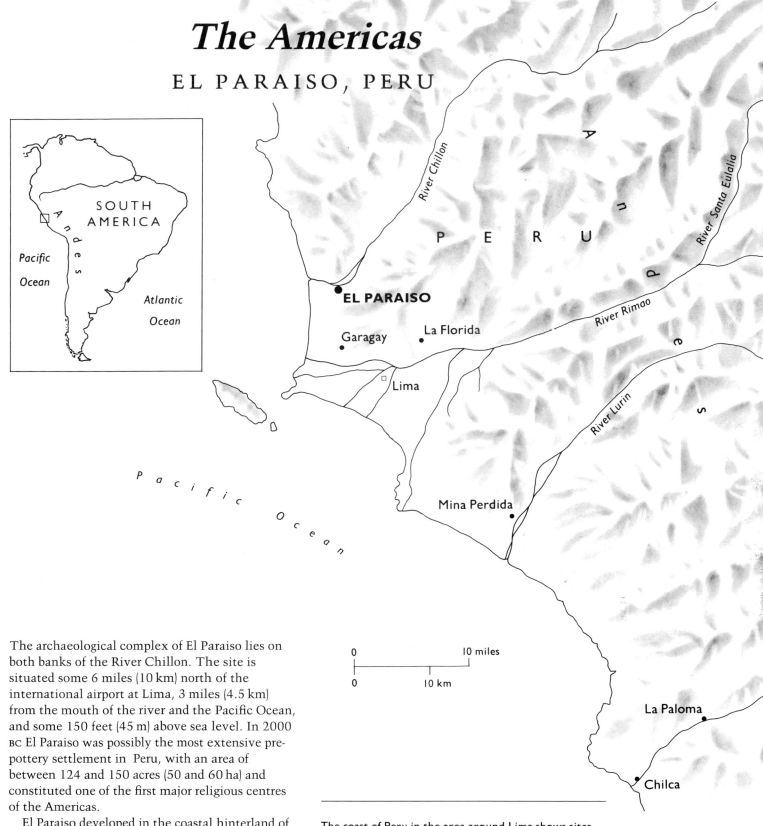

The archaeological complex of El Paraiso lies on both banks of the River Chillon. The site is situated some 6 miles (10 km) north of the international airport at Lima, 3 miles (4.5 km) from the mouth of the river and the Pacific Ocean, and some 150 feet (45 m) above sea level. In 2000 BC El Paraiso was possibly the most extensive pre-pottery settlement in Peru, with an area of between 124 and 150 acres (50 and 60 ha) and constituted one of the first major religious centres of the Americas.

El Paraiso developed in the coastal hinterland of Peru, which consists of a desert that is often fog-covered in the winter months and periodically crossed by rivers flowing down the west slopes of the Andes on their way to the ocean. It was in the river valleys near the coast that many of Peru's impressive prehistoric societies began to

The coast of Peru in the area around Lima shows sites that co-existed with El Paraiso. A large number of rivers flow down from the foothills into the Pacific, providing ideal sites for the early Andean civilization. River valleys flowing through desiccated regions often provided the geographical springboards for the development of complex societies. The Nile, Indus, and the Tigris and Euphrates are famous examples.

2000 BC

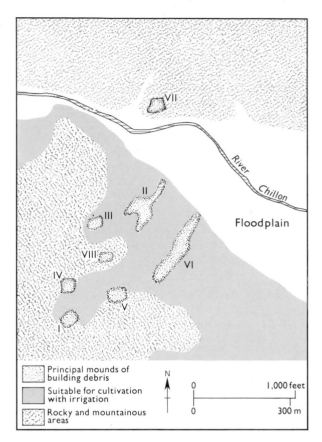

The remains of El Paraiso consist of eight mounds of
stone building debris; all but one are on the edge of the
high ground on the south side of the River Chillon.

experiment with irrigation agriculture, forming
larger centres of population and ultimately
constructing public buildings as well as private
houses. The coastal location also offered other
significant benefits to early communities.
Centrifugal winds radiate from the South Pacific
high-pressure zone situated near Easter Island.
Warm surface water is driven towards South
America, where it is forced to turn west, and near
the Peruvian coast it tends to veer away from the
shore, to be replaced by a deep, cold-water current.
The upwelling of cold coastal waters prevents
nutrients from sinking slowly to the ocean floor.
Birds, sea mammals and the whole marine
ecosystem is thus multiplied and the Peruvian
inshore waters teem with life. From the beginning
marine resources would have formed a crucial
element in the diet of coastal settlers.

The physical remains of El Paraiso consist of
eight mounds of stone building debris. Seven of
these are spread out along the lower edges of a
small valley on the south side of the Chillon; the
eighth is built on a terrace on the north bank. It is
likely that in 2000 BC more mounds existed. Not
all of the mounds are of the same size; two of them
(II and VI) are over 660 feet (200 m) in length and
seem to border a flattish area which opens out to
the river. Most are of similar proportions to mound
I, which has been excavated and subsequently
restored. Before excavation it took the form of a

A view of the reconstructed site at mound I, looking towards the River Chillon. There is an abrupt change between
the green of the irrigated fields and the harshness of unwatered, bare areas closer to the complex.

2000
BC

Staircases on the north-east side of mound I gave access to the rooms on top of the terraces. The stone steps were originally rounded and smeared with a covering of clay plaster.

square mass of rubble masonry measuring 165 by 165 feet (50 by 50 m), surviving to a height of 26 feet (8 m). Removal of the fallen rubble and subsequent restoration suggested that around 2000 BC this mound comprised a series of more than twenty interconnected rectangular rooms, laid out on top of a platform of terraces varying from two to four. The rooms were reached by stone stairs, the most monumental flight, and doubtless the front of the complex, being on the north-eastern side. This final form of the structure was evidently the culmination of a long process of construction, modification and redevelopment, incorporating five or even six phases. Earlier buildings had been partially levelled and filled with rubble to act as a foundation platform for the next phase of reconstruction. It seems likely that the rectangular building which projects from the north-western edge of the later monument belongs to one of the earlier phases.

It was in the third phase that the complex took on its present square shape and height. Clay floors were laid in rooms, now some 8 feet (2.5 m) above

the floor of the valley, and two fine staircases, with rounded stone steps smeared with clay plaster, gave access to the rooms on the north-eastern side. In the fourth phase important modifications were undertaken. Rooms were partly demolished and filled with earth and rubble, carried in baskets made of cane. These were thrown down intact with their contents and found sealed beneath the clay floors of the rooms from the fourth phase. Additional, narrower staircases were provided on the north-west and south-east perimeters. The staircases on the north-eastern side were rebuilt directly over their predecessors, with greater width being given to the westernmost of the two. The significance of this change was that the wider stairs led up to the religious heart of the building, the room where the first gods of the people of El Paraiso were worshipped. The names and powers of these gods, of course, will remain a mystery for ever since the community at El Paraiso was not literate; silent

Plan of part of the excavated and reconstructed complex of mound I, showing the 'temple' which is surrounded by terraces. With so few artefacts found it is impossible to decide whether this was a religious site or a residence, but it is known that the rectangular basin was the centre of a sacred area used for fire rituals.

Terraces

Terraces

Terraces

Rectangular basin

Smaller staircase

Stone stairs

0   60 feet

0   20 m

archaeological remains are therefore the only clues to their beliefs. The room contained a central rectangular basin, partly discoloured through the action of heat, surrounded by four pits, one at each corner, containing quantities of charcoal, indicating the presence of fires.

On the highest terrace, on the north-western edge of the monument, another obvious ritual room was discovered. This was much smaller, hollowed out of the rubble of the terrace, and was roofed by willow trunks. In it was a small female statuette of clay, painted red and wrapped in cotton. An offering of food had been placed in a calabash by her side, along with a basket containing a few blocks of limestone.

The various phases of the temple at El Paraiso were constructed largely of medium-sized blocks of sedimentary stone, bonded together in walls by a clay or mud mortar. Walls were formed of two vertical faces with a core of earth and rubble, blocks of which could exceed 7 feet (2 m) in length. A vast quantity of stone was thus quarried and transported to the site, either on matting or in cane

baskets. The priests of El Paraiso must have been able to command a sizeable workforce for this undertaking, and it is possible that the containers used represented measures in the unit of work assigned to each individual during the enterprise. In its final phases, the edifice achieved a considerable height and, since the walls were held together with mud, the builders must have encountered and overcome problems of stability. Crude solutions were adopted, such as the laying of a second, contiguous parallel wall to buttress the first wall, making a combined thickness of 8 feet (2.5 m) for these double walls. A rough plaster was applied to some of the walls, and painted using red and white pigments. In certain cases the varying thickness of the plaster was employed to correct the sloping faces of the stone walls and make them appear more vertical. Occasionally graffiti were scratched on to the plaster, and two examples seem to portray the sun and a group of vultures. In its final secular phase, when the rooms of the temple had been divided up into smaller houses, sun-baked mud bricks were utilized for repairs and in the

---

This rectangular basin, with a pit at each of its corners, was most likely the ritual focus of mound I. Charcoal found in the pits and discoloured stone from the basin suggest that fire played an important part in whatever ceremonies took place in this room.

2000
BC

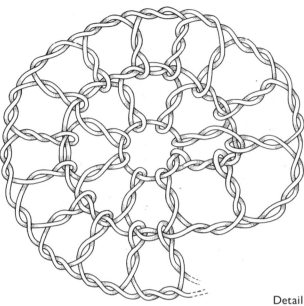

Detail of the construction of a basket made from rushes, preserved in the dry desert-like conditions that enveloped El Paraiso when it was abandoned shortly after this period.

The walls were constructed of medium-sized blocks of sedimentary stone, bonded together by clay or a mud mortar. Vertical rectangular holes (of unknown function) were built in the thicknesses of some of the walls.

2000 BC

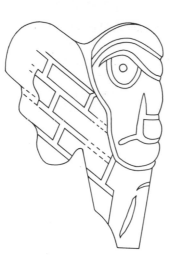

The bone pommel of a dagger or knife, decorated with an incised human face. The height of the pommel is 3 inches (8 cm).

The rooms of mound I at El Paraiso were laid out on top of three terraces. Barren hills to the south of the site limited the amount of land that could be cultivated.

construction of new walls which partitioned some of the larger rooms. In all its phases much uncertainty concerns the nature of the roofs. What is clear, however, is the enormous amount of stone, and therefore public endeavour, that went into the building of this temple at El Paraiso. The archaeologist who excavated the site calculated that approximately twenty blocks of stone were laid for every square foot, making a total of 20,000 blocks for a large room, and some 300,000 for the complete monument. The first gods and priests of El Paraiso must have possessed considerable powers, both sacred and secular.

But those powers did not last indefinitely. Ashes and charcoal on the steps of the final phase of the structure at mound I provided a radiocarbon date of around 1900 BC, suggesting that the complex did not survive much longer than that time. Some burials were found, presumably of the last inhabitants. Two were located in the rubble and two in kidney-shaped pits dug in front of the main north-east wall. One burial was found in an adjacent quarry. The body had been wrapped in cotton and then enveloped in a cane mat; a basket served as the last hat of the deceased. When the end of the complex at mound I came, it came suddenly. Possibly a major geological catastrophe,

2000
BC

such as an earthquake, was to some extent responsible. The highest parts of all the walls fell, scattering debris inside the rooms and on top of the staircases. Fine soil blown from the valley sides quickly began to cover both walls and rubble, and plants eventually took root in the newly laid sediments. But the abandonment was not restricted to mound I. All of the structures comprising El Paraiso were deserted seemingly at the same time. Given that the inhabitants were cultivating beans in the flat area between mounds II and VI, it is possible that the Chillon changed course, destroying the crop and precipitating famine conditions. In recent years the volume of water in the river, entirely dependent on the duration and amount of rainfall in the Andes, has fluctuated between 53 cubic feet (1.5 cubic m) per second and an alarming 4,240 cubic feet (120 cubic m) per second. The river was the lifeblood of the people of El Paraiso. They depended on it and prayed for its predictable and regular supply. Too much or too little threatened the livelihoods of the farmers, fishermen and hunters of El Paraiso and meant that their prayers had not been answered.

The overall interpretation of the site is fraught with problems, since only mound I has been excavated. That particular complex appears to have been a temple for much of its life, and perhaps the remaining square mounds of rubble may conceal religious centres. The two elongated mounds (II and VI), however, being a completely different shape, could, in contrast, contain the houses of the residents. The excavator of mound I calculated that about 1,500 people may have lived at El Paraiso. Assuming a double harvest of beans every year and an intake of 4 oz (100 gr) per person per day, he suggested that some 200 acres (80 ha) of cultivable land would be required to feed the populace. It is interesting to note that some 222 acres (90 ha) of land lie in the flat space between the two elongated mounds, and that these fields could be cultivated without irrigation solely by the annual flood of the Chillon. Such neat calculations, however, can be complicated by other unknown factors. It is possible that the rulers of El Paraiso controlled other adjacent territories and may have received tribute food from them. Alternatively, the construction of a simple dam and canal up-river from El Paraiso would have led water to the site at a level 17 feet (5 m) above the present bed of the Chillon, allowing a further 370 acres (150 ha) to be cultivated. What is not in doubt is that the rulers of El Paraiso were able to coerce or persuade a great number of people to build some of the earliest communal architecture in the Americas. It is inherently likely that such collective enterprises were undertaken and completed by religious

persuasion, where a small class of priest-rulers had managed to formalize their relationship as mediators between the fears and aspirations of the populace and the powers of the gods. The sacred leaders also became the repositories of religious and technical information that was essential for the well-being of the entire community.

Examination of earlier and contemporary settlements in coastal Peru suggests that in the centuries preceding 2000 BC population pressure and increases in social differentiation were giving rise to differences in the form and layout of buildings. At La Paloma, south of Lima, simple circular or oval conical houses were constructed, with bundles of matting or cane attached to a framework of willow and acacia to form the walls. Nearby, at Chilca, rectangular houses with more-developed plans were erected, while at the adjacent site of Asia to the south a rectangular structure, measuring 40 by 41 feet (12 by 12.5 m), and made up of rooms and passages, was excavated. Then again at Aspero, north of Lima, ritual mounds supporting structures formed by interconnecting rectangular rooms were being constructed as early as 2600 BC.

After 2000 BC significant technical developments took place in irrigation, the production of pottery and the widespread cultivation of maize. More formally planned religious centres appeared in the area around El Paraiso and their overall shape of a U-pattern can be traced back to El Paraiso. The U-plan of such sites as La Florida, Garagay and Mina Perdida now comprised a central mound or pyramid with projecting lateral wings. All of the complexes opened towards a source of water, and their orientation, between north and east, correlated with the course of an adjacent river. These new religious centres all lay on cultivable land which could be easily irrigated by inundation or by digging canals.

CONCLUSION

At all of the sites discussed in *Chapter I* there is considerable evidence for the importance of ritual and religion. This is nowhere more obvious than at Stonehenge, where, of course, the monument itself was entirely connected with the ceremonies of a populace which did not live in the immediate area around the stones. Indeed, there is plenty of evidence to suggest that Stonehenge stood at the centre of a sacred landscape and that settlements were not allowed in its immediate environs. The other four sites are different in that they did function as settlements, although key areas of those settlements were allocated for the construction of monumental religious buildings. The division between Stonehenge and the others is also underlined by the locations of each of the sites. All except Stonehenge were next to major rivers, and all the rivers shared the characteristic of periodically overflowing their banks and depositing fertile alluvium over fields. These were the situations that encouraged a large number of farmers to congregate in one place and provided the social opportunities for élite classes within society to emerge. This in turn led to the development of early states.

The five sites can, however, be divided according to other criteria. Stonehenge and El Paraiso were probably constructed by societies which existed at the chiefdom level. As we have seen, the chiefs who presided over such societies were able to manipulate the agricultural productivity of their people by encouraging some to produce a surplus. The surplus was then collected and used to feed a workforce that constructed large-scale public monuments, or was redistributed to the people at times of need or during periodic ceremonies. By such a redistribution chiefs were seen 'to feed the people' and so were valued because of their largesse. Often in these societies the only reason for accumulating wealth was that when necessary it could be given away again in the form of goods and food. If this redistribution was performed at large public gatherings, then the donors naturally earned considerable respect and prestige as a result of their actions. Ur, Thebes and Mohenjo-daro, on the other hand, were the products of a

different level of society. They were highly organized states, possessing such classic features as a written script, a class of bureaucrats, armies, a range of specialists and extensive trade contacts. Citizens of all three states had the use of bronze tools, whereas for the builders of Stonehenge bronze must have been a rare and exotic material in 2000 BC. For the farmers at El Paraiso metals and even pottery seem to have been unknown.

The first gods of these peoples governed most aspects of their daily lives. For the communities who worshipped at Stonehenge, the alignments contained in the setting of the stones strongly suggest that at least one of the gods must have been the sun itself. We have seen how important it was for agricultural peoples to try and understand the mechanism behind the movements of the sun, the heavenly body that was critical to the success of their annual harvests. It was reassuring for them to believe that the regular rising and setting of the sun could be controlled by priests and leaders at Stonehenge, and that as long as they provided the necessary food and goods to support these officials, then the cyclical regularity of their existence could be maintained. It is perfectly possible, however – and this applies to many societies at all levels of development – that household gods or spirits, worshipped within the confines of the home, were quite different in character from the gods honoured in public.

We are unlikely to know the names or nature of the gods worshipped either in the homes or on the temple mounds at El Paraiso, but the labour involved in the construction of the mounds and their considerable number suggest that the gods were very important for the people, and the ritual use of fire on the excavated mound implies that fire was a key element in religious ceremonies.

We are better informed about the Sumerians of ancient Ur. Although they believed in a pantheon of gods who were honoured throughout the empire, every city had its patron deity, which at Ur was the moon god Nanna. The citizens of Ur regarded Nanna as the real ruler of their lives, while the king and his ministers were merely his mortal representatives on earth. The summit of the ziggurat was a fitting place for the house of Nanna, emphasizing the god's separation from the merely

2000
BC

mortal populace. Astronomical knowledge played a significant role in the religion of Ur. Some of the heavenly bodies were personified as gods and goddesses, while such knowledge was used in establishing the correct orientation for the ziggurat itself. State religion seems to have been of fundamental importance for the functioning of the Sumerian economy. The priests and bureaucrats in the temples encouraged the production of surpluses, ostensibly so that the storehouses of the gods should always be full.

A sophisticated temple economy was also the mainstay of the ancient Egyptians. The pharaohs were considered to be the sons of a divinity, and temples throughout Egypt acted as huge storehouses managed by a hereditary priesthood on behalf of the ruling pharaoh.

At Mohenjo-daro the situation is altogether less clear, not least because the Indus script has so far resisted attempts to decipher it. There are hints of temples, stone icons and representations of goddesses in terracotta figurines. The Indus civilization may well have been largely supported by a temple economy, but convincing evidence for this has yet to be unearthed.

One further point of comparison can be drawn between the sites. The first gods from three of the locations, El Paraiso, Ur and Thebes, were housed in temple-pyramids. The pyramid form was developed independently and used at different times in distinct regions of the world for religious buildings. These areas were widely scattered and included Mesopotamia, Egypt, Peru and Central America. True pyramids, with four smooth sides culminating in a point, were restricted to Egypt, where the form replaced stepped pyramids around 2600 BC. They were closed structures which housed the bodies of the god-kings, while those of Central America, Peru and Mesopotamia were built to serve as raised temple platforms for the gods. In Mesopotamia and in the Americas the pyramid was of the stepped form. Some of the earliest temple mounds were constructed at Aspero in Peru around 2600 BC. At Aspero there are at least eight recognizable mounds, with six smaller mound-like structures. The mounds were formed of conjoined rooms eventually filled in to form a raised platform for another phase of multi-roomed construction – a situation that has some constructional similarities

with the mounds at El Paraiso. Pyramids and temple-pyramids were clearly independently invented in response to common ritual and symbolic needs. The tapering shape of a pyramid lent itself to structural stability while enhancing the impression of height. Height had a symbolic significance, distancing the gods from the mortals below. The very monumentality of these edifices emphasized the power of the religious establishment, the ruling élite and the first gods themselves.

Not even the first gods, however, could preserve their faithful followers from destruction. By 1000 BC Stonehenge, El Paraiso and Mohenjo-daro had long been abandoned, while the third dynasty rulers of Ur and the XIth dynasty of Egyptian pharaohs were the stuff of history. In the next chapter we will appreciate how some communities in Europe and the Middle East increasingly sought refuge in the force of arms, as the weapons deposited at Flag Fen and the fortified town of Megiddo demonstrate. Elsewhere in the world the natural environment still fed and clothed the hunters and gatherers at Kalemba and Roonka, illustrating that the pace of change was anything but constant. The first gods were still capable of surprising manifestations, however. Poverty Point, christened by some as an American Stonehenge, is the exception that proves the rule. Hunters and gatherers there apparently favoured gods associated with particular alignments marked out with mounds.

2000
BC

CHAPTER 2

WAYS OF LIFE

1000 BC

EUROPE
Flag Fen, England

WESTERN ASIA
Megiddo, Israel

AFRICA
Kalemba, Zambia

EASTERN ASIA AND OCEANIA
Roonka Flat, Australia

THE AMERICAS
Poverty Point, USA

1000
BC

INTRODUCTION

The central focus of this chapter is an examination of the economic, political and social contexts – the 'Ways of Life' – of five different communities around 1000 BC. Given the great longevity of human hunting and gathering, it seemed justifiable to include three sites occupied by such peoples: Kalemba, Roonka Flat and Poverty Point. They provide fascinating insights into three hunting and gathering societies which reached quite varying levels of social and cultural complexity, culminating in the scarcely credible earthworks and alignments of Poverty Point. Flag Fen offers us a glimpse of a society ruled by a chief or chiefs, some of whom probably exercised sacred as well as secular duties, and who were capable of mobilizing large numbers of people and ordering the effective destruction of valuable metal artefacts. Megiddo was included to contrast all four other sites with an urban way of life, and to provide a historical cross-reference to the Bible.

Even a cursory appreciation of the information from Kalemba, Roonka Flat and Poverty Point indicates that only the hunters of Kalemba might have been described as egalitarian. The occupants of the camp at Roonka Flat were divided by adherences to different totems and seemingly also by status and wealth, while the hunters at Poverty Point were part of one of the most highly developed hunting and gathering groups yet documented. The inhabitants of Megiddo, and to a lesser extent Flag Fen, demonstrate the increasing trend in Europe and the Middle East towards more militaristic societies.

So, three of the locations described here – Kalemba, Roonka Flat and Poverty Point – were inhabited in 1000 BC by groups of people who obtained their daily food through a mixture of hunting wild animals and gathering wild plants, nuts and berries. At two of them – Roonka Flat and Poverty Point – their diet was probably supplemented by fishing. In all three the notion of an agricultural economy, based on raising tame animals and sowing and harvesting crops, was probably unknown and certainly not practised. Hunting and gathering as a life style had been followed throughout the world for tens of thousands of years and in 1000 BC was still pursued in most of the Americas, in the greater part of Africa south of the Sahara and in Australia.

Anthropologists who have studied contemporary hunters and gatherers, who survive in isolated corners of the world, emphasize some key characteristics of their societies. Often groups tend to be small, comprising four or five families, and they lead a mobile existence, moving from camp to camp on a seasonal basis, taking advantage of whatever plants, animals or fish flourish or frequent that particular spot at that time of year. The hours spent in obtaining food are not excessive and clearly number less than the hours worked by peasant farmers. Detailed analysis of the contribution made by each sex suggests that gathering performed by women contributes far more to calorific intake than the occasionally successful hunts of the men. Sharing of food equally among group members is fairly common, as is also the absence of elaborate storage devices to conserve food for the future. Such egalitarian societies usually have no well-defined authority structures and decisions to move camp, for instance, tend to be taken by consensus.

A typical example of a contemporary hunting and gathering society is that represented by the !Kung of southern Africa, who live in the border region between north-west Botswana and Namibia, in the Kalahari desert. On average an adult !Kung spends between 2.2 and 2.4 days per week on subsistence activities. Men do most of the hunting and women most of the gathering, and although the men work up to a third longer, they manage to provide only some 30 per cent of the food requirements of the band. Men make most of the tools, although women are responsible for constructing the temporary shelters and for the majority of housework. Arrogance and authority are considered extremely anti-social among the !Kung and there is a positive assertion of the equality of all band members. Men have a greater role in decision-making than women. Adultery and conflicts between husband and wife are the most common causes of dispute and, in the absence of any external authority to encourage reconciliation, can easily lead to violence or a splitting of the camp to resolve a dispute.

The Tiwi hunters on the Melville and Bathurst

*Islands, off the northern coast of Australia,
illustrate a more complex hunter-gatherer society.
The same sexual division of labour is present, with
men hunting and women gathering, and the latter
provide most of the food. With respect to domestic
and manufacturing skills, women do the
housework and prepare the more utilitarian goods,
while men make ceremonial spears, canoes and
decorative graveposts, which are indicators of
wealth, status and prestige. Unlike the !Kung, the
Tiwi have a recognized authority structure, which
is focused on the two or three 'big men' who are
judged by public opinion to be the most admired
and influential in each band. In their polygamous
society such positions are obtained by an
accumulation of gathered foods and goods made
possible by a large number of wives, freeing the
head of the house so that he can make ceremonial
items and participate in public affairs. Control over
women is therefore one of the principal areas of
authority exercised by Tiwi males. Disputes are
resolved through a formal spear-throwing fight,
which is usually terminated when one of the
combatants suffers a surface wound. When reading
about the hunters at Kalemba, Roonka Flat and
Poverty Point, it will be instructive to see what
archaeological indicators there are concerning
social structure and whether the kind of society
hinted at fits the !Kung or the Tiwi model.*

*In 1000 BC in most of Europe, the Middle East
and large parts of Asia hunting and gathering as a
way of life had long since disappeared. At Flag Fen
in southern Britain, still a long time before
recorded history, late prehistoric farmers
constructed an extraordinary timber platform out
in the waterlogged fens. Excavations are currently
unravelling the unique story of a site that promises
to overturn our present conceptions of Late Bronze
Age Britain. Meanwhile, in the Middle East the year
1000 BC places us firmly on the historical ladder
with one of its most celebrated sites, Megiddo,
occupied by one of its most controversial leaders,
King David.*

1000
BC

Europe

FLAG FEN, ENGLAND

The Fens of East Anglia form Britain's lowest lying area. This vast water-logged countryside provided safety from invasion and ideal hunting grounds for the tribes that occupied the area.

Inset: Reconstructing buildings from the tangle of waterlogged timber uprights means assessing the characteristics of each timber. Here the excavators have marked with orange tape the principal wall posts.

The twin towers of Peterborough Cathedral in eastern England look out across a flat and peat-filled lowland basin that stretches without a break until it reaches the shores of the North Sea. Water is never far away in this landscape of expansive horizons and can be glimpsed or heard in the hundreds of channels and drainage dykes that lower the water table and make farming possible. It seems at first a harsh environment, the very flatness of the land offering no sheltering contour to facilitate escape from the bitter east winds. But those who live there come to love it, learning to appreciate the subtle variations of its skies and the vast openness of its landscape in a way that is quite beyond the visitor accustomed to more uneven terrain. This land is called the Fens, England's largest wetland, and around 1000 BC – long before the construction of Peterborough Cathedral – prehistoric inhabitants were

frequenting a remarkable timber platform built a little way out into the waterlogged Fens. They too must have appreciated the Fen country, for in building their platform they probably had to fell, shape, transport and position over 1 million timbers. It was an extraordinary undertaking, directed by individuals who could persuade or coerce a large labour force to help them construct the platform. The identity of these individuals, precisely why they chose such an unlikely place for their buildings and, indeed, what activities they undertook there are questions that leave us with all the makings of a first-rate archaeological mystery.

The construction of Flag Fen took place during a time of deteriorating climate. How quickly this climatic change happened is a matter of debate. Certainly some events were sudden. The eruption of Mount Hekla on Iceland occurred in about 1150 BC and released an estimated 9 cubic miles

(37.5 cubic km) of volcanic dust into the atmosphere, reducing sunlight and stunting the growth of plants and trees over large areas of the northern hemisphere. Other climatic effects followed more slowly but no less catastrophically: a decrease in average annual temperature by about 4°F (2°C), increased precipitation and stronger winds. Such widespread changes ushered in a prehistoric Dark Age to the British Isles. Upland farms and fields were deserted and the depth and extent of waterlogging in the Fens increased, pushing human settlements up on to more elevated ground. The greater number of bronze weapons from this period demonstrates that this was a time of inter-community friction. Tribes and chiefdoms may well have been increasingly dominated by bands of warlords and warriors, anxious to defend their loved ones and impress their potential adversaries.

It was one such group that ordered the construction of the wooden platform at Flag Fen. Large timbers were thrown down on to organic mud as a foundation. The site was carefully located at a point where the shallow water was at its narrowest, between higher ground to the west on the edge of the Fen and the slight elevation now known as the 'island' of Northey to the east. In 1000 BC the platform was probably surrounded by shallow water in the winter, perhaps drying out to

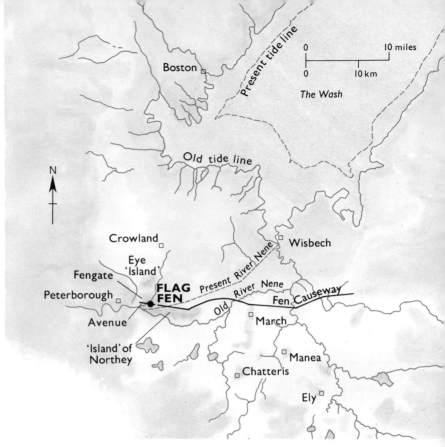

Flag Fen and 'upland' areas, such as March and Chatteris, which existed as islands prior to drainage in the seventeenth century AD. The Fen causeway is a Roman road constructed around AD 60.

The level of land in the Fens has risen and fallen dramatically since 1000 BC. Wetter conditions and subsequent flooding after 1000 BC saw a considerable rise; in this century drainage has caused a massive fall.

reveal muddy ground during exceptionally good summers. Around the edge of the Fen grew one or two alder trees and a few bushes that would tolerate wet conditions, but there would also have been large expanses of water, reed and even rank grass and sedge beds. On the fringes of the dry land grew stands of willow, poplar, ash and alder, many of which were coppiced or pollarded to produce suitable lengths of timber for woodworking. Behind the screen of trees was an open landscape of flood-free gravel lands, where cattle grazed in small, square fields.

The platform itself appears to cover an area of about 2½ acres (1 ha) and was formed by placing a lattice of horizontal timbers, trunks and branches

the foundation layers. The vertical timbers have sharpened points which have been driven about 1 foot 6 inches (50 cm) into the underlying mud.

But what did this building look like in 1000 BC? The recognition of mortise and tenon joints surviving on some of the oak timbers allows a tentative reconstruction. The outermost rows of posts seem to have risen about 1 foot 6 inches (50 cm) above the ground and probably supported the low eaves of the structure, which was aligned E–W. The innermost rows of posts were the principal load-bearing timbers for the roof and were staggered in their positions with respect to the eaves supports, their alternate spacing ensuring that a wall post occurred between every two eaves posts. The vertical timbers carried tenons, and horizontal timbers with mortises tied the tops of uprights together. Rafters, alternately resting on the tops of wall posts or eaves posts, were arranged to support a ridged roof, which was presumably thatched. The infilling of the walls consisted of longitudinal and horizontal roundwood laths, pegged into place between the main wall posts. It is possible that the laths were then treated with a coating of daub.

Whoever stepped inside the building was unlikely to lose their footing since the floor of the structure comprised numerous split oak planks covered with a deposit of white sand and fine gravel, no doubt laid down to prevent slipping on the wet timbers. In the north wall a doorway was

A scaffolding framework allows archaeologists to lie on modern wooden planks and reach down to the archaeological layers below.

directly on to the organic mud. Although its exact shape is unknown, it was probably surrounded by a boardwalk, constructed of horizontal planks and poles overlying timbers running at right angles below them. Excavations are ongoing and so far have concentrated in the area of the platform where a forest of upright timbers protrudes about 2 feet (60 cm) above several layers of horizontal wood and timber. Many of the vertical timbers, which are grouped into four parallel rows, are thought to be the eaves supports, wall and roof supports of a rectangular timber building approximately 20 to 21 feet 6 inches (6 to 6.5 m) wide and perhaps as long as 66 feet (20 m). The uppermost layer of horizontal timber is probably collapsed material from the building's roof and walls. Underneath the collapse lie one or two floors, while below these are

1000 BC

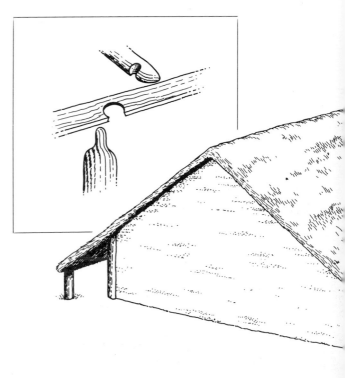

marked by a large threshold plank which lay transversely across the outer wall, and had been pegged into place at its sides. North of the structure was a yard with a surface of smaller timber and brushwood, perhaps divided by a fence that ran away from the building at right angles, and there was another yard to the south of the building. A door in its south wall was marked by a post with a short dowel-like protrusion that might have been a door pivot.

The initial seasons of excavation produced a small collection of finds from the floor of the structure. About 300 sherds of pottery were recovered, mostly from straight-sided or barrel-shaped jars, along with a few flints and some butchered animal bones. Putting the structure and finds together suggested that the building might have been a house. However, as is often the case, further excavation produced more questions than answers and the interpretation appeared less straightforward. More prestigious artefacts, such as a bronze dagger, a pin and fragments of broken shale bracelets were found. In addition the excavators were astounded when the complete skull of an ox was uncovered, placed within the timbers in what seemed to be a deliberate fashion. This could indicate no more than an elaborate ritual foundation deposit for the house, but it raised doubts all the same. Not far from the ox skull was a complete fine pottery jar, again carefully positioned underneath a large alder log.

Examination of the pottery fragments from earlier excavations showed that most could be reassembled to form near-complete pots, while the forest of vertical timbers seemed just too dense a forest to be accounted for by one rectangular building.

It was during this period of re-evaluation that the archaeologists made their most spectacular discovery. West of the platform two parallel rows of oak posts, forming an alignment some 33 to 40 feet (10 to 12 m) in width, were uncovered approaching Flag Fen. The tops of over 700 posts were recorded, stretching for a distance of over 330 feet (100 m). It seems entirely likely that this Avenue ran from the dry land across the shallow water to the platform

The builders of Flag Fen were experienced carpenters. An interpretive facility displayed at the Visitors' Centre shows how wooden planks were split by hammering in timber wedges.

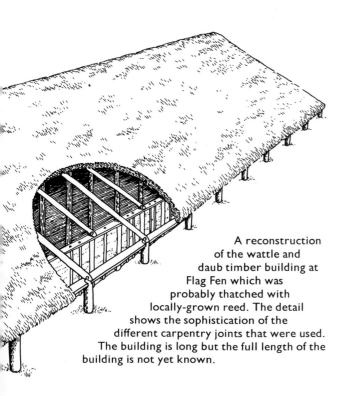

A reconstruction of the wattle and daub timber building at Flag Fen which was probably thatched with locally-grown reed. The detail shows the sophistication of the different carpentry joints that were used. The building is long but the full length of the building is not yet known.

and may even have continued across the site and on to the 'island' of Northey. If so, the total number of posts in the Avenue may have been as high as 2,000. Around some of them were scattered horizontal timbers, at least one of which had been pegged into the ground with a short peg driven through a mortise hole. The discovery of some physical connection between Flag Fen and dry land could have been, and was, anticipated. What came as a shock was the realization that hundreds of high-quality bronze weapons and tools seem to have been deliberately thrown from the Avenue into the shallow Fen waters by prehistoric visitors or residents of the site.

As well as pottery and broken shale bracelets, over 250 pieces of metalwork were found, many of them broken and deliberately placed in the water.

1000 BC

An imaginative reconstruction by Robert Donaldson illustrates the waterlogged Avenue, with the main platform of Flag Fen in the background. A Late Bronze Age priest or chief prepares to throw part of a broken sword into the waters.

The chronological range of the finds stretches for over 1,000 years, from about 1300 BC to 200 BC, but most of the artefacts were deposited shortly after 1000 BC. The metalwork included many high-status items and is dominated by weapons, such as swords, rapiers, daggers and spears, and ornaments, such as pins. Other items consisted of fragments of a bronze helmet, numerous rings of various sizes and a finely fashioned shale or jet armlet with an inlaid decoration of white metal, probably tin. The distribution of the objects also provided interesting information. Most of the artefacts were concentrated to the south of the Avenue, with a greater number towards its western end and the junction with dry land. One further type of find deserves mention and provides an entirely new dimension to the site. To the north of the Avenue a human skeleton was located, while loose human bones were frequently observed scattered around the timber uprights. Clearly, as people approached or left the platform at Flag Fen they did so via the Avenue. Did they row across the shallow water in some kind of coracle? Or did they wade through the water, their feet placed on horizontal planking as long as they kept within the lines of uprights? At some point they stopped and began elaborate rituals that culminated in the placing or throwing of costly metalwork and occasional human bones into the water. The key to the function of Flag Fen may well lie in the explanation of these expensive practices. So why did they do it?

The practice of depositing fine metalwork in wet places, such as rivers and bogs, was increasingly common in western Europe around 1000 BC. That these depositions occurred during elaborate rituals is clear, since once deposited, the items could rarely be recovered. It seems that the discarding of metalwork in this way was somehow connected to the decline of elaborate formal burials, since the metal artefacts formerly placed with the dead were now being thrown into rivers and were no longer available as grave goods. Concern for the dead, therefore, may have been replaced by different preoccupations, perhaps associated with new forms of worship. It should be remembered that the period around 1000 BC was one of crisis and change. Two centuries of climatic change, coupled with environmental degradation by prehistoric farming practices which had felled woodland and led to soil erosion and waterlogging, had brought about considerable dislocations in settlements,

1000 BC

with retreats from both very high and very low ground. Cloudy, rain-laden skies resulting in sodden, peaty soils and rivers flowing uncontrollably at full spate induced a new reverence for the powers of water. In addition, more people were forced to live and farm in a much smaller area, leading inevitably to friction and greater significance for the warrior in society.

It is against this background that we can imagine an eastern England in 1000 BC divided among tribes and chiefdoms anxious to defend their own territories and prone to raiding their neighbours' when the opportunity arose. The positions of authority in each tribe were gained by successful warriors and also reserved for the religious leaders. The latter had the responsibility of controlling the gods of water through placatory offerings. Such offerings, comprising sometimes exquisite metalwork thrown into rivers and bogs, were designed to show the community's reverence for its particular water deity, and to ensure his or her continuing powers of intercession on the community's behalf. The warriors too may have played a role in such rituals, anxious to display their impressive quantity of armaments by deliberately destroying a percentage of them during these ceremonies.

To go back to Flag Fen, if this site was a settlement, it was clearly a special one. Although it would have been perfectly possible to take a boat and trap wildfowl or fish from the platform, crops and farm animals would have to grow and graze on the dry land to the west. So most of the food for the inhabitants would probably have been processed first and then brought to the platform by boat. Elsewhere in Britain at this time some people were beginning to construct hill-top fortifications, for defensive reasons but also for prestige and status. The absence of any hills in the Fens precluded this option, and it is possible to see Flag Fen, established away from dry land and set apart as it was, as perhaps inspired by the same desires. If Flag Fen can be interpreted as the approximate equivalent of an upland hillfort, then it may well be that the site was only seasonally occupied by individuals of certain status, such as chiefs, warriors, priests and craft workers.

The discovery which caused most excitement was the remains of the Avenue. Prestigious Late Bronze Age artefacts, such as these swords, daggers and spearheads, were thrown periodically into the water near the Avenue, presumably during important rituals.

1000 BC

A map of Palestine showing the position of a number of ancient sites. The first historical mention of Megiddo is in the fifteenth century BC, when it appears as a place name in the inscriptions of the Egyptian pharaoh Thutmose III. Thutmose turned Megiddo into a major Egyptian fortress.

1000 BC

When the Israelites arrived in Palestine, the town of Megiddo was assigned to the tribe of Manasseh, one of the twelve tribes of Israel. The Book of Joshua (17, 11) reports that: 'In Issachar and Asher, Manasseh had Beth-shean and its villages, and Ible-am and its villages, and the inhabitants of Dor and its villages, and the inhabitants of En-dor and its villages, and the inhabitants of Taanach and its villages, and the inhabitants of Megiddo and its villages.' In the decade before 1000 BC Megiddo was captured by David, and under Solomon it became one of the royal cities of the short-lived Israelite empire.

Megiddo lies on the south-west edge of the extensive plain of Esdraelon, which provides one of the very few easy cross-country routes from the

coastal plain of Palestine to the Jordan valley and the Sea of Galilee. Despite the problems of drainage caused by the evenness of the plain, it is crossed by the River Kishon, one of the few perennial streams of Palestine, and, given the fertile soil and the ample rainfall, was extremely productive agriculturally. The hilly hinterland of Megiddo probably supported vines and olives and provided grazing. Water for the inhabitants of Megiddo came from two springs, one on the northern slopes of the settlement mound or tell and the other in a cave on the south-west slopes, both outside the fortification walls of the various ancient settlements.

The pear-shaped mound of Megiddo measures about 1,040 feet (315 m) from east to west and 760 feet (230 m) from north to south. The summit, a

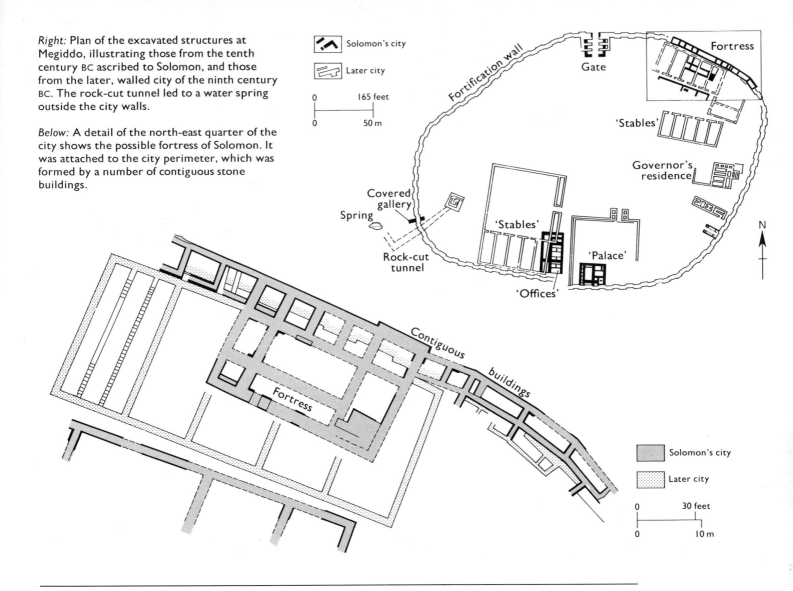

Right: Plan of the excavated structures at Megiddo, illustrating those from the tenth century BC ascribed to Solomon, and those from the later, walled city of the ninth century BC. The rock-cut tunnel led to a water spring outside the city walls.

Below: A detail of the north-east quarter of the city shows the possible fortress of Solomon. It was attached to the city perimeter, which was formed by a number of contiguous stone buildings.

Solomon's city

Later city

0   165 feet

0   50 m

Fortress
Gate
Fortification wall
'Stables'
Governor's residence
Covered gallery
Spring
Rock-cut tunnel
'Stables'
'Palace'
'Offices'
N

Contiguous buildings
Fortress

Solomon's city

Later city

0   30 feet

0   10 m

little under 12 acres (5 ha) in area, is highest in the south-eastern corner. Like many ancient tells, Megiddo was occupied by successive generations and peoples over a considerable period of time. The earliest settlement occurred around 5000 BC, when a small farming community became established on the hill, while its last major period of occupation was probably as a garrison town under Persian domination from the sixth to fourth centuries BC. Each generation and each new people at Megiddo added to the accumulation of building debris and artefacts at the site, demolishing earlier structures of mud brick and stone and replacing them with their own. Through such a process about 82 feet (25 m) of occupation deposits lie on top of the hill, and by carefully digging down through the mound and recording one layer after another, archaeologists have recovered some of the long history of the site.

The emergence of the Israelites as a military force in Palestine stemmed from the arrival of the Exodus contingent from Egypt, during the thirteenth century BC, and their gradual unification with other groups of a similar character who were either already resident in the area or had entered the land separately. At first the tribes of Israel were confined to the hill country, fearful of the chariot forces of the lowland cities of Canaan. They were also confronted by a new threat, the arrival of the 'Peoples of the Sea', among whom were an aggressive group known as the Philistines. It is the latter who might have been responsible for the destruction of Megiddo around 1150 BC and its subsequent reoccupation, which included a northern and southern city gate, a large palatial building in the northern part of the settlement and probably a protected water supply. Around 1100 BC the city was a flourishing Philistine outpost. Finds of silver earrings and pendants, bronze jugs, bowls and strainers and painted pottery indicate that

1000 BC

Megiddo enjoyed extensive trading contacts and had developed a highly skilled metal industry. The growing power of the Israelites, however, became more menacing during the subsequent century, and, shortly before 1000 BC, soldiers acting for King David stormed and burnt the city.

The city that the newcomers constructed was a pale reflection of its predecessor. In the southern part of the site several blocks of rectangular rooms possessing a common orientation were uncovered, but no clear street pattern came to light. The difficulties of revealing meaningful plans of David's city were greatly exacerbated as a result of the destruction of the first Israelite settlement by the foundations for the large, public buildings constructed subsequently by Solomon. Generally the stone foundations alone remained, with the mud bricks of the superstructure surviving only in a few places. Floors in David's city were either of beaten earth or of rubble. A small gate and an approach road from the north gave access to the settlement, which appears to have been undefended, or at least lacked a city wall. It is possible that houses on the perimeter of the mound formed a defensive ring, as was the case at some other early Israelite sites. The finds show that bronze was still the most widely used metal, although iron was increasingly employed for implements where sharpness was important, such as knives and arrowheads. There is no evidence to suggest that at this stage Megiddo occupied a position of political importance in the kingdom. Indeed, the Old Testament indicates that, despite some preliminary attempts at organizing the kingdom and the establishment of a court at Jerusalem, the essential tribal divisions of the people remained intact and the underlying major distinction between Israel in the north and Judah in the south was not overcome.

The eclipse of Megiddo's fortunes was only temporary, however. Under Solomon, who succeeded David around 970 BC, the city became

A general view of the pear-shaped mound of Megiddo from the east. The top 82 feet (25 m) of the mound were formed by the debris of successive eras: the position of Solomon's gate lies on the northern perimeter (mid-right).

1000
BC

one of the most important in a united Israel and was enriched with prestigious public buildings. The defences of the city remained as a row of continuous houses parallel to the edge of the tell, but the entrance in the north was strengthened with the construction of an impressive gateway. This was a rectangular structure 50 by 40 feet (15 by 12 m), massive in plan and built with some fine masonry. Two towers stood at the outer end of the entrance, with three matching chambers on each side of the roadway behind them. The roadway itself was some 14 feet (4.25 m) wide. Double doors closed off the entrance just inside the towers, while an outer gate was situated some 100 feet (30 m) down the slope. The space between the two gates was heavily defended, forming a kind of barbican. Other features of the gate complex included a stone drain that ran down the western side of the gate and a possibly subterranean stairway that led from just outside the outer gate to a spring north of the tell.

Inside the city a number of new buildings appeared. Close to the southern edge of the tell a rectangular structure measuring some 76 by 70 feet (23 by 21.5 m) was constructed. Only the foundation courses remained in place, but these showed that the walls were up to 5 feet (1.5 m) thick and capable of supporting a second storey. The layout of the building suggests that it is similar to the palace Solomon built in Jerusalem since it is possible to identify an entrance on the north side, an open court within the building and a throne or audience room. The palace itself stood within a large courtyard about 200 feet square (60 m sq.), which had a gatehouse in its north-east corner. West of the palace was a long rectangular building. The excavators found nothing to indicate its function, but its proximity to the palace suggests that it might have been offices for the administrators of Megiddo. Other contemporary buildings inside the city included a structure near the south-eastern perimeter and a possible fortress

The remains of the outer sections of Solomon's gate, through which passed a road into the settlement. Two towers stood guard at the outer end of this gateway, with three chambers on each side of the entrance passageway.

1000 BC

A detail from an ivory carving from Megiddo, dating to the period between 1400 and 1200 BC. The engraving, showing heavy Egyptian influence, depicts a ruler seated on a throne receiving a victory procession after battle.

that was linked to the chain of contiguous buildings which formed the defences of the city. Great care was taken during Solomon's reign to ensure adequate supplies of water for the inhabitants during potential sieges. To this end a covered gallery was constructed underneath the western defences of the city which led to the spring in the cave further down the slope. Between the public buildings lay some of the houses, shops and workshops of the populace. These were rectangular structures largely of mud brick, separated by rubble-paved streets. The majority of the citizens, however, may have dwelt on the slopes below the defences.

Solomon's rule, while creating the secure conditions necessary for a united Israel, had been an oppressive one, keenly felt by his subjects at Megiddo. On his death around 920 BC, the kingdom once again split into Israel in the north and Judah, with its capital at Jerusalem, in the south. An additional devastating blow was an Egyptian invasion under Sheshonq I, who stormed and took more than 150 towns in Palestine, including Megiddo. Fortunately for the Israelites, he was not able to follow up his advantage and re-establish an Egyptian empire in Palestine due to internal problems in Egypt. Megiddo's fortunes were again painstakingly rebuilt after these upheavals. In the ninth century BC the city enjoyed a renewed period of prosperity and security. A solid city wall was built for defence around the top of the slope. It was some 12 feet (3.6 m) thick and constructed of finely hewn stone, almost certainly taken from earlier monumental structures. The wall was unusual, being laid out in sections about 20 feet (6 m) long which were alternately offset, either forward or backward from each other, by about 18 inches (45 cm). This may have provided extra access for flanking fire along the recessed

sections of the wall face. Associated with the fortification wall was a slightly smaller city gate, incorporating two chambers on either side of the entrance passage. It was built on top of, and replaced, the gate of Solomon. In the eastern part of the city lay the governor's residence. This consisted of a large building set in its own courtyard. Its stone foundations supported a superstructure of at least two storeys, made from mud brick and cedar beams. The plan of the complex indicates that there was probably a tower at the north-east corner, from which extensive views over the plain of Esdraelon could be had. No doubt it was covered, like most of the buildings in Megiddo, with a flat, plastered roof.

Two of the largest complexes of buildings in ninth-century Megiddo were the so-called Southern Stables and Northern Stables. Both contained arrangements of long, narrow rooms, which were in turn divided into five units of three rooms each. Rows of stone pillars separated the central from the adjacent rooms on either side. The excavators conjectured that the central rooms formed aisles, allowing the stable staff to walk between rows of horses which were tethered and fed in mangers between the pillars. However, not everyone is satisfied with this explanation. Some archaeologists have argued that if these buildings were stables, horse trappings would have been found in the vicinity, but they have not. Others have said that there is little evidence for the use of stables for horses in the ancient Near East (the present-day Middle East), proposing instead that these complexes were probably barracks or storehouses. Yet others have taken the opposite view, arguing that there is a good deal of contemporary archaeological and textual evidence for stables, even saying that smaller stables did exist at Megiddo under Solomon. The matter is clearly far

1000 BC

from resolution and will no doubt be debated for some considerable time to come.

The most impressive feat of civil engineering at Megiddo concerned improvements to the water supply. In the south-west part of the city a vertical shaft was sunk and connected to a horizontal rock-cut tunnel that led underneath the city defences to the cave containing the spring at the foot of the mound. This huge undertaking allowed the inhabitants to draw water safely from outside the city during times of siege. As a finishing touch to this great project, a stone wall was built across the mouth of the cave. As a result, the spring was accessible only from within the city, thus preventing a besieging enemy from poisoning or otherwise contaminating the water supply.

Military defeat had been the catalyst for Israelite political reform. The crisis that had brought the Israelite tribal confederation to an end came in the latter part of the eleventh century. The Philistines had become increasingly more aggressive, developing a strong military tradition, with a monopoly on the use of iron for weapons and also making use of the chariot in warfare. The decisive blow was struck at some time after 1050 BC near Aphek on the coastal plain. The army of Israel was cut to pieces, the priests who bore the Ark were

killed and the shrine itself was destroyed. In such a national emergency, the Israelites were forced to elect a more permament ruler, and this was Saul, who had gained prestige in the old-fashioned way as a charismatic leader. Saul's reign was spent almost entirely at war, defending the land of Israel, and he made little change to the internal structure of the country. The tribal organization was left in place, no bureaucracy was developed and no capital or splendid court was established. Despite his ceaseless campaigning, Saul was not able to destroy the Philistines. Shortly before 1000 BC he was forced to face his enemy in the plain of Esdraelon, where their chariots could manoeuvre freely. The outcome was a foregone conclusion. The Israelite forces were routed, Saul's three sons were killed and he himself, severely wounded, apparently took his own life.

David was cast in a similar mould to Saul, being a military hero elected king in an hour of need. According to the Bible he was a native of Bethlehem, a skilled musician, and had gained fame by his early exploits, in particular the killing of the Philistine giant Goliath. David managed to bring together the two halves of the kingdom, Israel and Judah, in a united Israel. He countered the Philistine threat in a series of battles that began

A view of one of the 'stables' at Megiddo. Some scholars think that horses were tethered to the pillars and fed from the troughs; others dispute the use of stables at this period in the ancient Near East.

1000
BC

near Jerusalem, ultimately destroying the enemy by taking the struggle into their own territory. He cemented the union of the new Israel by moving the Ark of the Covenant to Jerusalem and establishing the city as his religious and political capital. The nature of Israel now began to change from a tribal confederacy of purely Israelite populations to a geographical entity which embraced people of other nations. David's increasing use of iron weapons and his introduction of the chariot helped fuel his wars of expansion, so that Israel soon became an imperial power. In the later years of his reign rebellions at home took up most of his attention, as the tribal framework of Israelite society exercised its divisive influence one more time. But the fragile monarchy weathered the storm. David had fathered a son, Solomon, as a result of his affair with Bathsheba and he had promised her that Solomon would succeed him.

Solomon took the throne at some time around 970 BC and was faced with an entirely different set of problems from his father. Not for Solomon the life of a warrior, extending the bounds of Israelite rule. Instead, his task was to hold the fledgeling state together and to consolidate the gains of his predecessor. Key cities, such as Hazor, Gezer and Megiddo, were fortified and turned into military bases and the chariot contingents of the army were greatly expanded. But the real genius of Solomon

An extraordinary feat of engineering produced the rock-cut tunnel that led beneath the city's defences to a spring, so that water could be obtained safely in times of siege.

A scene from a decorated Philistine jug from eleventh-century BC Megiddo. The Philistines defeated the Egyptians but were themselves defeated by King Saul and King David.

lay in other areas. He developed trading contacts to an unprecedented level, including his famous dialogue with the queen of Sheba; he spent huge sums of money on public buildings, the most famous of which was the Temple at Jerusalem; and he promoted the arts, so that during this period some of the masterworks of the Old Testament were written. None of this was achieved without cost. Heavier taxation and increasing use of conscripted labour gradually alienated the population. The Israelites recognized that their tribal independence had ended and that the effective base of social obligation was not the covenant of Yahweh but the state. However, neither David nor Solomon had managed to overcome all the inner tensions of the new state. When Solomon died, the structure erected by David fell apart and was replaced by two rival states of second-rate importance, Judah and Israel. These lived side by side, at times at war with one another, at times at peace, until the northern state, and Megiddo, was destroyed by the Assyrians some 200 years later.

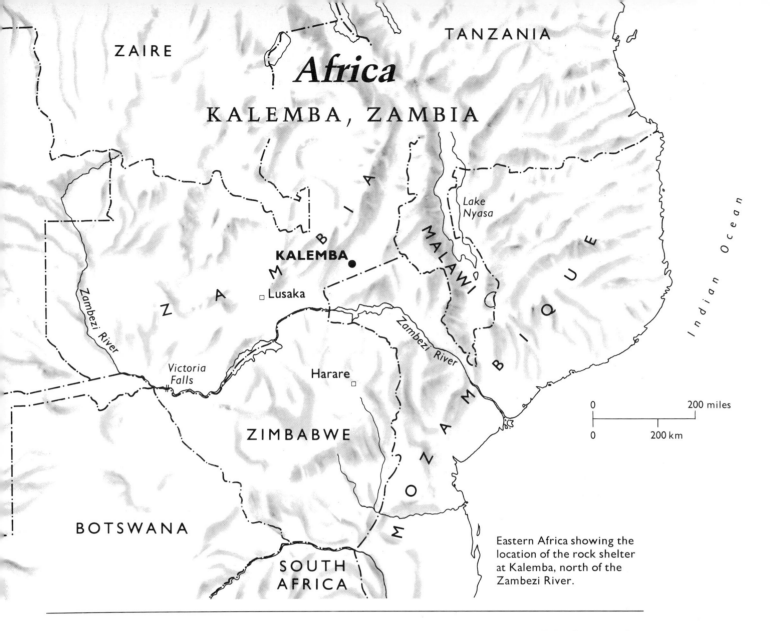

Africa

KALEMBA, ZAMBIA

ZAIRE

TANZANIA

ZAMBIA

KALEMBA ●

Lake Nyasa

MALAWI

□ Lusaka

MOZAMBIQUE

Indian Ocean

Zambezi River

Victoria Falls

Zambezi River

Harare □

ZIMBABWE

BOTSWANA

SOUTH AFRICA

0 — 200 miles
0 — 200 km

Eastern Africa showing the location of the rock shelter at Kalemba, north of the Zambezi River.

The overhang of the rock shelter at Kalemba protrudes like a claw from the bush-covered hillside. Kalemba is one of the largest rock shelters discovered in Zambia.

A few miles to the north of the border between Zambia and Mozambique lies Kalemba, one of the largest rock shelters discovered in Zambia. It is situated at an altitude of over 3,300 feet (1,000 m) above sea level in stony hill country which is covered with dense bush. Geologically the area is characterized by domed granitic hills, and rock shelters are a frequent occurrence. Kalemba looks out to the north-west, over the upper reaches of the Chipwete River. Although herds of buffalo and large antelope once grazed in the valley, the local villagers now farm the high, well-watered plains, growing maize, pumpkins, bananas, plantains and tobacco, and raising cattle, goats, pigs and chickens. Their agricultural way of life is a relatively recent introduction and dates back to the early first millennium AD, when iron-using peoples arrived in the region, bringing with them domesticated animals and seed grain. A much older tradition is represented by the bands of

Above: A detailed location plan of the Kalemba rock shelter and the numerous adjacent and contemporary rock shelters and rock-painting sites. Land over 3,500 feet (1,060 m) is shaded.

Right: The rock shelter was formed from an outcrop of granite gneiss. Archaeological deposits are usually better preserved in rock shelters and caves as they are less prone to disturbance than those in 'open' sites.

hunter-gatherers who occupied the rock shelter at Kalemba and may have witnessed the arrival of these pioneer farmers, because excavations have demonstrated that Kalemba was home to successive bands of hunters for at least 30,000 years.

The rock shelter is formed by a massive outcrop of granite gneiss, over 100 feet (30 m) high, jutting out from the hillside. On its north-west side, facing the valley, a finely domed overhang with a maximum height of 15 feet (4.5 m) extends outward for a distance of 23 feet (7 m), protecting an open, flat area measuring some 30 by 36 feet (9 by 11 m). The uninterrupted floor is further protected by a steep slope of the hillside to the north-east. To the north-west and south-west lie additional outcrops, the tops of which can be reached only from the living space of the shelter floor. These provided extensions to the occupation areas and also served as vantage points from which to observe game in the valley below. A second, smaller overhang is situated at the south-west end

of the main shelter. Throughout its long prehistory, and certainly around 1000 BC, Kalemba must have been occupied as one of a number of camps that were frequented by band members in their search for seasonal foods. Local people today have given the name Kalemba, meaning the painted place, to the shelter because of the series of rock paintings that are preserved on the rear wall of the main shelter and in a smaller panel beneath the south-western overhang. The long frieze of numerous human figures, painted in white, is now the only obvious indication that Kalemba was once a place of importance.

Excavations through the deposits on the floor of the shelter soon suggested that the human occupation at Kalemba had been a long one. The archaeologists were not always able to excavate exactly where they wanted. A massive fallen boulder, with its top about 1 foot 6 inches (50 cm) below the surface and weighing around 25 tons, obstructed one part of the trench and the archaeologists were compelled to dig around it.

1000
BC

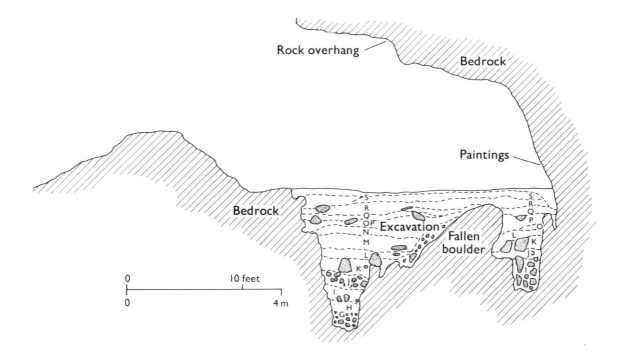

A plan of the rock shelter at Kalemba, indicating the extent of the overhang and the area of the excavation; the paintings are positioned at the back. As is often the case, the ground level of the site rose over successive generations as each one discarded its rubbish on to the floor. The letters refer to these various levels of occupation.

Despite the problems, forty-seven layers were removed, comprising mixed deposits of soil, ash, charcoal, stone implements, debris from the manufacture of stone tools, artefacts of bone and shell, animal bones, plant remains, pottery sherds (upper levels only), and fragments of rock fallen from the roof of the shelter. The excavation terminated at a depth of 14 feet (4.3 m) for reasons of safety, although it was clear that deposits containing older implements continued downwards. For the purposes of analysis and description of the finds, the forty-seven layers were grouped into thirteen 'horizons', with Horizon S being the surface and latest deposit and Horizon G the deepest and oldest.

The characteristics of each horizon varied considerably. For instance, at some time during the formation of Horizon P, a group of large rocks had fallen from the shelter roof. These seemed to form a favourite stone-knapping area for one or more of the hunters, since the gaps between them were filled with large quantities of quartz flakes and many knapping-hammers. The hunters also knew how to keep warm. In the south-east part of the excavation an ash-filled fire pit some 5 inches (13 cm) deep was discovered, with the surrounding deposits scorched to a reddish-brown by the heat.

It is likely that the huge boulder fell from the roof during the accumulation of Horizon K. It is also probable that during the period covered by Horizon K, and similarly throughout the periods represented by Horizons M and H, occupation of the cave by humans may have been interrupted. The large numbers of stone artefacts and waste flakes were not evenly distributed throughout the shelter, either in terms of horizontal or vertical space. Densities of worked stone were much greater in the north-west part of the excavation and decreased as the rear shelter wall was approached. Numbers of stone implements were actually increasing during the excavation of Horizon G, the lowest in the shelter. The greatest frequencies of tools were located in Horizons S, P, M and I; in Horizon I artefacts of bone and shell also reached their highest quantity.

The hunters and gatherers at Kalemba probably carried out a range of everyday tasks in the shelter, such as stone-working, the processing of food, cooking, the making and repairing of implements and the preparation of skins. They also undertook more ceremonial activities, such as painting the walls and burying some of their dead. Four separate burials were discovered during the excavation, three associated with Horizon O and one with

1000 BC

Horizon Q. The three in Horizon O comprised an adult and two infants. In each case only the skull bones were located, and in one instance it was evident that the skull pieces had been broken and separated before burial. In Horizon Q a small pit, only some 8 inches (20 cm) in diameter, was identified. This had been scooped out of the underlying deposits and used for the interment of much-fragmented human remains. Some of the bones of an adult male, who probably died in his third decade, had been carefully placed in the pit. Three pieces of the pelvis and one fragment of skull were used to line the sides. In the middle were piled two halves of a mandible, a heap of vertebrae and rib fragments, a few bits of shattered long bone, two pieces of the temporal bone and a few animal bones. Radiocarbon dating of charcoals and bones from many of the layers suggested that the deposits comprising Horizon Q were formed around 3,000 years ago, and one of the activities we can date to around 1000 BC is the final burial of the bones of this dead hunter.

The rock shelter at Kalemba was not abandoned by the hunters when the first farmers arrived in the region. Eventually, however, after a period of co-existence, the two ways of life proved incompatible and the last band members probably withdrew into less well-occupied areas or were absorbed into the society of the farmers.

The radiocarbon dates from Kalemba clearly demonstrate that the shelter was utilized by hunter-gatherers over a period of more than 30,000 years and that it is to the deposits of Horizon Q that we should look if we wish to reconstruct some aspects of life around 1000 BC. However, it is only by comparing the artefacts and materials from Horizon Q with those of preceding layers that a true picture of a slowly developing indigenous life style can be appreciated.

The manufacture of stone tools, by preparing blades and flakes from a stone core and then producing a cutting edge by the removal of minute flakes (a process known as retouching), appears to have become more sophisticated through time. Certainly the materials left over from tool production, such as the cores and the redundant

Along the base of the rear wall of the shelter is a horizontal frieze of human figures, painted in white. Hunting people have always relied on the power of cave paintings and these figures suggest that Kalemba was an important place for the generations of hunter-gatherers who lived there.

flakes, gradually became smaller as the millennia passed, implying a more efficient and skilled working of stone. The amount of retouching on the edges of implements also increased over time, and there are more examples of artefacts where the non-cutting side or back has been especially blunted. The finished stone implements mostly comprise scrapers and a variety of points, presumably needed for the working of skins and for the tips of spears and arrows used in hunting. Tools such as retouched blades also occur and could have been used for a range of tasks to do with cutting and serrating anything from skins to plant foods. The overall trend is also towards smaller implements, so that well before 1000 BC the inhabitants at Kalemba were manufacturing microliths, very small retouched tools that could be used singly as arrowheads or hafted in multiples to produce composite cutting artefacts. A sticky material made from resin and gum was used to fix the stone microliths in grooves cut in their wooden hafts. Some larger implements were utilized by the hunters around 1000 BC. Four examples of

knapping-hammers and one pounding-stone were recovered from Horizon Q, along with one example of a rubbing-stone on which some material was regularly polished or smoothed, leaving a slightly concave depression. The most exciting larger stone from Horizon Q was a grindstone, some 7 inches (17 cm) across with a dished depression at its centre. It was evidently used for a considerable period until it eventually broke. Its last use was to grind red pigment and this strongly suggests that it was the property of the rock painters of Kalemba.

A few artefacts of materials other than stone were found in Horizon Q. Three complete pins, made from the long bones of a large bird, presumably relate to the making of clothing and ornamentation, as do a bone point and a bone needle, complete with a small perforation at its butt end. Two beads of shell give a further hint of decoration. Large numbers of animal bones were found during the excavations and, as most of these are likely to represent creatures killed by the hunters and brought to the site, they give some indication of a changing diet. There was a

This view from the side of the shelter demonstrates the impressive size of the living area underneath the vast rock overhang. The gradual decline in height towards the rear meant that occupation was restricted to the area nearer the front.

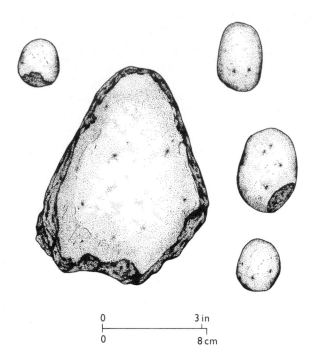

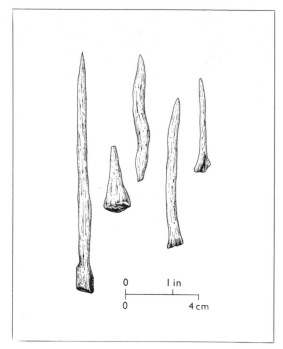

Left: A grindstone, with traces of red pigment, from Horizon Q. The pigment would have been used in the creation of rock paintings. The grindstone is surrounded by a selection of knapping-hammers used for making stone tools from Horizons K, L and M.

Right: A selection of bone pins and points from different horizons, used for piercing leather hides and stitching skins.

preponderance of bones from large game, such as zebra and wildebeest, in the lower layers. This suggests that the shelter may have been surrounded by more open country than it is at present, and that the hunters relied on taking these animals from herds. In the more recent layers the number of small animals increases in frequency and variety, and comprises such creatures as galago, genet, hyrax, small antelope, hare, porcupine and lizard – all characteristic of the dense bush presently surrounding the site – with a corresponding decline in wildebeest and larger antelope. In addition, at least one of the delicacies consumed at the shelter was the giant land snail.

The band of hunters and gatherers at Kalemba in 1000 BC, therefore, was heir to a way of life that had been established tens of thousands of years before. But it was not an unchanging life style. By 1000 BC the hunters had become more skilled in the manufacture of stone tools and had succeeded in making a wider range of implements, including microliths. To a considerable extent the development of smaller tools was a response to the gradual disappearance of extensive herds of sizeable animals and an increasing reliance on a variety of smaller game. This development is typified by the discovery in Horizon Q of a blunt-tipped arrowhead

known as a *petit tranchet*, which was almost certainly used for shooting down birds. New techniques of hunting were probably evolved and there must have been a greater emphasis on trapping. The discovery of bone and shell artefacts in the later deposits in the shelter suggests that the material culture of the hunters was becoming more and more sophisticated.

Another feature that the hunters would be confronted with in their daily lives was, of course, the rock paintings on the rear wall of the shelter. Although none of the extant paintings at Kalemba is likely to be as early as 1000 BC, it is probable that the tradition of rock art goes back further and the discovery of pigments in Horizon Q may attest to the longevity of the practice. The development and meaning of other rock paintings in eastern Zambia can throw some light on the probable paintings that the band members at Kalemba in 1000 BC would have been familiar with. More than forty rock-painting sites are known from eastern Zambia, with Kalemba demonstrating at least two major periods. The later period covers the main series of white paintings depicting grids, circles and lines and many stylized human figures. Underlying these are red schematic paintings, including three grids and two crude animals in a buff colour.

1000 BC

Dating of these paintings is extremely difficult, but it would seem that the white paintings may be quite recent, perhaps from the eighteenth and nineteenth centuries, and, on comparison with present customs, they may be associated with ceremonies marking the initiation of young people into adulthood. The red schematic paintings are older and most probably connected with the arrival of farmers in the region during the first millennium AD. Although the farmers would not have inhabited the shelter, they too would possibly have utilized rock paintings in initiation ceremonies and perhaps in rituals concerned with rain-making. An earlier style of rock art, not represented at Kalemba, uses red paint in a naturalistic format. Two of the three paintings in this style known from eastern Zambia portray the eland, an animal that occupied a special place in the religious and spiritual life of the later stone-tool-using societies of southern Africa. Among the San Bushmen the eland is seen as a symbol of potency, and during trances designed to harness the forces of the supernatural, the role of the shaman is frequently identified with the eland. It seems possible that the hunters at Kalemba in 1000 BC may have viewed the portrayal of elands on the rear of their shelter with a mixture of reverence and fear.

Above: A red painted eland from another Southern Africa site. The eland was a magical animal for many hunters and gatherers in the region.

Below: It seems likely that this wall would have been repainted regularly by successive generations, with later depictions masking the earlier ones.

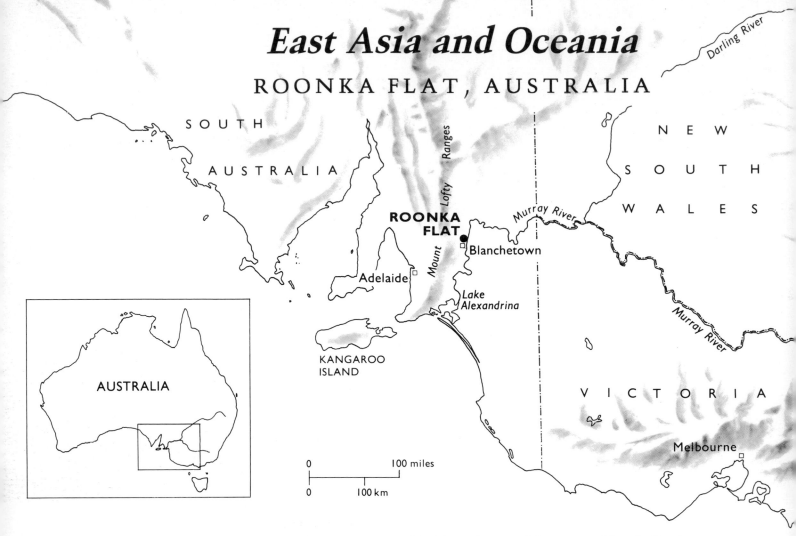

East Asia and Oceania
ROONKA FLAT, AUSTRALIA

A map showing the course of the lower reaches of the Murray River, and the position of Roonka Flat. Access to food resources of the coast, the river and neighbouring uplands made it a favoured location for hunters and gatherers.

1000 BC

The summary descriptions by European explorers and settlers usually fall woefully short of portraying the true complexity and sophistication of Aboriginal life. The ancestors of the men who confronted Captain James Cook in 1770 had arrived in Australia at least 40,000 years before from the north, when that continent was joined by a land bridge to New Guinea. Gradually they spread and multiplied throughout the country, adapting their hunting, gathering and fishing life style ingeniously to the new plants and animals, and the often inhospitable environments they found. By 8,000 years ago rising sea levels had flooded extensive coastal plains, severing Australia from New Guinea and isolating the population of Tasmania. About 5,000 years ago sea levels had reached their maximum heights, creating a rich inshore environment of lagoons and estuaries which supported prolific amounts of

marine life, especially shellfish. The gradual desiccation of the interior led to more concentrated settlement in the river valleys, where occasionally native millet was harvested and processed with grinding-stones. Around 1000 BC the Aboriginal population had evolved a complex social organization, long-distance exchange networks and elaborate ceremonials. Ritual life was centred on sacred sites such as painted rock shelters, associated with the concept of Dreamtime, a mythical golden age independent of the passage of time. Excavations at Roonka Flat on the Murray River, some 94 miles (150 km) north-east of Adelaide, have provided a remarkable picture of the development of Aboriginal society.

The Murray River in this area of south Australia was a permanent stream, flowing along the bottom of a broad, shallow gorge. Floodplains, lagoons, dunes and terraces of alluvium were scattered along

Above: This is one of the plates forming part of *South Australia Illustrated*, an early colonial album of lithographs of natural and cultural scenes by George French Angas, published in London in 1847. The scene can be reliably identified as Roonka Flat, looking across the river to the east-bank cliffs.

Left: A detailed map of the Murray River around the area of Roonka Flat near Blanchetown. Throughout its history the river has changed its course on the floodplain, sometimes forming creeks and lagoons and periodically inundating extensive areas.

the bottom of the gorge, which rarely exceeded 2 miles (3 km) in width. The profusion of gum forests, woodland, swampland, sedges, grasses and shrubs within the river basin contrasted sharply with the aridity of the scrub-covered plateau on either side of the gorge. Concentration of such resources in a narrow, confined area meant that the locality was always attractive to Aboriginal hunter-gatherers, and the archaeological record demonstrates that communities have lived in this area for the last 20,000 years. During much of the later period of occupation the climate consisted of cool winters and hot, dry summers. Throughout the winters fish and game supplies in the valley would be low and communities may have had to move away to hunt and forage in the scrub. The Aboriginals were very resourceful in their search for food, however. The name Roonka was derived from a local word for the larvae of a species of moth which was extracted from its burrows in the root systems of box trees with a long, flexible, hooked stick made from a polygonum bush. In the light of the common Aboriginal penchant for giving names to places on the basis of their most useful product, it seems safe to assume that the principal value of Roonka Flat lay in the quantity of these grubs.

1000 BC

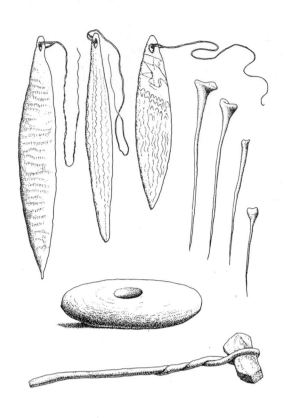

The trunk of an Australian River Red Gum, showing a scar caused by stripping a sheet of bark, cut to the shape required to make a canoe.

Nineteenth-century illustrators drew these artefacts: sacred pieces of wood, spun at night to produce a noise, needles, a stone for pounding roots and a axe.

Excavations at Roonka Flat have concentrated on examining an elongated dune west of the river. Aboriginal communities seem to have regularly settled here, and for the last 7,000 years have also buried their dead in the dune. At least 142 people were interred, their bones and grave goods offering a unique insight into the health and social organization of the community. Of the 142 burials, twelve were more than 4,000 years old and seem strikingly different from later interments. The majority of the earliest burials were in shaft tombs, with the deceased placed vertically in the grave. In a few cases the bones had been rearranged at a later date, and most were accompanied by grave goods of some kind. These included drilled animal mandibles, perforated shells and bone pins; human infants, evidence of the practice of infanticide, were also occasionally interred with the deceased, seemingly as grave goods. The later burials exhibited a variety of characteristics, but all consisted of extended or contracted interments. Around 1000 BC the dune at Roonka Flat was well established as both an important residence camp and a final resting-place for some of the hunters.

It is the burials, however, which are so

fascinating at Roonka Flat and allow us a rare glimpse of the individuals of prehistoric Australia. The dead were placed in longitudinal, circular or oval graves. The grave goods accompanying the deceased fall into three categories: tools, ornaments and offerings. The tools were made of stone, bone and teeth. In one instance, they seemed to represent the personal tool kit of the deceased: quartz and bone hammering implements were associated with partly made projectile points of stone and bone. Ornaments were fashioned from shell, as well as bone and teeth. These ranged from caches of bone points that were used to fasten hair, while other ornaments included headbands, ear pendants, neck pendants, necklaces, cloak pins and pubic coverings. Offerings in the graves consisted of parts of animals, including the jaw bones of dingos, freshwater mussel shells and, in one case, a fish.

The positions of the bodies varied considerably. Many individuals were laid out full length on their backs. The close proximity of ankles and feet suggested to the archaeologist that some persons may have been buried in a bound state. In other graves the deceased were placed face down.

1000 BC

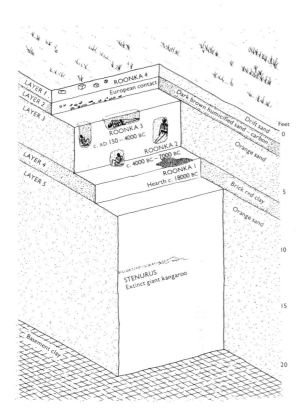

A cut-away drawing of the layers of soil in Trench A at Roonka, showing the relative depths of the burials, and the principal soil horizons.

Tool types can sometimes change little over several millennia, as indicated by these three bone pins from three tombs of very different dates.

Another favoured arrangement was for the body to be contracted, with arms and legs drawn up against the chest. Contracted bodies were found on their sides but also upright, suggesting that the dead person had been buried in a sitting position. In addition, three cremation burials were recorded. Analysis of the bones demonstrated the age range of the people buried at Roonka Flat. Of a sample of 120 individuals, twenty-six died before they were six years of age, while sixty-three died between the ages of twenty-one and fifty; only seven survived their fiftieth year.

Closer examination of the bones provided more detailed and intriguing facts about the health of the hunters at Roonka Flat. Males were slightly taller than females, with average heights of 5 feet 6 inches (1.67 m) for males and 5 feet 2 inches (1.56 m) for females. Over 70 per cent of the population seem to have been free from any osseous disease or evidence of congenital abnormalities. In dental health only one individual was afflicted with caries, while six demonstrated excessive wear of a sort characteristic of hunter-gatherers, where the teeth are used to finish tools, prepare fibrous vegetable material for cordage and

masticate fibrous and gritty foods. Seven adults, however, suffered from arthritis of the elbow, probably as a result of repetitive throwing of a spear or boomerang. Fractures were observed in eight individuals. As hunter-gatherers are known to have been very agile by modern standards and less prone to accidental injuries, most of these fractures may have been caused by combat. Breaks noted in four ulnas might be explained by the victim's raising a forearm to protect the head in a confrontation and then being struck on the arm by a weapon. One incidence of amputation of the arm was recorded, and it is possible that euthanasia was practised on a pregnant mother to relieve her suffering during a very difficult birth. Signs of bone infection were observed in six individuals, probably caused by bacterial infection. The overall impression given by the analysis is one of a predominantly healthy people.

In some instances infants seem to have been deliberately interred with adult males. The discovery of one such infant body, concealed within the thorax of an adult male, was made when the adult skeleton was being cleaned in the laboratory. Intentional concealment of this kind

1000 BC

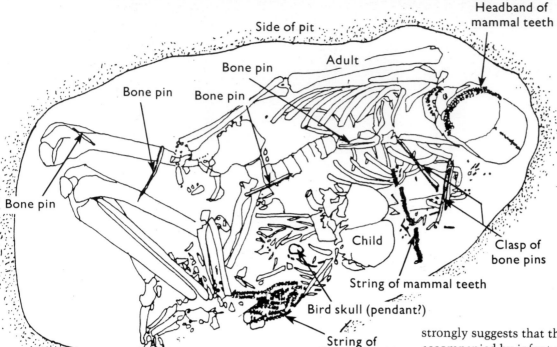

Side of pit

Headband of mammal teeth

Bone pin

Bone pin

Bone pin

Adult

Bone pin

Child

Clasp of bone pins

String of mammal teeth

Bird skull (pendant?)

String of reptile vertebrae

Above: A plan view of the burial (photographed below) of an adult male (top) and child (below, with skull flattened) both in contracted positions. Various pins, pendants and necklaces accompanied the dead for use in the afterlife. Some of the deceased were buried in an upright position – these were among the earliest burials on the site – but the majority of the remaining burials were of the contracted or extended variety. The incidence of an infant being buried with an adult is rare, and it is likely that the adults involved had special status.

Below: The body of the man, arranged in 'recumbent contracted' position and supporting the body of a small child of between seven and fourteen years. The male has a two-string fillet, or headband, of wallaby incisor pairs across his forehead.

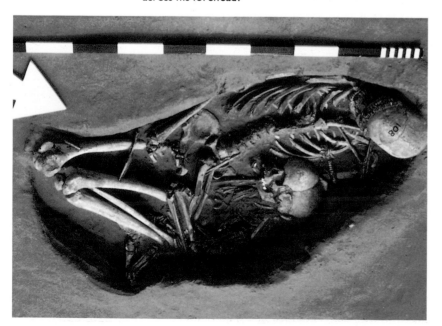

strongly suggests that the individuals accompanied by infant offerings possessed some special status or office in life. Although infanticide was reported by later Europeans as a common aspect of mortality in Aboriginal communities during periods of nutritional stress, the placing of infants in adult graves was something unexpected. In life members of Aboriginal communities were divided into various age grades and descent groups, separated into different sets according to their ritual association with certain animals or totems, and could hold additional offices connected with the performance of prophecy, curing and leadership in battle. It seems likely that these special adult graves at Roonka Flat were connected with one or several of these distinctions.

Study of the orientation of the burials indicated that they could point to most parts of the compass. Inferences drawn from European descriptions of Aboriginal societies suggest that the direction of orientation of the deceased could mark the final destination of the spirits of the dead. Some of the graves had clearly been reopened by mourners or later inhabitants at the site. Sometimes fires had been lit in the graves, while in other cases tombs had been re-entered, in order to retrieve specific bones, and then resealed. Grave pits were lined either with plant material or with bark. The filling of the grave pits clearly suggested a link with the living, since deposits covering the bodies often contained debris from the adjacent settlement. Earlier graves were either forgotten or no longer considered inviolate, because later interments often disturbed neighbouring graves and frequently penetrated underlying burials.

The evidence from Roonka Flat was, of course, not just restricted to these extraordinary burials.

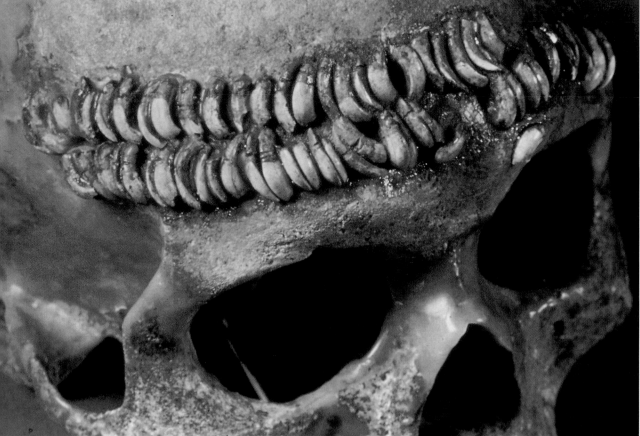

Detail of the headband of wallaby incisors. The band is two-stranded, but does not extend completely around the skull, implying that the teeth were attached to some form of plaited or woven string band.

Although no hut floors were located, two principal types of fireplace were recorded. In one an irregularly shaped spread of cobbles rested on the original ground surface. The gaps between the stones were filled with ash and charcoal, and fragments of mussel shell were occasionally found. They seemed to have functioned as hot plates and were interpreted as being low platforms of heated stones, surrounded by embers, upon which shellfish could be placed to grill or broil. The other fireplace form consisted of a shallow pit filled with stones and ash. These were probably earth ovens, in which carcasses or layers of vegetables were cooked between heated stones. Hearths, intended more for warmth than for cooking, took two distinct forms as well. They appeared either as shallow, circular areas of ash and charcoal or as linear masses of ash. The latter type is best interpreted as a burning log, or sleeping hearth, providing warmth at night.

The long period of settlement and burial at Roonka Flat could well be seen as a microcosm of Aboriginal development in Australia. Around 10,000 years ago the climate began to improve, gradually changing from cold and dry to warmer and more humid conditions. Some 5,000 years ago, as the sea level reached its maximum extent, humidity decreased; thereafter sea levels began

slowly to fall. The population throughout this period seems to have grown in number, despite the fact that the range of foodstuffs consumed at Roonka Flat showed little change over the millennia. There are changes in other aspects of daily life, however. Stone-tool technology improved considerably, with the manufacture of smaller and more specialized implements, including ground and hafted artefacts. The art depicted at sacred sites evolved from abstract, geometric motifs and footprints to a more figurative style, illustrating humans, trees and animals. There are eight such art and mythological sites from the Roonka Flat region, and ethnographic accounts suggest that they may have been located at the boundaries of a community's territory. Here they perhaps played a role in bringing neighbouring communities together to indulge in trade or wife exchange, or simply to dispel mutual suspicions. An alternative explanation is that the changing art may reflect an increasing focus in Aboriginal religion on a supreme deity or father of creation whose domination over animals was unquestioned. The most dramatic evidence from Roonka Flat, that of burial practices, demonstrates increasing variety through time, so that by 1000 BC four different burial modes are in existence: extended in the grave on the back; extended in the grave on the

1000 BC

front; contracted and lying on the side; and contracted and sitting up. It is tempting to infer from these four types of burial that each was reserved for a specific section of the community.

To reconstruct the lives of those advanced hunters who camped and periodically buried their dead at Roonka Flat requires a disciplined imagination. The Aboriginal mind did not perceive the material world in the same way as the European colonists did. It did not differentiate between the physical and supernatural qualities of substances. For example, the everyday world of animals, plants, land, waters and sky was real enough, but the appearances of design and variation in the surface texture of a tree trunk or in the colour of a flower could be taken as proof of their supernatural origin, and the justification for rituals whose repeated performances were believed to ensure that they continued to grow.

It was probably through such rituals and ceremonies that the Aboriginals at Roonka Flat around 1000 BC felt secure in their world. They comprised a small band of hunter-gatherers who utilized several other temporary camps in a defined territory. They were linked to other such bands by the sharing of a common language and to even larger tribal groupings through ceremonial obligations that were undertaken at specific locations and at appointed times during the year. These ceremonies fulfilled a number of minor functions, including the settlement of disputes, the regulation of long-distance trade and the punishment of offenders. But their principal roles were to initiate men into the corporate life of the ceremonial community and to organize and confirm the exchange of women as marriage partners. Exchanges of woman produced ties between neighbouring bands, while the initiation of men into the religious community introduced them to the knowledge of the supernatural. Such knowledge gave them a belief in their ability to control their daily lives.

At Roonka Flat the Aboriginals probably believed that the source of all power was vested in a supreme being, resident in the sky, creator of all things and host to the spirits of the dead. The works of this being were to divide the diversity of the plant and animal world into categories and to separate the individuals within human communities into corresponding sets. The supreme being also established the rules by which each human set was linked to a category of animal or plant that became its totem. As a result of this, each member of a hunting band claimed identity with one or more categories of living species, a relationship that was traced through the mother. Membership of these totemic classes determined

from which natural-species categories of other groups a future spouse would be drawn. Therefore, in a band like the one resident at Roonka Flat, it was entirely possible for there to be representatives of several totemic groups within the same community. Through time and as the population numbers increased, it seems that each of these totems became equated with its specific land-owning band. Territorial frictions between neighbouring communities probably explain the greater emphasis placed in some areas in later years, up to the arrival of the Europeans, upon rule through clan councils. Such associations clearly promoted the appearance of distinctions of personal rank. However, for the people of Roonka Flat in 1000 BC, older and earlier ways prevailed and it is more likely that the four different burial rites corresponded with a more evenly balanced and widely shared set of categories linking marriage between communities to the perceived subdivisions of the totemic universe. These distinctions were of critical significance for the social and spiritual vitality of the hunter-gatherers on the Murray River.

Drawing of nineteenth century illustrations of contemporary artefacts on the Murray River include a skin for carrying water, a container net, a leather bag and a basket.

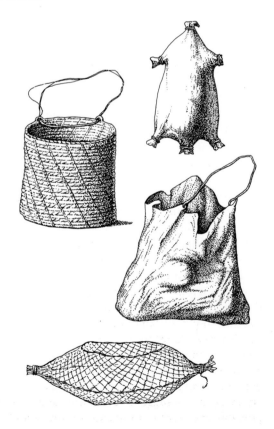

1000
BC

The Americas
POVERTY POINT, USA

The southern United States showing the Mississippi delta.

Around the world the life styles of communities that lived by a mixture of hunting, gathering and fishing have been reconstructed by archaeologists and recorded by anthropologists. With some exceptions, the general picture that emerges from such studies is of a way of life in which small groups of people moved from camp to camp to exploit various seasonal food resources found in a particular locality. Such a life style, committed to an ordered but mobile existence, demands the minimum of portable belongings, little investment in non-functional structures and a social system that promotes cooperation and egalitarian relations between band members. Imagine the controversy, therefore, when it was proposed that one of the most complex systems of earthworks in North America, containing ample evidence for built ritual alignments and producing a range of artefacts that is suggestive of status and rank, was probably the work of indigenous hunters and gatherers. The site in question is Poverty Point in north-east Louisiana, and the investigations of its earthworks are providing an extraordinary insight into a way of life 3,000 years ago.

Poverty Point reached the zenith of its development around 1000 BC. The site itself is in the Lower Mississippi valley and was constructed on top of an escarpment known as the Macon ridge, which looks out to the east over the floodplain of the Bayou Macon, a small stream flowing through an abandoned arm of the Arkansas River. The principal feature of the complex was a huge, semicircular enclosure delimited by six artificial earthen embankments that formed concentric arcs. The scale of the earthworks is staggering. The embankments were from roughly 3 to 6 feet (1 to 2 m) in height and were separated crest to crest by a remarkably uniform distance of around 142 feet (43 m). Between these embankments or ridges were low areas or swales from which most of the

1000 BC

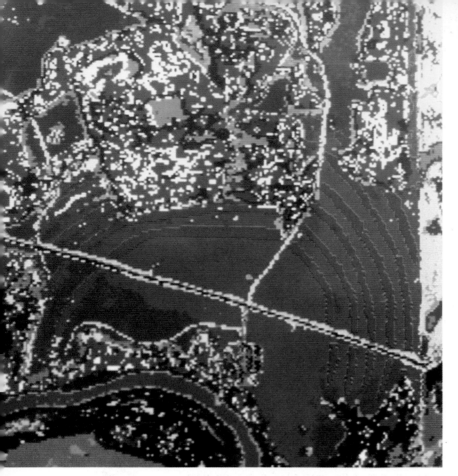

A satellite image of the banks and ditches that form the focal point of the Poverty Point complex.

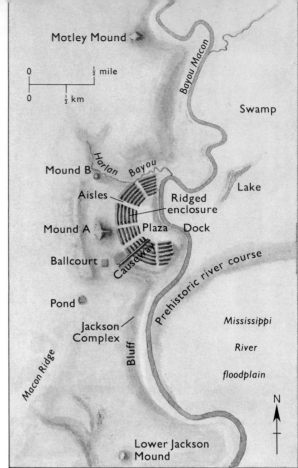

At the centre of the complex lies the concentric ridges and intervening ditches or swales.

1000 BC

construction material had been obtained. From one end of the outermost arc to the other was a distance of some ¾ mile (1.2 km), while opposite ends of the innermost arcs were about 2,000 feet (600 m) apart. Excavations on the west perimeter of the site suggest that a seventh ridge had been planned but for some reason was never constructed. The ridges enclosed a central area or Plaza, and all terminated at the edge of the bluff, from where there was a drop of about 20 feet (6 m) to the stream that flowed alongside the entire eastern side of the earthwork.

The ridges were divided into six sectors by five aisles or corridors. These ranged from 33 to 165 feet (10 to 50 m) in width. While they all led into the Plaza, they neither converged on the same point nor divided the encircling embankments into sectors of equal size. This suggests that formal geometric symmetry was an important but secondary consideration in the construction of the earthworks. What was obviously more significant was the lie of the land and the practical function of the embankments and swales. An additional feature ran across all the ridges to the south of the south-western aisle. This consisted of a built-up causeway which led from the Plaza across the

concentric embankments and south-west to a mound known as the Ballcourt (because its summit bore two slight depressions at either end, reminiscent of the worn areas underneath outdoor basketball goals; it is not to be confused with the more formalized Ballcourts that occur on certain central American sites).

The Plaza appears to have been a deliberately landscaped feature and not just an open space. Some areas in the 37 acres (15 ha) surrounded by the embankments had been artificially levelled by filling in small depressions to the height of adjacent elevated areas. Small-scale excavations in the Plaza have provided tangible evidence of human activity and constructions. Two pits were discovered under a knoll in the south-central part of the enclosed area. The first measured some 2 feet 7 inches (80 cm) in diameter and about 1 foot (30 cm) in depth and contained numerous amorphous baked clay objects, indicating that a fire had once burnt in the pit. The second feature comprised a ring of baked clay objects and clay balls lying in a shallow pit, almost certainly a cooking pit in which hot clay objects, placed in an earth oven, had been used to cook food. In a separate excavation evidence has been recovered which confirms the presence of

An aerial view of Poverty Point. The banks and ditches around the site were never designed to form a complete circle, but instead terminated on the bluff overlooking the Bayou Macon and the Mississippi floodplain.

timber uprights and probably also structures within the Plaza. While some of the post holes are relatively shallow, others are of such size that we have to imagine timber constructions of massive proportions. One was over 6 feet (1.8 m) in depth and broadened out at the top to more than 3 feet (1 m) in diameter. Deposits filling the hole indicate that the post, at least 1 foot 6 inches (50 cm) in diameter, probably rotted in place and was so large that when it was hauled into position, its point of entry into the pit had to be widened and gradually inclined. On the western side of the Plaza a group of unusually large post holes are claimed by excavators to be the settings for an arrangement of towering timbers that might have represented a kind of American Stonehenge, markers for ritually significant days, such as equinoxes and solstices. Another focal point of the Plaza may have been the area now known as the Dock, situated on the edge of the bluff at the south-eastern termination of the innermost arc. This is the only place in the vicinity where the slope down to the water is gentle rather than sheer. Given such access it would have been here that the people of Poverty Point landed their catches of fish or their cargoes of traded goods from rafts or boats before hauling them up to the Plaza.

Outside the central area were other earthworks. Just beyond the western sector was the huge Mound A, which has an unusual shape that reminds some experts of a gigantic bird. It stood over 70 feet (21 m) in height, with a 'wingspan' of 643 feet (195 m) and a length from 'head to tail' of 713 feet (216 m). The flattened or so-called 'tail' section of the monster structure was actually built in a pit some 13 feet (4 m) deep. Another similar but slightly smaller mound, Motley Mound, was constructed just over a mile (2 km) north of the main complex. Some archaeologists believe that it is unfinished and was also originally designed to resemble a bird.

Three more structures were positioned along a N–S line that passed through the central 'bird' mound. To the north stood a conical mound, Mound B, which covered a possible cremation burial. To the south lay the square, earthen structure known as the Ballcourt. Core samples of the mound indicated that it was a naturally formed eminence that had been trimmed into an artificial-looking shape, unlike all the other mounds, which were built from piling up basketfuls of soil. About a mile (2 km) further south along the same axis stood a second dome-shaped mound, the southernmost

1000 BC

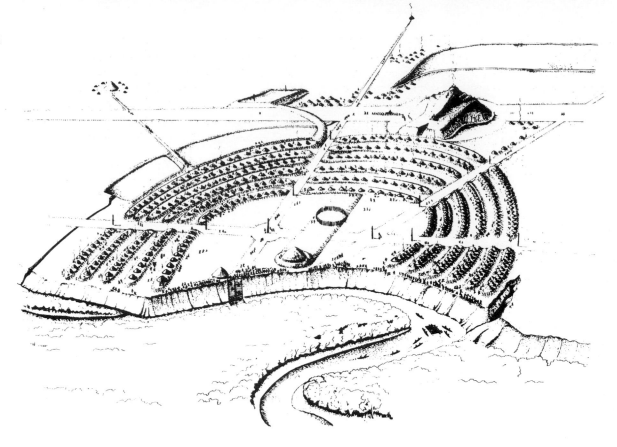

A reconstruction of Poverty Point as it might have looked in 1000 BC. Timber houses are shown on the top of concentric earthwork banks. The circular setting of vertical timbers in the central Plaza is sometimes referred to as the American Stonehenge. A prepared incline from the Plaza leads down the edge of the bluff to a dock area on the riverside.

structure of the Poverty Point complex. Other, more problematic, mounds occur. To the south of the main embankments lies the Jackson complex, a comma-shaped ridge and at least one mound. Artefacts found after these structures were levelled by the plough suggest they are of Poverty Point age.

When people were resident at Poverty Point the majority apparently lived on top of the semicircular ridges. Excavations have not yet been extensive enough to reveal detailed plans of houses or domestic furnishings, but it seems from isolated examples that structures were circular and small, averaging between 13 and 16 feet (4 and 5 m) in diameter, or rectangular. One possible house at Poverty Point, destroyed by fire, appears to have been a semi-subterranean dwelling, framed with bent poles and covered with cane thatch and daub. Not all the inhabitants lived on the ridges, however. There were a number of suburbs situated on the edge of the bluff, north and south of the main area.

The scale of the earthworks at Poverty Point prompts some obvious questions. How long did they take to build? And how many people were involved in their construction? Approximate

calculations of the amount of spoil in the embankments and mounds suggest that between 8 and 12 million basketloads of earth went into their construction and perhaps 5 million or so person-hours. By expressing the labour in terms of numbers of workers and time worked, the magnitude of the undertaking can be more easily grasped. By presuming that one person in five, or one-fifth of the population, constitutes the labour force, we can arrive at a rough estimate of the total population. Equations using a sliding scale for the numbers of workers indicate that a workforce of about 100 (implying a total population of around 500) could have built Poverty Point in about twenty-four years. This, of course, presumes that the population was resident at Poverty Point all year round and that other members of the group managed to procure all the necessary subsistence requirements. At the other end of the scale, the equation demonstrates that 1,000 labourers (implying a total population of around 5,000) could have constructed the complex in just over two years. Such estimates cannot tell us how long the process of construction actually took, but they do illustrate that even with 100 people, working for just three months of the year, Poverty Point could have been constructed in less than a century.

The way of life represented by the Poverty Point site was not just restricted to this key complex. It was part of a widespread culture followed by certain Indian peoples in the Lower Mississippi valley between 2000 and 700 BC. The area occupied by these peoples covered parts of Louisiana, Arkansas and Mississippi and its influences reached as far afield as the eastern coast of Florida and up the valley to Tennessee and Missouri. They were not a unified people, either socially, politically, ethnically or linguistically, but they shared some common cultural traits. One was participation in a far-reaching system of trade, manufacture and the use of certain artefacts. Some of these typical artefacts included clay cooking-balls, clay figurines, small stone tools (microliths), plummets (plumb bobs) and finely crafted stone beads and pendants. Two particular features distinguish Poverty Point artefacts: one is the decided preference for materials imported from other regions; the other is an emphasis on ground and polished stone ornaments.

A map of the Lower Mississippi valley in 1000 BC reveals some interesting settlement patterns. Clusters of sites appear in at least ten concentrations, with these densely inhabited zones separated from each other by many miles. In the more sparsely settled areas the inhabitants do not seem to have participated in the Poverty Point trading networks. Another highly significant characterstic was that each population concentration was linked by waterways. They were all tied into the Mississippi River, and although the Mississippi itself did not run through every concentration, one of its major tributaries did. These interconnected streams and rivers were the highways that carried people, trade goods and ideas. Most of the people resided in camps along these streams. There were small, medium and large camps, extending from 2½ to 100 acres (1 to 40 ha) in size. At least one large camp in every Poverty Point territory was embellished with public construction works, usually mounds and embankments. The embankments were raised by a combination of building activity and the incidental accumulation of living refuse. Not all the ridges served as foundations for houses and there was evidently no standard architectural arrangement involving mounds and ridges, although semicircular patterns occurred most frequently.

Poverty Point culture had many unique objects, but perhaps the most important were its artefacts of personal adornment and symbolic meaning. A variety of stone beads and pendants was worn, often fashioned in deliberate geometric or

zoomorphic shapes. Predominant designs were those representing birds, bird heads, animal claws, foot effigies and turtles. Perforated human and animal teeth have been dredged from the silts of the bayou below the Poverty Point site, suggesting that much more ornamentation from perishable materials has disappeared. Almost certainly religious and symbolic purposes were served by stone pipes. Their presence suggests that they might have been the first calumets (peace pipes) used by south-eastern Indians. Calumets were the most sacred symbols of inter-tribal relations, used to proclaim war and peace and to honour and salute important ceremonies and visiting dignitaries. Other sacred objects included crudely

Bows and arrows were unknown to Poverty Point people and javelins or spears were the main hunting devices. Spears, which were tipped with a range of stone points, could be cast further and with greater power by the use of an *atlatl*. These were held in the throwing hand, with the hooked end inserted into a shallow socket in the butt end of the spear. Hurled with a smooth, gliding action, the spear was released towards the target while the *atlatl* remained in the hand.

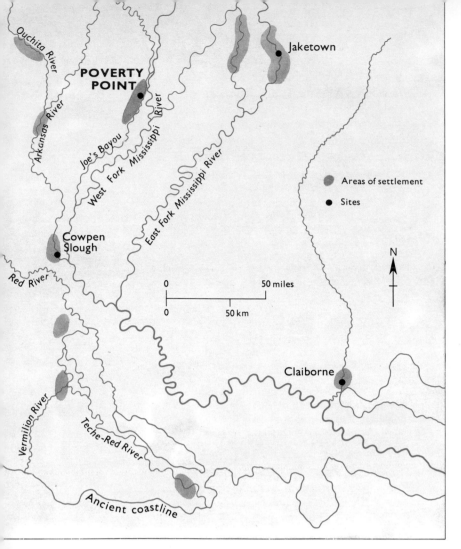

Location map of the old route of the Mississippi, showing Poverty Point at the centre of a number of sites sharing the same culture. Similar clusters of sites appeared in at least ten concentrations in the Lower Mississippi valley around 1000 BC. Each population concentration was linked by waterways, either the Mississippi or its tributaries. The delta has spread into the Gulf of Mexico since this period, and the coastline shown is contemporary for Poverty Point.

moulded clay figurines, often depicting seated and pregnant women. Few of these symbolic objects have a widespread distribution among all the Poverty Point population. This suggests that there was not a uniform religion but rather independent systems of worship based on the veneration of a great number of human, animal and nature spirits.

Long-distance trade, dealing primarily in rocks and minerals which were needed for stone-tool production, was a hallmark of peoples sharing common cultural traits described by archaeologists as the Poverty Point culture. Rocks do occur in the area of Poverty Point but only as outcrops of soft sandstones and ironstones; harder rocks were imported from the north, and from Poverty Point itself some of them were shipped by river further south, all the way to the Gulf of Mexico. It seems most likely that the materials changed hands between neighbouring communities through exchange ceremonies at regular festivals. What might have been given in return by the hunters who lived in the rockless areas of south Louisiana and south Mississippi is unknown, but it may be that perishable goods were traded from south to north. The complexity and extent of the trading system strongly suggest that the social structure of the Poverty Point peoples was highly developed.

As to the earthworks themselves at Poverty Point, their form may be better understood but their function continues to baffle archaeologists. A completely new dimension to the inquiry is offered by the idea that the swales between the ridges could have been flooded by damming the bayou, and might therefore have been designed as an elaborate system of water management, the long, curving canals serving as fishponds. Whatever their purpose, the mystery of Poverty Point will endure, and with less than 1 per cent of the earthworks archaeologically examined, many more surprises lie waiting to be unearthed.

1000 BC

Pendant owl effigies of stone had special significance in the Poverty Point culture, while more ordinary stone spearheads were manufactured in a variety of sizes and shapes.

CONCLUSION

It is an intriguing exercise to compare the studies of anthropologists with the results of archaeological excavations. Some archaeologists have always claimed that it is impossible to reconstruct social structures from the post holes, pits and stone tools often discovered in camps occupied by hunters and gatherers thousands of years ago. Others, frustrated by the routine classification of stone implements, which can sometimes become a necessary but uninspiring end in itself, have sought to go beyond the limits of what can essentially be proved as fact and try to reconstruct the daily lives of hunters from the objects that have survived them. So we can now contrast the anthropological ideal of an egalitarian hunting band, as evidenced by the !Kung, and see which of our excavated sites might match their example.

Of the three excavated sites, perhaps the occupants of the Kalemba rock shelter came closest to the egalitarian ideal. The artefacts that they left behind suggest an easily produced range of hunting and gathering tools with few surviving items that could be taken to indicate differences of prestige or rank. There are pitfalls in such an interpretation, however. Unless they encounter exceptional conditions of preservation – for example, waterlogged or very dry sites – archaeologists cannot recover artefacts made from organic materials such as leather or wood. It is entirely possible that the organic range of products made by the hunters of Kalemba would illustrate the potential for personal distinctions. Another shortcoming of archaeological evidence concerns varying rates of survival. It would be incorrect to link rock shelters exclusively with hunting and gathering camps. The Kalemba people may have moved to various open grassland, woodland and river-bank locations during their seasonal round, perhaps with only minimal annual use of their rock shelter accommodation. Caves and rock shelters dominate the archaeological record of hunters and gatherers simply because those places are where the fragile archaeological deposits are best preserved.

The hunters at Roonka Flat and Poverty Point do not conform to the egalitarian model. The former, divided by adherence to totemic groupings and with signs of variable status and wealth, seem to be a more unequal society, their differences perhaps akin to those seen now in the society of the Tiwi on islands off the north coast of Australia. The seasonal residents of Poverty Point belonged to a highly organized society, with a clear and compelling authority structure, capable of directing huge earth-moving operations. Variations in prestige were perhaps governed by possession of ritual knowledge and by access to rare, traded goods, with the most powerful no doubt controlling their circulation. Poverty Point, with its emphasis on complex earthworks, trade and the possible use of astronomical sightlines, attests the potential for cultural development of societies existing with the simplest technologies and the most direct methods of obtaining food.

The three groups of hunters at Kalemba, Roonka Flat and Poverty Point did have one shared attribute. They were all manufacturing small stone tools or microliths, multi-purpose tools used either singly, as the tips of arrowshafts, or in hafted multiples as knives or scraping implements. They do seem to reflect a worldwide, although not simultaneous, trend towards the replacement of large stone artefacts with smaller, more finely worked, stone tools, suggestive of a move away from the hunting of large mammals to the trapping of a greater variety of much smaller game. They also are indicative of increased ingenuity and foresight in implement manufacture and use, and are often taken as typical of societies described as 'advanced hunters'. Such hunter-gatherers possessed a detailed knowledge of their environment and of the growth and movement of plants and animals which lived in it. They planned ahead and with care for their subsistence requirements, and manufactured a range of non-utilitarian items for display and personal adornment. They engaged in various ritual activities, most notably expressed thousands of years earlier in the vivid cave paintings of south-west France and northern Spain. Some thoughts on life after death had been formulated, as is demonstrated by the care of the Roonka Flat population for its dead.

1000 BC

The existence of hunter-gatherers was already under threat by 1000 BC. Population grew exponentially after the successful transition to an agricultural way of life some 10,000 years ago. From the different parts of the world in which farming sprang up, it spread through the hunting and gathering peoples like bushfire. By 1000 BC more than half the world's population had shifted to a new way of life, and by 200 years ago, hunters had dwindled to perhaps 10 per cent of the population. The descendants of the inhabitants of Kalemba, Roonka Flat and Poverty Point would one day face extinction or assimilation as a result of the new life style.

By 1000 BC the spread of farming right across Europe from the Middle East (the ancient Near East) was already ancient history. It had reached the British Isles some time after 5000 BC, when groups of families had set sail from continental Europe, bringing with them domesticated livestock and primitive strains of wheat. The colonists followed a way of life that was not compatible with the resident hunters and gatherers. The farmers had to commence clearing the forest cover by fire and with stone axes, but the forests provided the woodland habitats for many of the plants and animals on which the hunters depended. The farmers also had to stake out claims to particular territories, since they needed to ensure that they could reap the harvest that they themselves had sown months earlier. Gradually a patchwork of farms, fields and trackways stretched across the landscape, confining the hunting bands to smaller and more fragmented areas. Hunters and gatherers clung on to their life style in the remote corners of the islands, or on high or in densely forested land, but they were fast becoming an endangered species.

By 1000 BC, 4,000 years of farming had produced an intensively settled countryside which was showing increasing signs of over-exploitation. A slowly worsening climate and the widespread availability of bronze weapons provided the conditions for the rise of warlords and the emergence of fortified hill tops. Old religious practices were abandoned and in their place a cult which centred on reverence for water, springs and wells offered a new focus. The site of Flag Fen was constructed during this period of change. Situated in a very low-lying region, it demonstrated its status and importance not by seeking out any relative rise in ground for its position, but by its construction as an artificial island surrounded by shallow water. The power of the water cult is amply illustrated by the quantity of costly metalwork thrown into the water on either side of the Avenue there.

The centuries either side of 1000 BC were ones of crisis and change in both the British Isles and the Middle East. The eastern Mediterranean had been thrown into turmoil during the late thirteenth century with the commencement of raiding by the 'Peoples of the Sea'. It was during this period of insecurity that Moses was able to lead a group of Israelites from their slavery in Egypt into the land of Canaan. In the twelfth century Egypt was subjected to a massive series of assaults by these 'Peoples of the Sea', at the end of which the country lay in a state of exhaustion, from which its empire never recovered. Lacking the strength to eject some of the invaders from Palestine, Egypt was forced to make a virtue out of necessity by allowing peoples such as the Philistines to settle there as its vassals. The power vacuum was accentuated by the contemporary eclipse of Assyrian might and by the disappearance of the Hittite empire, again swept into oblivion by the destructive raiding of the 'Peoples of the Sea'. In the Aegean the fall of Troy and the collapse of the Mycenaeans had plunged Greece into a Dark Age. Famine in Turkey during the thirteenth century led to emigration westwards over the sea, and Sicily, Sardinia and Etruria are all named after contemporary Middle Eastern peoples. In such uncertain political conditions David was able to seize his opportunity and create a unified Israelite state, with its capital at Jerusalem.

Shock waves from the Middle Eastern epicentre must have reached the British Isles, perhaps in the form of increased folk movements from continental Europe. It is quite possible that some refugees from the mainland crossed to Britain in order to settle there. The political disturbances of the ancient world found an echo in the natural world with the eruption of Mount Hekla on Iceland around 1150 BC. The volcano released an estimated 9 cubic miles (12 km) of volcanic dust into the atmosphere, reducing sunlight and having a major

1000 BC

impact on the growth of trees. The effect was felt in Ireland, for example, where the widths of oak tree-rings decreased significantly around this time, reacting to conditions that some have claimed resembled a 'nuclear winter'. Flag Fen and Megiddo were linked: both were the products of triumph in adversity.

Whether volcanic eruptions caused widespread environmental changes is still a matter of debate. Yet the centuries after 1000 BC were ones of considerable change, particulary in the northern hemisphere. Flag Fen was abandoned some time during the first millennium BC; certainly it never achieved again such a period of prestigious use. Megiddo's final occupants were Persian garrisons between the sixth and fourth centuries BC. The earthworks of Poverty Point were deserted after 700 BC. Only successive generations of hunters and gatherers from the less complex societies at Kalemba and Roonka Flat survived, apparently without interruption, in the same locations.

Out of the dislocations of the last centuries BC arose some powerful imperial forces to create new networks of domination and control. The Roman and Han civilizations were the super-powers of the classical world, dwarfing the smaller empires based on Petra, Meroe and Monte Alban. These five sites will form the basis of our study of empires in the following chapter.

1000
BC

CHAPTER 3

EMPIRES OF

AD 1

OLD

AD
1

INTRODUCTION

Empires could be large or small in terms of territorial extent. Certainly, by AD 1 some very large and some very small ancient empires had already disappeared. An empire can be defined as an aggregate of peoples and territories under the rule of a single person, oligarchy or sovereign state. The five sites in this chapter highlight variations on the theme of empires, thus demonstrating the heterogeneity of the word 'empire'. The Han empire, administered from its capital at Chang'an, was one of the largest the world has seen, in AD 1 or indeed at any other period, while the Roman empire, in its relentless subjugation of one rival power after another, grew to become the dominating force in Mediterranean politics. The empires based on Petra, Meroe and Monte Alban were much smaller, although all three brought foreign peoples under their control. Together, the five cities discussed here allow us to explore the similarities and differences between ancient empires.

These comparisons will illustrate that the sustaining factors behind empires were quite diverse. The Roman empire was held together just so long as its military cohesion and superiority endured, while the Han empire owed its rapid gestation to its inheritance of Shang, Chou and Ch'in territories and traditions. Isolation and the fertility of the Nile provided the twin foundations of Meroitic supremacy, while trade was the key to Petra's success. A militant and perhaps ruling priesthood, achieving a monopoly of prestige trade items, probably kept the faithful of Monte Alban content and the territories under its control intact.

By the year AD 1, then, many empires had already flourished and decayed, leaving behind them abandoned cities that could be resettled by newcomers or plundered for their building materials and robbed of their buried riches. Permanent villages and towns whose inhabitants lived by cultivating nearby fields and grazing animals had been a feature of the landscape for thousands of years in many parts of the world. In Central America and on the western seaboard of South America civilizations such as the Moche in north-western Peru had demonstrated

sophisticated levels of cultural achievement and organization, as evidenced by the great temple mounds of mud brick, such as those of the sun and moon near Trujillo, and the fabulous goldwork and mould-made pottery faces on some of their vases. Some of the greatest empires in history were history themselves. The ziggurats of the Sumerians gradually weathered away, slowly becoming amorphous mounds of mud brick situated among abandoned buildings and dried-up irrigation channels. Some of the imposing city mounds of the Indus civilization lay deserted. The river system that once gave them life was capricious by nature, either coming too near and flooding their defences or meandering away, leaving their fields slightly higher and certainly drier. Along the Nile the pyramids of the pharaohs stood as a reminder of the greatness that was once the Egyptian empire. Many of these tombs had long since been robbed by the inhabitants of a land that was already ancient. Further east the capital of the Persians, Persepolis, had lain in ruins for over three centuries. The Mauryan empire of Asoka in northern India was already past its peak, while Han rule in China was but a successor to the preceding dynasties of the Shang, Chou and Ch'in.

Not all the world was inhabited by quite such complex cultures, however. Much of North America and Australia was still populated by groups of hunter-gatherers, content to follow their own life styles and oblivious to developments elsewhere. The steppes of central Asia were home to tribes of nomads who led an organized but peripatetic existence, following large herds from pasture to pasture and occasionally trading with or raiding the more settled states to the south. In the South Seas intrepid island sailors continued to make voyages of discovery, seeking out the furthest landfalls in Polynesia. And Bantu-speaking peoples spread throughout Africa, bringing with them the knowledge of farming and iron-working – but also disruption to the hunters who had lived there for hundreds of thousands of years.

With so much history already passed, the citizens of some of the empires of AD 1 were able to study the origins of their own and other peoples' cultures, with if not an objectivity that we would appreciate today, then at least a biased curiosity.

AD
1

The writings of Homer told of the fall of Troy and the wanderings of Odysseus, while later Greek historians such as Herodotus and Thucydides documented the emergence of that remarkable phenomenon, Greek democracy, and the various wars of the Athenians and Spartans. At least some of the more inquiring Roman soldiers invading southern England might have pondered on the function and age of Stonehenge; Tacitus certainly did, dismissing the ancient inhabitants of Britain as barbarians. The Chinese had for centuries realized the necessity of developing their contemporary ideas about society within a traditional framework laid down in various chronicles, including, of course, the teachings of Confucius. The developed regions of the world, therefore, clearly were conscious of their histories, both through the written and spoken word and through the remains of abandoned cities and tombs that lay littered across the landscape.

AD
1

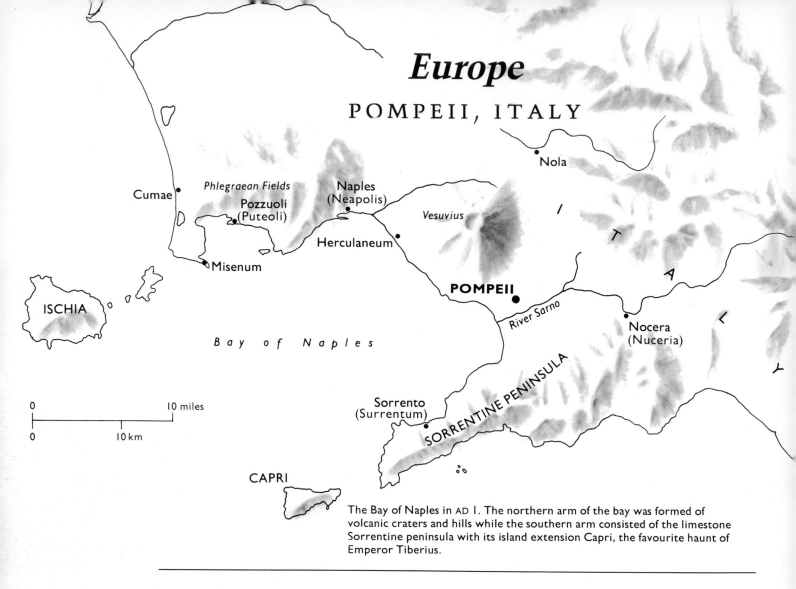

Europe

POMPEII, ITALY

The Bay of Naples in AD 1. The northern arm of the bay was formed of volcanic craters and hills while the southern arm consisted of the limestone Sorrentine peninsula with its island extension Capri, the favourite haunt of Emperor Tiberius.

AD 1

By AD 1 the Roman emperor, Augustus, had ruled the empire for nearly thirty years. The government of Rome was able to control the administration of a vast area centred on the Mediterranean basin. From the Euphrates to the Atlantic, and from the Nile to the Rhine, towns, villages and farms gradually conformed to the Roman model. Some 160 miles (250 km) south of the capital lay the riviera of the Roman world, the Bay of Naples. Here, in a fertile landscape dominated by the majestic summit of the volcano Vesuvius, many officials of the state built their luxurious second homes, often deciding to construct villas that enjoyed a view over the sea. During the summer, to escape the oppressive heat of Rome, they relaxed in the cultured atmosphere induced by towns like Naples, where Greek was still the language of the aristocracy. This was a legacy from the times when Greek colonists founded many of the towns in southern Italy; indeed, some of the earliest settlers in Pompeii in the sixth century BC were probably Greek. By AD 1, however, it was a thoroughly Roman town.

It is ironic that Pompeii was built over the very material that was eventually to engulf it, for the ancient town was situated on a solidified stream of volcanic material that had been thrown out in successive prehistoric eruptions by Vesuvius. The strip of land between the volcano and the bay was narrower in antiquity and was cut by rivers flowing westwards from the Apennine mountains. One of these rivers was the Sarno, and Pompeii was located just to its north, about 2,310 feet (700 m) from the ancient coastline. The river would certainly have been navigable as far as Pompeii, although the port installations for the town have not yet been discovered. The northern arm of the bay is formed by a collection of volcanic craters and hills known as the Phlegraean Fields. At the

The eruption of Vesuvius in AD 79 brought a cataclysmic end to the prosperous city of Pompeii. Thousands of its citizens fled, but many died, leaving their bodies transfixed for all time in a final agony.

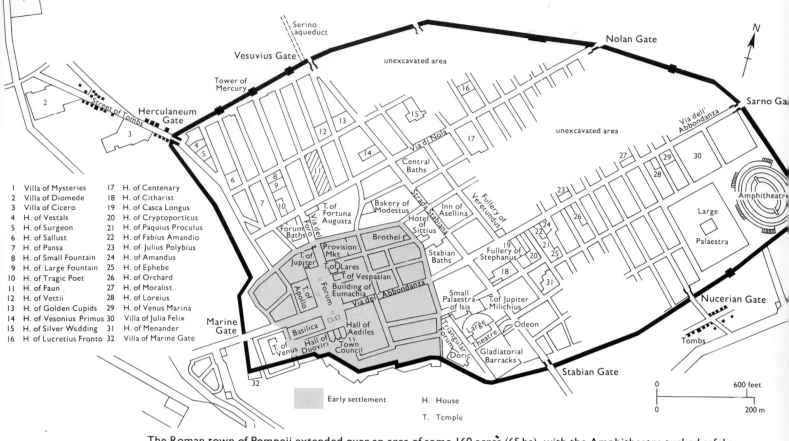

Serino aqueduct
Vesuvius Gate
unexcavated area
Nolan Gate
N
Sarno Ga
Tower of Mercury
16
Via dell' Abbondanza
Herculaneum Gate
Street of Tombs
2
3
4
5
13
12
15
14
Via di Nola
17
unexcavated area
Central Baths
27
29
30
6
8
9
7
10
T. of Fortuna Augusta
Bakery of Modestus
Inn of Asellina
23
28
Amphitheatre
Strada Stabiana
Forum Baths
T. of Jupiter
Provision Mkt
Brothel
Hotel of Sittius
Fullery of Verecundus
26
Large Palaestra
T. of Apollo
T. of Lares
Building of Eumachia
T. of Vespasian
Stabian Baths
Fullery of Stephanus
24
22
21
25
Forum
19
20
31
Via dell' Abbondanza
18
Marine Gate
Basilica
Hall of Aediles
Small Palaestra
T. of Jupiter Milichius
Nucerian Gate
T. of Venus
Hall of Duoviri
Town Council
T. of Isis
Large Theatre
Odeon
Triangular Forum
T. Doric
Gladiatorial Barracks
Tombs
32
Stabian Gate

1 Villa of Mysteries
2 Villa of Diomede
3 Villa of Cicero
4 H. of Vestals
5 H. of Surgeon
6 H. of Sallust
7 H. of Pansa
8 H. of Small Fountain
9 H. of Large Fountain
10 H. of Tragic Poet
11 H. of Faun
12 H. of Vettii
13 H. of Golden Cupids
14 H. of Vesonius Primus
15 H. of Silver Wedding
16 H. of Lucretius Fronto

17 H. of Centenary
18 H. of Citharist
19 H. of Casca Longus
20 H. of Cryptoporticus
21 H. of Paquius Proculus
22 H. of Fabius Amandio
23 H. of Julius Polybius
24 H. of Amandus
25 H. of Ephebe
26 H. of Orchard
27 H. of Moralist
28 H. of Loreius
29 H. of Venus Marina
30 Villa of Julia Felix
31 H. of Menander
32 Villa of Marine Gate

Early settlement   H. House
                    T. Temple

0   600 feet
0   200 m

The Roman town of Pompeii extended over an area of some 160 acres (65 ha), with the Amphitheatre tucked safely away in the poorer south-east corner, since gladiatorial contests often led to civil disturbances.

AD 1

western end stood Misenum, the naval base for the Augustan fleet. The southern arm consists of the limestone Sorrentine peninsula, which ends in the island of Capri, favourite haunt of Emperor Tiberius.

The Sarno valley around Pompeii was wide and fertile, with grain, fruit and vegetables growing in abundance. During its long history the region was often called upon to send grain to feed the population of Rome. On the more elevated slopes and the lower flanks of Vesuvius grew vines that produced a strong, sweet wine, while higher up there will have been olive groves and some pasture for sheep. The wall paintings of Pompeii, which throw so much light on various aspects of the lives of the town's inhabitants, depict a number of local fruits, including grapes, apples, pears, figs, pomegranates, cherries and peaches. Meat delicacies shown are suckling pig, kid, hare, chicken, geese, peacock, guinea fowl, squab and several other game birds. The region also held valuable sources of building stone, ranging from the limestone of the Sarno valley to the lava of Vesuvius, used in grain mills and olive pulpers. From slightly further afield came white limestone from Caserta and tuff from Nocera. It was in such a

favourable environment that the town of Pompeii – less worldly, less fashionable and not quite so historically significant as some of its illustrious neighbours – flourished, and it is Pompeii that was preserved for future generations as a perfect example of a town of the early Roman empire.

By ignoring the latest buildings at Pompeii buried by the eruption of Vesuvius in AD 79, we can describe the city as it might have looked in AD 1. The walls of the town enclosed an irregular, oval area, the long axis (NE–SW) being some 3,960 feet (1,200 m) in length, the short axis (NW–SE) some 2,376 feet (720 m). For about half of their circuit the walls were essentially a terrace built against the volcanic deposits underneath the town, but on the north and east sides they were of a more complicated form. Along this stretch a composite fortification was constructed, consisting of two walls of stone with a fill of earth between and a sloping bank of earth on the town side. There were probably about a dozen towers on the walled circuit. The best preserved lies to the west of the Vesuvius Gate. The towers were square in plan and projected out beyond the face of the fortification wall. They contained three storeys, each roofed by a barrel vault and connected by interior stairs. On

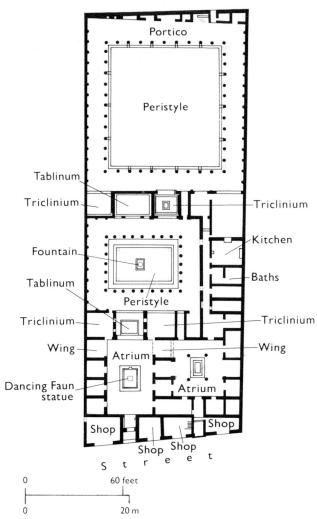

The House of Faun, one of the most sumptuous of private dwellings ever excavated, was built in a rich district near the Forum Baths. It possessed two entrances on its street side, each leading into separate atria; these were entrance halls, with basins open to the sky. The left atrium led to a tablinum (hall), with a dining room on either side. Across a colonnaded garden (peristyle) lay a further hall, beyond which was a secluded garden surrounded by a portico. Despite its richness, the house still had shops along its street front.

(Plan labels: Portico; Peristyle; Tablinum; Triclinium; Triclinium; Kitchen; Fountain; Baths; Tablinum; Peristyle; Triclinium; Triclinium; Wing; Wing; Atrium; Atrium; Dancing Faun statue; Shop; Shop; Shop; Shop; Street; 0 — 60 feet; 0 — 20 m)

the top storey was positioned the defensive artillery, while the middle storey allowed access to the wall walk on both sides. In the basement storey narrow slits on the tower face provided some light, and a postern door in the side of the tower functioned as an egress point for the sorties of defenders.

At least eight major gates pierced the walls. The nearest to the Forum was the Marine Gate, where visitors to the town could ascend a steep paved road under the barrel vault of the gate to enter the town. To one side of the main carriageway was a corridor walled off for pedestrians while on the opposite side stood a guardroom. The street pattern

Tower of Mercury, best-known of probably twelve defensive towers.

of Pompeii was probably laid out in a series of staged developments. Like most classical town plans, the arrangement of streets is a grid, dividing the areas for buildings into rectangular blocks. The principal arteries were the Via dell'Abbondanza, the Via di Nola and the Strada Stabiana. Even the new street plan could not entirely hide the older, and more irregular, streets of the original nucleus of the settlement in the south-west quarter.

Water for the fountains, baths and private houses of Pompeii was brought to the town by the great Serino aqueduct. This enormous construction was some 60 miles (96 km) in length. It took its waters from a source in the hills above Avellino and fed the towns of Naples and Pozzuoli. Subsidiary channels led off to many towns, including Pompeii, Nola and Cumae. The aqueduct entered the town just to the west of the Vesuvius Gate, the highest point of the enclosed area, and was distributed from there by pipes. Much of the water went to the public fountains, of which there were more than thirty in the town's streets. Indeed, the quantity of water piped to houses was small and most citizens obtained their drinking water from a public fountain. Additional supplies were obtained by collecting rainwater in cisterns, which were fed from gutters or from shallow stone basins inside the atrium (courtyard) of houses. Furthermore, there were a number of wells and standpipes, which helped augment and distribute the supply. There was a limited system of sewers beneath the streets of Pompeii. Many latrines in the town depended on

AD
1

water brought by hand or piped from roofs for flushing, while most were not connected to the sewer system but drained into pits.

In AD 1 anyone entering the southern side of the Forum would have been confronted by the majestic façade of the Temple of Jupiter, Juno and Minerva at the northern end of the public square, framed against a backdrop of Vesuvius. These three deities were the protectors of the Roman state and their worship in Pompeii, as in other towns of the empire, symbolized the embracing nature of Roman rule. The temple sat on a high platform which was approached by a flight of steps. A deep, colonnaded porch eventually led to a single chapel, whose walls were painted in imitation of marble. In the basement of the temple were rooms containing sacrificial offerings and the public treasury. Both private and public religion played an important part in the lives of the inhabitants and ten temples to a variety of deities have been discovered in the town.

Many of Pompeii's significant public buildings were constructed at private expense and given to the town by wealthy officials, who were no doubt keen to improve their political standing among the people. Two particular politicians, Marcus Porcius and Caius Quinctius Valgus, constructed places of public entertainment for the masses: the Small Theatre and the Amphitheatre. The Small Theatre consisted of a broad rectangle, 92 by 99 feet (28 by 30 m), which was covered by a great gable roof. A semicircular arrangement of raked seats housed the spectators, who looked down on the rectangular platform of the stage. When full, the auditorium must have housed between 1,000 and 1,500 people who could witness refined spectacles such as concerts and recitations. More boisterous performances were staged at the Amphitheatre, a huge oval arena which occupied the south-eastern quarter of the town and had seating capacity for nearly the whole population. Here the performances that the masses loved were staged – gladiatorial combats, which often resulted in deaths, and savage confrontations between wild animals. Violence was not confined just to the field. In AD 59 a particularly nasty brawl broke out in the Amphitheatre between citizens of Pompeii and visitors from neighbouring Nocera. A considerable number of fatalities occurred and, as a result of a government inquiry, the Amphitheatre was closed for ten years.

Another form of relaxation for the citizens was to attend one of the two public baths in the town. The Forum Baths lay to the north of the Forum and provided separate suites of baths for men and women. The men's rooms included an exercise yard, a changing-room and then the usual sequence of cold, warm and hot rooms. The women's suite was essentially the same except for the omission of an exercise area. The baths were normally opened at midday, when the furnaces were lit. Bells, gongs

Much of Pompeii is laid out with an almost grid-like street pattern, though the south-west corner is irregular and bears the imprint of an earlier fifth to sixth century settlement.

and the cries of slaves would have broadcast the opening to the inhabitants. Bathers were expected to bring their own oil and soda, strigils (scrapers) and towels. Bathing in the Roman empire was, of course, a social occasion at which much else besides cleanliness was achieved; many a business deal or the hint of a scandal probably surfaced first in the baths. The Forum Baths were obviously open at night, since over 1,000 lamps were discovered in the complex.

One of the most significant architectural legacies of ancient Pompeii is the large number of private houses that have been uncovered through excavation. Some were spacious complexes and give an extraordinary insight into life in the Roman home. A few houses in Pompeii covered large areas, sometimes 7,535 square feet (700 sq. m) or more, and were usually one storey high. Like many Arab houses, the rooms were meant to be lit from within; the bustle and noise of the street were kept firmly outside. Most substantial houses consisted of rooms arranged around a sky-lit atrium. On the floor of the atrium was a basin to collect rainwater from the ridged roofs. Often the houses incorporated gardens, which would be surrounded by rectangular colonnades. One of the most sumptuous of these houses is the House of the Faun, which extended over some 31,284 square feet (3,000 sq. m) and occupied the whole of one block. It possessed two entrances on one of its shorter sides, both leading into separate atria. From the larger atrium a guest proceeded to the tablinum (hall), which was flanked on either side by dining-rooms known as triclinia (the name refers to the three couches which were usually found in each dining-room; the diner would lean on his or her left elbow, supported by a cushion, with the feet stretching away from the square table and perhaps resting on a small footstool). Beyond this suite of rooms lay a colonnaded garden (the peristyle), on the far side of which was another hall again, flanked by dining-rooms. This particular hall was paved with an exceptionally fine mosaic, depicting Alexander the Great in battle against Darius III at Issus in 333 BC. A corridor led on to a further and larger garden, surrounded by a portico. The living-rooms and bedrooms were arranged around the two atria, while along a corridor on the eastern side were the baths and the kitchen. The house had four dining-rooms in all, one for each season. Those of the autumn and winter faced south, while the spring and summer rooms were turned to northern breezes and the shade.

The town walls divided the living from the dead. Burial and cremation were forbidden within settlements by Roman law. At Pompeii two roads, one leading from the Herculaneum Gate and the

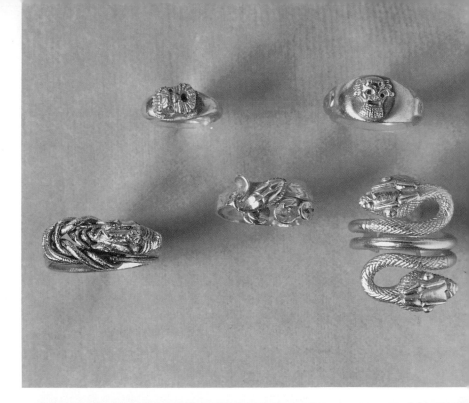

Top: Although all Roman citizens were allowed to wear the toga, status was defined very clearly by style and colour, and by the richness and type of jewellery worn.

Above: The interior of the Hot Room in the Forum Baths. Here slaves scraped and oiled the skin of citizens, while business deals were clinched and gossip exchanged.

AD
1

other from the Nucerian Gate, were lined with an uninterrupted sequence of monumental tombs. The oldest tomb appears to be that of M. Porcius outside the Herculaneum, the same Porcius who helped finance the construction of the Small Theatre and the Amphitheatre. Most of the tombs were square or rectangular in plan, with façades and sides decorated by applied architectural detail. The interiors of the tombs could be lavishly painted and contained expensive grave furniture, such as urns, lamps, wine jars and bottles of scent. There was a comfortable relationship between the living and the dead. Many tombs had benches fitted to their outsides on which relatives, friends or descendants of the deceased would sit and sometimes eat.

Further down the road from the Herculaneum Gate lay the Villa of Mysteries, one of a group of over 100 villas from the countryside around Pompeii. The Villa of Mysteries had developed by AD 1 into an elegant complex of over sixty rooms, arranged around a peristyle and an atrium. The villa is famous for the room filled with a series of remarkable murals illustrating the mystic cult of Bacchus. Out in the countryside the remaining villas can be divided into three categories. First, there were the rich country houses which formed the centres of agricultural estates; these were owned by landlords who dwelt in the town and used bailiffs to run their agricultural investments. Then there were villas inhabited by owner-occupiers, who sometimes offered country produce to visitors and must have served a similar function to country inns. Finally, there were villas owned by absentee landlords, managed by bailiffs and worked by slaves.

Pompeii continued developing as a town after AD 1. The east side of the Forum was almost totally

Above left: An evocative reminder of everyday life in Pompeii are the lava millstones, used for grinding grain. The arch of the oven can be seen in the background.

Above right: A reconstruction of the same bakery, showing how donkeys turned the millstones. Note the flagstones (to stop the floor wearing out), the awning over the oven and the well set into the floor.

AD
1

Above: The Temple of Apollo is the largest of four temples set around the Forum. The temple's 'drum-built' fluted columns surround an inner sanctum.

Below: Into the ports along the shores of the Bay of Naples came cargo ships carrying exotic animals to perform or fight in the amphitheatres of Italy. Such beasts inspired local mosaic manufacturers.

rebuilt, with a series of monumental edifices replacing an earlier line of shops. Many public and private buildings were damaged by an earthquake in AD 62 and the Pompeiians were left with the massive task of rebuilding some of the town, including areas in and around the Forum. Some parts of the town, however, still resembled a building site when Vesuvius erupted in AD 79.

For Pompeii and for many Pompeiians that summer of AD 79 was to be their last. On the morning of 24 August Vesuvius began to erupt, causing one of the worst catastrophes of the ancient world. Pliny the Younger described the eruption in graphic detail. At first the solidified matter stopping the throat of the volcano was blown skywards, descending as a rain of pumice pellets which ranged from the size of a small pea to the size of a large plum. This phase of the eruption probably lasted about eighteen hours and during this time there were clearly some organized attempts to evacuate the town. By early the following morning, the plug in the throat of the volcano had completely disintegrated and heavy, liquid magma shot up in repeated explosions, to fall back on the town as a thick layer of ash. It appears that many Pompeiians would have been killed by the heat of the ash. Electrical storms accompanied the eruption and several places in the town were struck by lightning. After two days the eruption was complete, and Pompeii lay buried beneath nearly 13 feet (4 m) of pumice and ash. The survivors returned to a nightmare landscape of cooling volcanic matter pierced only by the highest remaining walls, such as the fortifications. They must have desperately sought out their relatives and later their valuables by digging through the overburden. The precise number of fatalities from those two last days of Pompeii is still unknown.

AD 1

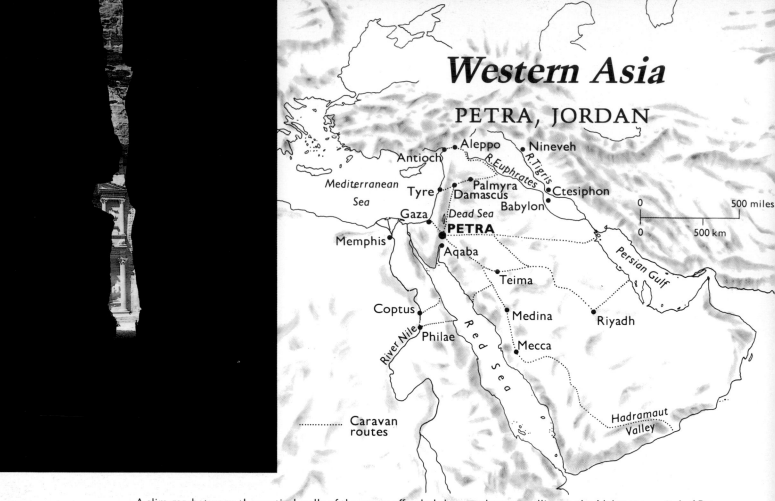

Western Asia

PETRA, JORDAN

Caravan routes

A slim gap between the vertical walls of the gorge afforded the merchant travelling to the Nabatean capital of Petra his first sight of that most celebrated monument, the Khazneh.

The Nabatean capital of Petra (meaning 'rock') was at its most prosperous in AD 1. It lay on either side of a wadi known as the Wadi Musa (wadi of Moses) and was surrounded by towering cliffs of multi-coloured rock, banded in different colours: red, yellow, white and mauve. The architecture of the city centre comprised elegant, free-standing buildings ranged along a principal street. As the ground gradually rose away from the centre, however, and as buildings made more use of the underlying sandstone, terraces were cut into the live rock and basement walls consisted of geological strata rather than laid courses of stone. Finally, as the vertical walls of the cliffs constrained the area for building, the cliff walls themselves were carved in elaborate façades and rooms tunnelled into the cliff face behind them. The Nabateans became masters of two very contrasting methods of building. The free-standing structures were constructed in the usual manner, from the foundations upwards, but the façades sculpted from the rock were fashioned from the top downwards. The overall effect is stunning. As the sun rises and falls over the basin of Petra, the colours of the façades at first dazzle, then deepen through various

shades of red and brown until they are silhouetted in sharp shadow. The buildings carved from the rock seem to be emerging from the strata, struggling to free themselves from their perpetual, geological guardians. But the struggle is a vain one, as the sun sets on the rose-red city yet again and, suddenly dark, Petra stills itself.

In AD 1 Petra was a bustling, commercial capital which owed its success to its location at the junction of several important trade routes. It was sited on the eastern flank of the African Rift Valley, about half-way between the Dead Sea to the north and the Red Sea at Aqaba to the south. It was able to profit from control of goods between the great cities of Mesopotamia and those of Egypt. It also acted as a successful intermediary in the movement of exotic products from the Arabian world, such as frankincense and myrrh, to its powerful western neighbour, the Roman empire. The fame of Petra spread even further afield and spices, silk thread and cloth must have regularly entered the city at the termination of the long land routes from China and India. Surprisingly, some types of cloth, including gauze and damask (respectively from Gaza and Damascus), were exported from the Near

AD 1

The classic image of the rock-cut Royal Tombs at Petra. From left to right: The Palace Tomb, the Corinthian Tomb, the Silk Tomb and the Urn Tomb. Petra was surrounded by towering cliffs which constrained the area available for building but which were used to ingenious effect by the stonemasons of the city.

East to China. On most days at Petra, therefore, the narrow and winding gorges that thread through the mountains surrounding the city must have echoed to the sounds of camel-caravans and their merchants bringing goods to the great warehouses.

The merchant coming to Petra from the east would first enter the gorge known as the Bab as-Siq and begin tracing a serpentine course towards the city centre. Among the monuments carved into the sides of the gorge, two on the left cliff face would immediately catch the eye: the so-called Obelisk Tomb and, underneath it, the Bab as-Siq Triclinium. The two unrelated façades are strikingly different. The front of the Obelisk Tomb is dominated by the four rock obelisks that stand above the doorway. In between the two middle obelisks is a recessed niche with two pillars flanking a central figure. Inside the doorway is a single rock-cut room, with two burial chambers on either side and a further burial chamber in the rear wall. Smaller obelisks can be found throughout the Petra area and it may be that the pillars represent the spirits of the dead. The façade of this tomb is unique, however, because the obelisks suggest that the architect of the tomb had some familiarity with Egyptian buildings. The front of the Bab as-Siq Triclinium could not be a greater contrast. It has a two-storey façade, the lower storey comprising six engaged pilasters carrying an arched pediment while the upper consists of six very squat pillars supporting broken pediments. It is typically Nabatean in design. The central doorway gives on to a single chamber, surrounded on three sides by long benches – a characteristic triclinium arrangement. There are over 500 tombs in Petra, of which about twenty-five possess triclinia. These clearly provided the setting for meals held in memory and honour of the dead.

AD
1

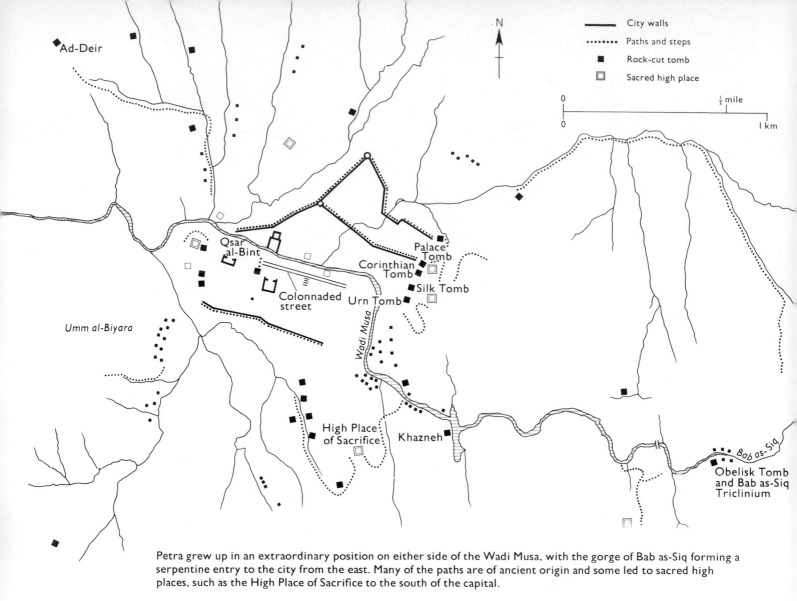

Petra grew up in an extraordinary position on either side of the Wadi Musa, with the gorge of Bab as-Siq forming a serpentine entry to the city from the east. Many of the paths are of ancient origin and some led to sacred high places, such as the High Place of Sacrifice to the south of the capital.

AD 1

In AD 1 the waters of the Wadi Musa flowed through the gorge and down towards the city. The merchant could meander down the Siq before suddenly catching sight, through the slim gap between the walls of the gorge, of a section of Petra's most celebrated monument, the Khazneh. The deeply cut façade of the tomb has been called the most perfectly preserved frontage in antiquity, and no visitor can fail to be impressed by the quality of the architectural detail. Its name in Arabic, Al-Khazneh or Khaznet Phar'oun, means Treasury or Pharaoh's Treasury, deriving from a local legend that tells of vast treasures contained in the urn on top of the façade. Close examination of the urn reveals that it is riddled with bullet marks. For centuries it has been the target of marksmen attempting to break open the urn and reap a showering harvest of gold and silver coins for their troubles.

The façade of the Khazneh consists of two superimposed storeys, both with Corinthian capitals. The lower section comprises a row of six columns, of which the two in the centre are free-standing. A decorated pediment is supported on the four central columns. The upper storey has a circular structure or tholos at its centre, surrounded by columns and flanked by two small rectangular buildings, each capped by a broken pediment. On top of the roof of the tholos is a Corinthian capital which, in turn, is the base for the nearly 13-foot-tall (4-m) urn. Behind the broken pediments of the rectangular buildings the bases of two massive obelisks rise the short distance to the rock-roof of the frontage. The tomb is unusual in Petra in that the façade carries an enormous number of human and animal carvings, including representations of Medusa, satyrs, male equestrian figures that watch over the dead, dancing Amazons, victory figures, eagles and sphinxes or lions. In addition, the surviving scaffolding putlog holes on the façade of the tomb demonstrate the system of carving and construction from the top downwards.

Two great obelisks, near the High Place of Sacrifice, were formed by carving away the top of a rock ridge, leaving two exposed cores that were then worked into pyramid-like pillars. One example (right) is illustrated here.

The internal plan of the Khazneh is that of a monumental tomb. Passing between the columns you reach a portico with two richly decorated doorways leading into differently shaped side chambers. Perhaps both chambers served the clergy in some manner. A staircase from the portico leads up to the 26-foot-high (8-m) doorway of the principal chamber of the Khazneh. The doorway was clearly once equipped with double wooden doors, since the jambs for them can still be seen in the floor. The main chamber of the monument is an almost exact 40-foot (12-m) cube, with framed and pedimented doorways in the end and side walls giving access to three small burial chambers. The rear chamber seems to have been the most important and may have held the stone coffin in which lay the remains of the person for whom the tomb was carved. It is argued that the deceased was the Nabatean king Aretas III, who ruled from 86 to 62 BC. He had enlarged the Nabatean empire to include southern Syria and Damascus, from where stylistic ideas and craftsmen could have been obtained to design and sculpt a façade so foreign to Petra itself.

Turning to the right past the Khazneh the merchant would continue on down the Siq, passing an extraordinary number of tombs arranged on different levels, before emerging from the gorge at the eastern end of the major E–W street of Petra. At this point the alternating silence and echoes of the Siq, and its association with the dead, were replaced by the continuous bustle of the city and its lively citizens. The main public buildings lined this street, but between the public structures there were glimpses in the distance of rising ground covered with houses. At the far end of the thoroughfare an arched gate spanned the road and separated a sacred and quieter area of the city from the clamour of its commercial quarters. Through the gate a 660-foot-long (200-m) temenos or sacred courtyard gave eventually on to the most important Nabatean temple at Petra, the Qasr al-Bint, probably built during the reign of Obodas II, who ruled from 30 to 9 BC. The temple was aligned N–S and was, of course, built as a free-standing structure, using local sandstone blocks set in mortar. The main temple building, some 92 feet (28 m) square, had squared pilasters at each of its corners. Extensive traces of plaster on its west and south external walls indicate that a finely detailed ornamental stucco once covered the whole building. Worshippers approaching the temple from the open-air altar (which was originally covered in marble and must have gleamed in the sunlight) to the north ascended a monumental staircase before passing between the four marble-clad columns to enter the portico. A doorway on the south side of the portico gave access into the cella, the principal internal chamber in the temple. High windows in the east and west walls allowed sunlight to play on the decorated and painted plaster that once lined the cella walls. At the rear of the cella were three chambers, the central and most sacred of which was approached by a flight of steps and no doubt

AD
1

This colonnaded principal street in the centre of Petra was excavated in the 1950s by Jordanian and British excavation teams.

Left and above: External and internal reconstructions of the most important Nabatean temple at Petra – the Qasr al-Bint – probably built during the reign of Obodas II between 30 BC and 9 BC. The temple was constructed as a free-standing structure using local sandstone blocks. Worshippers were restricted to practising their rites at an open-air altar, outside the temple. The temple itself was the domain of the priests and housed the temple treasures.

housed the Nabatean deity Dushara, represented perhaps simply by a block of stone.

The religious structures of Petra were not confined to the centre of the city. It appears that many of the cliff tops that surrounded the built-up areas carried important and sacred monuments, including the massive rock of Umm al-Biyara, which towers over central Petra from the south-west; an elaborately carved processional way led up to the summit. South of the Siq, near the High Place of Sacrifice, stand two obelisks, approximately 100 feet (30 m) apart. They are both over 20 feet (6 m) in height and are unadorned except for some typically Nabatean diagonal hatching. However, the extraordinary aspect of these obelisks is that they were built up not from cut blocks of sandstone but from live rock. The whole surface of the ridge around them must have been lowered to leave them so prominent. The two obelisks almost certainly represent the two key Nabatean deities, Dushara and Al-Uzza.

Close to the obelisks on the Attuf ridge was the most important sanctuary of the Nabateans, known as the High Place of Sacrifice. The sanctuary comprised a large central court with a raised platform, two altars, a pool and associated

The Garden Temple complex is a typical example of rock-cut architecture at Petra, situated just to the west of the High Place of Sacrifice. Part of this area was thought to be a garden and has given the monument its name.

Qasr al-Bint, showing the positions of four marble columns giving access to the portico, and from there to the principal internal chamber of the temple. From here stairs led up to a room for the cult statue or stone.

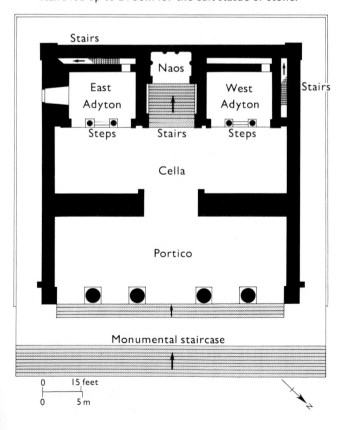

drains, all carved out of the mountain top. It seems likely that animal sacrifices took place on the altars, with the water tanks providing a supply of water for ritual cleansing. Among the heights on the opposite side of the city, Petra's largest and most impressive rock-cut façade, Ad-Deir, marks another Nabatean religious structure, almost certainly a temple. The frontage measures 165 feet (50 m) in width by 148 feet (45 m) in height, and boasts a 26-foot-high (8-m) doorway, which gives access to a single internal chamber. The architectural style of the exterior owes much to the Khazneh, as it consists of two storeys, the upper formed by a central tholos topped by an urn. Although the legacy of Petra today is largely one of monumental public buildings and tombs, in AD 1 the thousands of houses of its inhabitants would have filled the landscape, from the banks of the Wadi Musa to the crests of the encircling mountains.

Where did the Nabateans come from? The first historical mention is in an account of an attack against them in 312 BC by the ruler of Syria, Antigonus, who was one of Alexander the Great's former generals. That attack was probably directed

AD 1

The largest and most impressive rock-cut façade at Petra is the Ad-Deir, a Nabatean religious structure, most probably a temple. The architectural style of the exterior owes much to the Khazneh.

against a fortress that stood on Umm al-Biyara, to the immediate west of Petra. The Nabateans had originally come from northern Arabia, some time after the sixth century BC, and spoke an Arabic dialect. By the late fourth century BC they had adopted an Aramaic-related script which was widely used between the Red and Dead Seas for commercial transactions. Initially they had relied for subsistence on livestock, and on the trade in frankincense and myrrh, but once settled at Petra, the variety and quantity of their trading activities grew considerably, and they successfully experimented with irrigation agriculture. They were quick to defend their advantageous trading location against any threat. When maritime trade along the Red Sea threatened to bypass Petra, the Nabateans resorted to piracy to disrupt it. Nabatean control seems to have extended to Gaza on the Mediterranean coast and to Damascus, which was captured by them in 84 BC.

Trade was the source of Petra's prosperity and the Romans dealt a commercial blow to the city by developing alternative routes from Mesopotamia, through Palmyra, to the north of Petra, and on to the Levantine ports. Yet in its heyday the warehouses at Petra must have been packed with exotic materials such as henna, cloth, silk, damask,

glass, gold, silver, frankincense, myrrh, perfumes, ginger, pepper, cotton and sugar. In order to handle the volume of trade Petra had developed its own coinage by the first century BC. The Nabateans were an industrious people, apparently with few slaves, who also manufactured goods on their own account and produced particularly fine pottery. They were, of course, ruled by kings. Yet the Greek geographer Strabo suggested some form of token democracy when he wrote of the Nabatean king submitting his financial accounts to the people, and also allowing his private life to be scrutinized. The Nabateans were guarded by their two principal deities, Dushara and Al-Uzza. Dushara derived his name from the mountains of Sharra to the north of the city, and it was therefore appropriate that many of his sanctuaries should be the high places on mountain tops. He was frequently represented at Petra as a block of stone, owing to the generalized abhorrence the people possessed for life-like idols. Al-Uzza was the goddess of springs and water, and was especially revered in Petra, where the management of water both for the welfare of the city and also for its surrounding irrigated fields was so important. No deity, however, could prevent the conquest and incorporation of Petra into the Roman province of Arabia in AD 106.

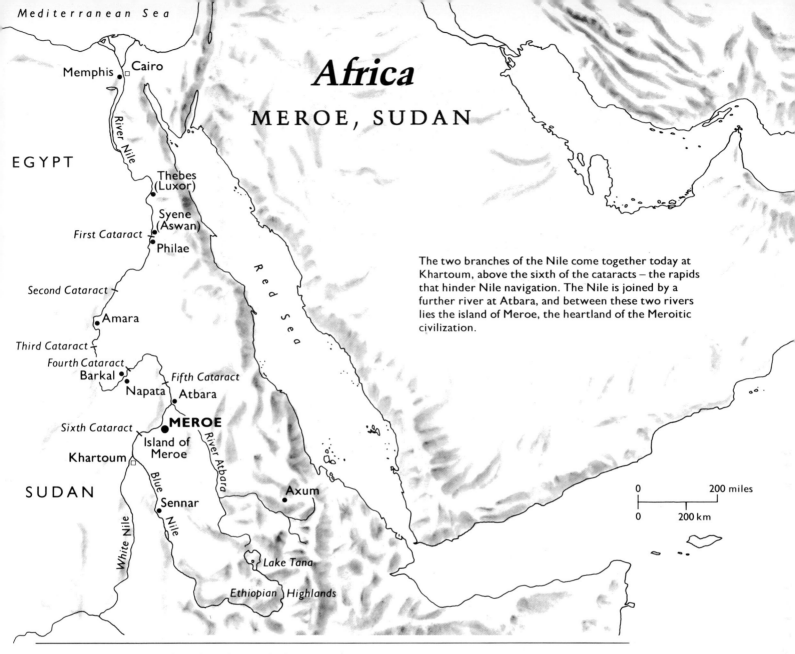

Africa

MEROE, SUDAN

The two branches of the Nile come together today at Khartoum, above the sixth of the cataracts – the rapids that hinder Nile navigation. The Nile is joined by a further river at Atbara, and between these two rivers lies the island of Meroe, the heartland of the Meroitic civilization.

Two branches of the Nile – the White Nile from the lakes of Uganda, the Blue Nile from the highlands of Ethiopia – come together at Khartoum, the capital of the Sudan. Together they form an enormous body of water, destined to trace a long and serpentine course across rocky cataracts and through desert landscapes on its voyage to Egypt and eventually the Mediterranean. About 188 miles (300 km) north of Khartoum the river passes the small town of Atbara and joins forces with another body of water, supplied by the river after which the town is named. In the triangular area of land south of this confluence, lying between the rivers Atbara and Nile, lies the so-called Island of Meroe. The region takes its name from the ancient town of Meroe, situated on the east bank of the Nile. In AD 1 Meroe was the capital of a state that controlled territory from its northern border with Egypt to the lands south of

Khartoum. Meroitic civilization was a unique blend of classical Egyptian and African influences, typified, for example, by the way in which human figures on Egyptian-style temple reliefs show features such as facial scarification or portray decidedly plump women.

Like its neighbour to the north, the Meroitic state was centred on the river, but the area was certainly more wooded in the last millennium BC than now. Higher annual rainfall across the plains of the Island of Meroe made possible the cultivation of millet and sorghum in the beds of wadis, while extensive grasslands enabled the pasturage of predominantly humpless shorthorn cattle and some sheep. Horses, and in late Meriotic times camels, offered alternative modes of transport to that provided by the Nile.

Meroe was not the original capital. Before 600 BC the royal family had resided at Napata, near the

AD 1

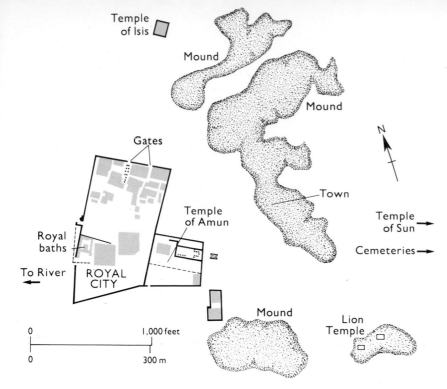

Temple
of Isis

Mound

Mound

Gates

Town

N

Temple
of Amun

Temple
of Sun →

Royal
baths

Cemeteries →

To River ←

ROYAL
CITY

0 ——————— 1,000 feet

0 ——————— 300 m

Mound

Lion
Temple

Meroe comprised a Royal City, the town proper and cemeteries to the east. Between the Royal City and the cemeteries, heaps of slag and mounds indicate the respective locations of iron factories and houses.

walled precinct. Other temples, such as those to the lion god, the sun and Isis, stood either in or close to the town. To the east of the Royal City numerous mounds covered with red-brick fragments indicate the presence of the homes of the population. Six large mounds of slag on the western and southern edges of the built-up area suggest the location of the iron factories. A few miles further east the dead were laid to rest. For the bulk of the populace there were relatively simple graves; for the members of the royal family there were small but steep-sided pyramids.

The largest single building known at Meroe is

Steep-sided pyramids mark the graves of Meroitic kings, queens, princes and priests. Small funerary chapels, containing inscriptions and reliefs, were attached to the

Fourth Cataract and much closer to Egypt. The move to Meroe may have occurred around 600 BC, possibly prompted by an Egyptian invasion in 593 BC which apparently reached as far as Napata. The transfer of the capital further south was to prove of lasting significance, marking an effective break from dependence on Egypt, and the more fertile surroundings of Meroe provided the basis for a larger population. It also made more accessible a plentiful supply of timber, which would prove so necessary as fuel for the important iron-smelting industry that was to develop. And finally, it opened up the possibility of Meroitic merchants using new trade routes. Instead of directing exports down the Nile, they could now be taken across the desert to ports on the Red Sea, or indeed along the Atbara and into the Ethiopian highlands, where a developing urban-based civilization centred on Axum had created a new market. Symptomatic of the political and cultural independence of Meroe was the emergence of a local cursive script (at present undeciphered, apart from the phonetic values of the signs and the names of people and places), which gradually replaced Egyptian as the language of monumental inscriptions.

The city of Meroe lay on the east bank of the Nile and can be divided into three separate elements: a Royal City, the town proper and the cemeteries. The Royal City lay nearest the river and comprised a complex of temples and baths in a

AD
1

the Temple of Amun, which was probably erected in the first century BC, on the site of an earlier temple, and clearly showed its derivation from Egyptian models. It was approached through a small kiosk or shrine and the walk from there to the temple was flanked by four stone rams, the sacred animal of the god. The temple was constructed of mud bricks and only those used in the facing were fired. Dressed blocks of sandstone were used to face columns, doorways and the entrance pylons at the eastern end of the structure. Inside the temple a long columned hall contained a small stone shrine bearing the names of

Netekamani and Amanitare, king and queen of Meroe (these monarchs ruled between approximately 12 BC and AD 12). To the west of the shrine a stone pulpit carried engraved scenes of bound and kneeling prisoners captured by the Meroites. Further halls led to the sanctuary at the western end of the temple, which contained an altar and, no doubt, a statue of Amun.

Excavations undertaken between 1910 and 1914 uncovered a number of presumed palaces and temples in the Royal City. One of the most remarkable structures was an elaborate swimming-pool consisting of a large brick-lined tank supplied by a complicated system of water channels from a nearby well. A ledge running around the upper part of the bath was decorated with plaster medallions and figures, as well as water spouts in the form of lion heads. It was here that members of the royal family sought relief from the searing summer heat. Of particular interest was a small temple which contained a bronze head of the Roman emperor Augustus. This was almost certainly a trophy that the Meroites had carried back triumphantly from a successful attack on Roman Syene (Aswan). They were later made to pay for their audacity in challenging the might of Rome. Before 20 BC Publius Petronius, the Governor of Egypt, invaded with 10,000 infantry and succeeded in sacking Napata. Although Meroe remained unscathed, the Romans felt that they had delivered sufficient warning and withdrew to the north. The Meroites may well have looked upon the captured head of Augustus with slightly more ambivalence after that.

Over ½ mile (1 km) east of the town stood the Temple of the Sun. This was surrounded by a perimeter wall of fired brick with stone-faced doorways. Inside this enclosure a ramp led up to a platform on which a colonnade enclosed the sanctuary. The outside wall of the platform was decorated with a series of reliefs which demonstrate the expansionist aims of the Meroitic state at the end of the last century BC. The scenes include victory processions, soldiers with prisoners, the king receiving a long line of women, a chariot with four horses, bound captives beneath the royal foot and inscriptions which are likely to mention captured peoples or countries. The sanctuary itself was approached by a flight of stone steps, and its floors and walls were covered with blue-glazed tiles. It is possible that some kind of religious or ceremonial avenue linked the Temple of the Sun with the Temple of Amun. Other contemporary temples included one possibly dedicated to Isis, lying north of the Royal City, and a shrine to Apis just over a mile (2 km) south of the town.

The most spectacular remains at Meroe are the

eastern side of each pyramid. Meroitic civilization formed a unique blend of Egyptian and African influences.

AD 1

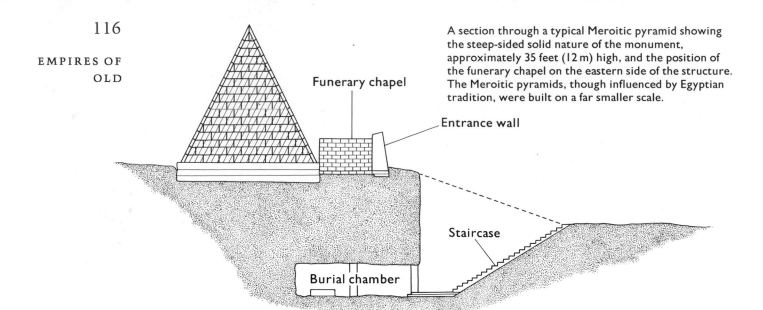

Funerary chapel

Entrance wall

Staircase

Burial chamber

A section through a typical Meroitic pyramid showing the steep-sided solid nature of the monument, approximately 35 feet (12 m) high, and the position of the funerary chapel on the eastern side of the structure. The Meroitic pyramids, though influenced by Egyptian tradition, were built on a far smaller scale.

Slag heaps of iron-working debris, which lie alongside the modern railway track linking Khartoum with Egypt, are the principal remains of Meroe's iron industry.

AD
1

small, steep-sided pyramids that dominate a low range of sandstone hills to the east of the city. There are three separate groups of pyramids known as the northern, southern and western cemeteries. The western cemetery comprised some pyramids and a great number of simple rock-cut tombs covered with a mound of sand or gravel. No tomb of a ruling king or queen has been located in this cemetery and it seems likely that those buried were distant relatives of the royal family. It was in the northern cemetery that the rulers of Meroe were laid to rest. The pyramids were constructed from a rubble core faced with dressed sandstone blocks.

Against the east face of the pyramid a funerary chapel was built, usually housing inscriptions and reliefs, from which the identity of the deceased has often been discovered. In the case of Queen Amanishakhete, who ruled in the second half of the last century BC, the chapel reliefs depict a plump woman with decorative neck wrinkles and face scars, wearing a fringed garment over her right shoulder, complete with tassels and beads. The burial chamber was dug into the rock below the pyramid and was approached by a stairway, the entrance to which lay some way to the east of the chapel. When the ruler's body was placed in the burial chamber the entrance to the grave was blocked and concealed. The burial chambers usually consisted of three compartments for a king and two for a queen, and the deceased were accompanied by a variety of grave goods. Between these imposing pyramids and the town the commoners were buried in rectangular graves surmounted by mounds.

Accompanying the dead were some of the finest products of Meroitic civilization. The range of pottery vessels, in particular, clearly demonstrated two distinct technologies. First, there was a variety of fine pottery, made on a wheel and decorated with stamped motifs or painted with floral patterns or animal and human figures; some of these are specifically local in inspiration, featuring such scenes as an African being eaten by a lion. Then, there was the ordinary domestic pottery, hand-made and manufactured from the porous mud of the Nile, containing small fragments of mica and abundant remains of chopped straw and grass. This pottery was much softer than the finer vessels;

Folding wooden stools have been found in some of the graves at Meroe and give a rare insight into domestic items that would have furnished the town's houses.

Meroe once enjoyed a higher annual rainfall, with millet and sorghum grown in the beds of wadis and large herds of cattle feeding on the extensive grasslands.

unlike them, it was not fired in a kiln but probably in a bonfire lit in a shallow hole in the ground. The shapes were based on gourds or bags and decoration was restricted to geometric forms filled with white, and more rarely red, pigment.

The manufacture of jewellery, especially from gold, must have been one of the most prestigious crafts in Meroe, judging from the precious objects found in the royal tombs. The items include earrings, bracelets and finger-rings, often enhanced by a semiprecious stone such as carnelian. Inspiration for much of the jewellery was obviously Egyptian: rings, both of gold and silver, carry a number of engraved Egyptian symbols, including the head of Hathor and the figure of Isis. The only local use of glass at Meroe was in the manufacture of beads, but a range of glass vessels and beads, as well as some distinctive faience amulets, were imported from the north. Although there are no naturally occurring deposits of copper in the Nile valley, some bronze containers were produced locally, presumably from imported metal ores. An unusual piece is a beaker from Meroe with an incised scene of two elephants holding what appears to be a number of rings in their trunks. Some of the most common bronze finds are bells, which were possibly used as cow bells. These would, therefore, have been valued objects in a society where cattle played such an important part in the local economy.

The reigns of Amanishakhete and her successors, Netekamani and Amanitare, who were ruling jointly in AD 1, formed a period of great prosperity, to judge from the amount of building that was taking place. The last two particularly are

better known for religious and public buildings than any other Meroitic rulers. They reconstructed the Temple of Amun at Meroe, repaired the Temple of Amun at Barkal, which had been devastated by the Roman army, constructed the Temple of Amun at Amara and built two temples at Naqa, the Lion Temple and the Temple of Amun. Two of the most important inland settlements of this period were Naqa and Musawwarat as-Sofra, both situated along wadis, where they could make use of any seasonal water, and about one day's camel or donkey journey east of the Nile, emphasizing their role as staging-points along the trade routes to the east. At Naqa are the remains of a town, a number of temples and two large cemeteries. The Lion Temple is simple in plan and, like Egyptian examples, had two entrance pylons at its eastern end. These carry scenes showing the king and queen destroying their enemies. The rear wall of the temple shows the royal family standing before a god who has three lion heads and four arms. On the sides of the entrance pylons the lion god is depicted with the body of a serpent. Although the royal figures are executed according to Egyptian artistic conventions, with the faces shown in profile, the queen is distinctly plump, in marked contrast to Egyptian taste, and plentiful neck wrinkles, still a sign of beauty in parts of Africa today, are indicated.

Some 9 miles (15 km) north-east of Naqa lay the town of Musawwarat as-Sofra. The main feature of this site was one enormous enclosure which surrounded a number of walled enclosures, dominated by a central temple erected on a

AD
1

The so-called Kiosk Temple at Naqa, an important town to the south-west of Meroe. The local sandstone provided good building stone, easy to cut and carve.

A detail from the left-hand pylon of the Lion Temple at Naqa – Queen Amanitare holding a group of enemies in her left hand while wielding a sword in her right.

platform. Outside the temple the enclosures were connected by a series of corridors and ramps, and the depiction of elephants in the reliefs and sculptures at the site may suggest that these animals were reared and trained in the enclosures, either for military or for ceremonial purposes. Excavations uncovered evidence for another temple dedicated to the lion god – known as Apedemek – thus illustrating the antiquity of this cult, for the temple was associated with a king who ruled at the end of the third century BC. Non-religious structures at Musawwarat as-Sofra included a device for water storage made by constructing a large earthen rampart with an opening which faces the direction of rain run-off from the hills. No Meroitic settlements are known west of the Nile at present, but it is likely that they will be found in the future. To the south the sites of Soba and Sennar on the Blue Nile seem to mark the southern extent of Meroitic civilization.

Since the Meroitic language cannot, on the whole, be understood, our reconstruction of the society must be drawn from its material remains. Meroe was the capital of an organized state and, from the reliefs depicting its monarchs conquering unknown places and peoples, it can be assumed that it was the centre of an empire. It was ruled by kings and queens and, if we follow the Egyptian model, we can assume that they were regarded as divine. Judging from their prominence in temple reliefs, queens played an important role in government and it may be that succession to the throne and property was transmitted through the female line. The status of priests and military leaders is uncertain, although the number of temples would suggest that the priesthood had considerable influence.

The predominance of the Meroites over other contemporary peoples in AD 1 may have owed something to their mastery of iron-working which developed quickly at this time. They were fortunate to live in a region where ironstone was plentiful and where acacia trees could supply abundant charcoal for simple furnaces. The Meroitic troops were armed with iron swords, axes, spears and bows and arrows, thus having a marked advantage over adversaries who fought with copper and stone weapons. Despite the growth of the iron industry, bronze implements continued to be made, including adzes, hoe blades, axes and chisels, as well as many smaller items, such as the little metal rods which were used for applying antimony to the eyes. Merchants from Meroe must have exported a considerable quantity of iron goods, along with ivory skins, ostrich feathers, ebony and gold. Imports included copper and bronze and a range of luxury items from the Roman world.

AD
1

Colossal figures stand on either side of the entrance to the north-east temple at Musawwarat as-Sofra. The inner jambs carry representations of a snake, while the foreparts of two lions project from the wall between the jambs and the giant figures.

Meroitic civilization lasted for about 1,000 years. It was a distinctive amalgam of Egyptian and African elements that reached its zenith around AD 1. The dual nature of its origins was nowhere more manifest than in its religion, where Egyptian gods such as Amun, Isis and Osiris were rivalled by indigenous deities such as Apedemek and Sebewyemeker and the cult of the elephant. But although its emergence was protracted, its decline was relatively swift. The date usually accepted for the end of Meroe and its empire is AD 350, when the Axumite king invaded the Island of Meroe.

Right: A ram of granite rears up from the swirling sands at Naqa. Representations of rams, the animal sacred to the god Amun, were common in Meroitic times and frequently lined the approaches to temples.

Far right: The Lion Temple at Naqa was constructed to a simple plan with two entrance towers, or pylons, at its eastern end. On the sides of the pylons the lion god is depicted with the body of a serpent.

AD 1

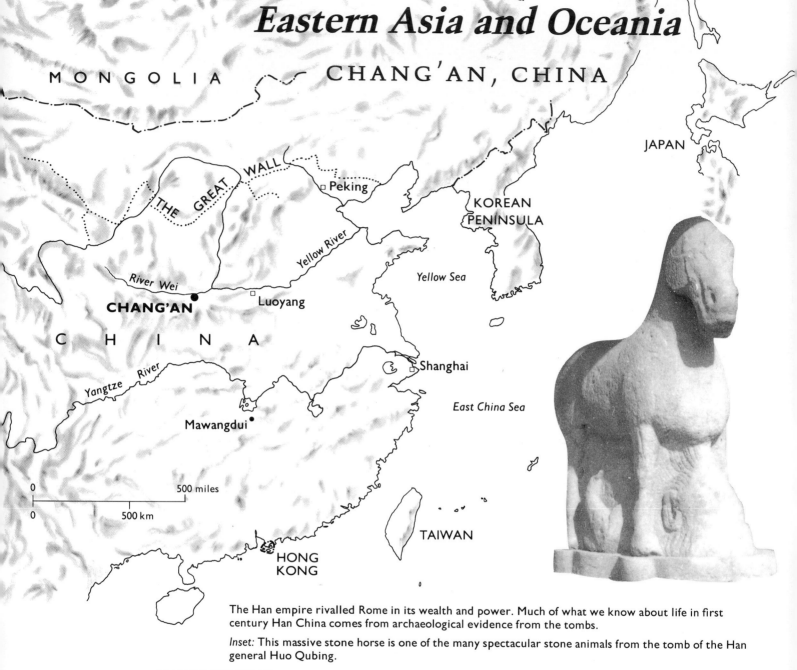

Eastern Asia and Oceania

CHANG'AN, CHINA

MONGOLIA

THE GREAT WALL

Peking

JAPAN

KOREAN PENINSULA

Yellow River

River Wei

CHANG'AN

Luoyang

Yellow Sea

CHINA

Yangtze River

Mawangdui

Shanghai

East China Sea

0   500 miles

0   500 km

TAIWAN

HONG KONG

The Han empire rivalled Rome in its wealth and power. Much of what we know about life in first century Han China comes from archaeological evidence from the tombs.

Inset: This massive stone horse is one of the many spectacular stone animals from the tomb of the Han general Huo Qubing.

AD 1

In AD 1 the imperial city of Chang'an and its hinterland, near the River Wei, contained a population of some 250,000 people and, according to official sources, was at the centre of an empire of around 57 million citizens. The lands administered by the Han officials stretched from the eastern ranges of the Himalayas to the shores of the Pacific, and from the Korean peninsula to the jungles of Vietnam. By any standards it was a vast empire, rivalling in extent, organization, wealth and military might the empire based on Rome. In AD 1 the two great powers were probably unaware of each other's existence, although trading contacts

had been established through the export of Chinese silk along the fabled Silk Road. Yet Han Chang'an was not to be as enduring as its Mediterranean counterpart. A few years after AD 1, imperial Han rule was subject to a short period of interruption, during which Chang'an was pillaged and the capital was re-established further to the east at Luoyang.

In AD 1 the monumentality of the city of Chang'an would have amazed any visiting provincial official. The length of the city walls, the width of the streets and the size of the palaces were all quite remarkable. Had an intrepid merchant from the eastern provinces of the Roman empire

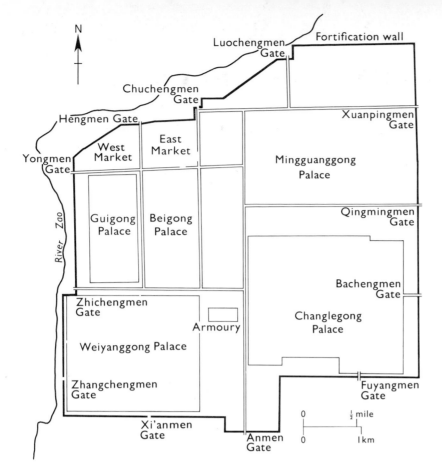

Chang'an's impressive fortification walls surrounded a city occupied by imperial palaces. The irregular alignment of these walls on Chang'an's north-west side kept the River Zao outside the city perimeter. The city had twelve gates, three to each wall. Each gate then had to have three gateways, the central one used only by the Emperor.

reached Chang'an, he would have recognized as familiar the grid pattern of the streets but not the character of the city. For unlike Rome or Pompeii, where a range of different public buildings was surrounded by extensive areas of private housing, in Chang'an possibly two-thirds of the internal area were taken up by imperial palaces, and the city had the appearance more of a royal court than a working capital. The imperial palaces consisted of enormous enclosures, surrounded by walls of rammed earth and containing elaborately decorated pavilions.

The plan of the city was approximately square, with the principal streets oriented according to the cardinal points, thereby relating the works of the city-planners to the movements of the heavenly bodies. The city basically faced south, shielded from supposed evil northern influences, so the emperor when in his audience chamber would also face south. It was particularly important to establish such links as the emperor was regarded as the Son of Heaven. The city wall of Chang'an was started in 194 BC, after the construction of two of the southern palaces, the Changlegong and the

Weiyanggong, and was planned to incorporate the palaces. However, it could not follow a straight course on its southern side since the southern walls of the two palaces were not on the same alignment. The northern and western perimeters also changed direction several times to take account of the meanders of the Zao River, a tributary of the Wei. The lengths of the walls are impressive: the north wall was some 4½ miles (7 km) long, while the west wall ran for 3 miles (5 km); in the south the wall was 4¾ miles (7.5 km) in length, while the only straight side, on the east, was 3¾ miles (6 km). In total the walled circuit was over 15½ miles (25 km), and enclosed an area of about 12 square miles (36 sq. km). The fortifications were constructed with hundreds of thousands of men drawn from conscript labour provided by local farmers and from prisoners sent by dependent lords and princes. The wall was not made with bricks or stone but with rammed layers of yellow earth. Its height was over 40 feet (12 m), as was its width at the base usually. Outside of the wall was a moat, some 26 feet (8 m) wide and 10 feet (3 m) deep, and wooden bridges crossed the moat to give access to the city gates.

AD
1

All that now remains of the defences of the Han imperial capital at Chang'an are stretches of wall, made up of rammed earth, with sometimes a water-filled ditch in front of them. The defences proved weak and the city was sacked shortly after this period.

There were twelve city gates, three to each wall. In their writings scholars had prescribed the form for gates. Each was to have three gateways, and each gateway was to be 20 feet (6 m) wide. The central access was to be for the emperor alone, while the lateral gateways were for the use of the commoners. The distance between gateways was some 13 feet (4 m) for the Xuanpingmen Gate on the eastern side of the city and the Zhichengmen Gate on the western wall. However, the gateways in the Bachengmen Gate and Xi'anmen Gate were separated by 46 feet (14 m), making them much more impressive, perhaps because they gave access to two important palace areas. Eight major avenues divided the interior of the city into huge rectangular blocks. The longest led to the Anmen Gate and was some 3½ miles (5.5 km) long. Although their lengths varied, the avenues were the result of deliberate city-planning and each was about 148 feet (45 m) in width, this great width being necessary to accommodate the movements of the emperor. The central carriageway was

separated from the lateral sections by two drainage ditches. The tripartite division of the major avenues corresponded, of course, to the three gateways of each gate.

About half of the internal area of the city was taken up by the Changlegong and Weiyanggong palace enclosures. They were themselves enclosed by ramparts over 26 feet (8 m) wide at the base. The irregular outline of the Changlegong enclosure was a result of the rebuilding by the Han rulers of an earlier summer palace of the Qin dynasty. The total area of the Changlegong was around 2⅓ square miles (6 sq. km) and, according to chroniclers, the enclosure had four doors, one on each side. The Weiyanggong was a construction of the Han period alone and was therefore regular in outline. The enclosing walls encompassed an area of 2 square miles (5 sq. km), one-seventh of the size of Chang'an. The emperors remained for long periods within these palace enclosures, conducting lengthy rituals and ceremonies away from the prying eyes of the commoners. In the centre of the

AD
1

Weiyanggong enclosure stood an Audience Hall measuring some 1,155 feet (350 m) from north to south by 660 feet (200 m) from east to west. Between these two great palaces was situated the Armoury, an enclosure some 1,060 feet (320 m) long. A partition separated the interior into two courtyards; a total of seven buildings lay within the courtyards and most were used for the storage of weapons, on wooden racks. Those that survived the destruction of Chang'an and were discovered by archaeologists this century include iron body-armour plates, halberds, spears, swords, knives and arrowheads.

There were nine markets in Chang'an and these were all located in the north-west corner of the city. Here archaeologists found many pottery figurines and moulds for coins, suggesting a craft and market area. Most of the ordinary people, including the officials, resided in the north-east corner of the city, near the Xuanpingmen Gate. It is clear that the planners of imperial Chang'an tried to make their city conform with the ideal plan described by earlier writers. The Zhouli kaogongji, (a section of the text in the Rites of Zhou which discusses the principles of town planning), describe the ideal city of the Zhou dynasty (1027–256 BC) as follows: 'Its area is 9 li square, with three gates on each side; within the city are nine longitudinal avenues and nine latitudinal avenues . . . ; the ancestral temple is located on the left and the earth altar on the right; the Audience Hall faces south and the market is in the north.' It is obvious that, although Chang'an differed significantly from this model because of historical and geographical factors, the Han planners tried to accommodate these earlier traditions in their design.

Across the Zao River a vast area to the south-west of Chang'an was developed as a royal park. In the park birds and animals for the royal hunt were reared, and several dozen resort palaces were erected. A great number of eaves tiles have been found bearing the name of the park, Shanglin. An artificial lake was added to the park in the year 120 BC by the emperor Wu Di. As well as enhancing the landscape, water from the lake also helped alleviate water shortages in the capital. The site of the lake can still be discerned as a depression nearly 4 square miles (10 sq. km) in area. Many palaces stood around the shores of the lake and some elevated ground in the northern part of the depression appears to have been an island, no doubt supporting another building.

To the south of Chang'an a series of ritual structures was erected during the period when the Xin dynasty interrupted Han rule in AD 9. According to Confucian rituals, the Pi Yong is a place where the emperor performed various rituals

Today the vast interior of the imperial capital is largely given over to agriculture. Peasant farmers and the ubiquitous bicycle now frequent the lanes between the fields.

AD 1

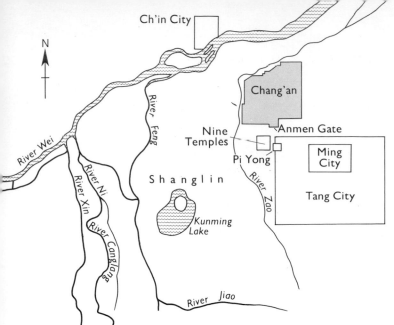

The position of the old imperial capital of Chang'an under the Han dynasty, showing its relationship to the earlier Qin capital north of the River Wei, and the later Tang and Ming cities to the south.

---

and played music; the ancient texts describe such buildings as being circular outside and square inside. Just such a structure was located south of the Anmen Gate, where a square building was surrounded by a large, square enclosure, some 775 feet (235 m) on each side. The building sat on a circular platform nearly 200 feet (60 m) across, while the square enclosure was contained within a circular ditch 1,188 feet (360 m) in diameter. The juxtaposition of circle and square was supposed to signify the complementary powers of Yin and Yang, which were responsible for the creation of the world. The circle enclosing a square signified the circular universe enclosing a square earth. Circle and square likewise accommodated symbols

of the five major elements of the universe: fire, water, metal, wood and earth. These elements were also associated with other objects, qualities or directions which could be divided into five. Chinese beliefs stressed that the proper state of man on earth depended on maintaining a correct balance between these forces. To the west of the Pi Yong a rectangular enclosure possibly contained the remains of ritual structures known as the Nine Temples, again designed in accordance with Confucian regulations.

Warfare was common throughout the Han period. During the first part of the dynasty internal conflicts had to be won to ensure unification. These were followed by wars of expansion, which took the rule of Han-dynasty China to the borders of modern Mongolia and the delta of the Mekong. The Great Wall, built by the previous Qin emperor, had not prevented disturbances from the northern nomads and the emperor Wu Di resolved to attack them from behind with a force of over 50,000 cavalry supported by a greater number of infantry and supply troops. Chinese cavalry remained at a disadvantage, however, when confronting the nomads, for the Chinese horses were much slighter. It was only after Han conquests in the north-west in central Asia that a supply of larger horses was ensured. Such horses were held in high regard and were immortalized in fine bronze castings and ceramics placed in some tombs. The principal weapon in the army was the long steel sword, more durable than the shorter bronze swords used previously, although crossbows became increasingly more important.

The enormous population of Han China and its huge army were fed by the products of farming. In the region around Chang'an the primary crops were millet and wheat, while in the south, near the

The ritual buildings of Pi Yong. Note the interplay of a circular enclosure surrounding a square building, and the extensive use of courtyard space, an important element in traditional Chinese architectural design.

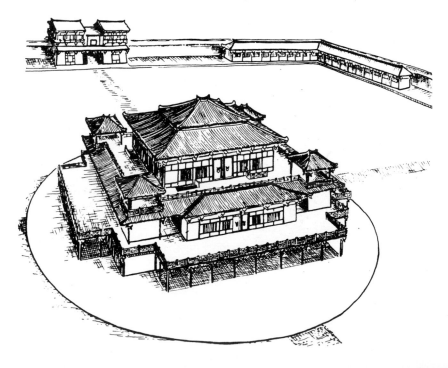

AD
1

Yangtze River, rice was the most significant staple. A variety of fruits and of nuts was also cultivated, including hemp for weaving cloth. One of the great technological achievements of Han China was its extensive refinement and use of iron. Iron ploughshares were fastened to wooden ploughs, equipped with mould boards for turning the furrow, and drawn by oxen. Other agricultural implements included the harrow, the seed machine and a bar for levelling the soil. Irrigation was widely practised and water was obtained from wells or canals. Furthermore, some canals were constructed for transport. One such canal, over 78 miles (125 km) long, linked the Huang (Yellow River) with Chang'an and was used to bring supplies of grain to the capital. Large millstones and water-driven tilthammers were employed in grinding grain. The animals kept included cows, sheep, pigs and dogs, as well as different types of domestic fowl. Camels were also used in the north for transportation. The most famous product of the farming economy was silk, obtained from silkworms fed on a diet of mulberries. Mechanization in the form of draw-looms helped to increase the quantity of silk manufactured. It was this brilliant material that reached the Roman world and drew the flow of western merchants along the Silk Road.

Technological developments in Han China were many. For example, multi-storeyed buildings were quite common. The system of roof construction, in single-storey structures, was completely unlike that developed in western countries, where a triangular truss dictated the ridged form of the roof. In China a multitude of columns, which could spread over the interior of a building, supported purlins, which could be arranged in straight or curved lines. The use of complicated brackets to transfer roof load to column meant that roofs could take curvilinear forms, emphasized by overhanging eaves. Considerable strides were made in the production of wooden or hard-fabric vessels that were decorated with lacquer. These became very precious objects, sometimes valued at ten times the amount of similar bronze containers. Most of the lacquered vessels produced were reserved for the nobility, either in life or in death. Production was increasingly controlled by the state and some lacquered cups and dishes were made at Chang'an. Rectangular fired bricks first appeared during the Han period and some of them were utilized in the construction of subterranean drains in Chang'an.

The bronze industry, like the silk, ceramics and lacquer industries, was highly developed under the Han emperors. These three bronze pieces are all exquisitely decorated; the one at the bottom left depicts Taoist figures.

The tombs of the western Han Emperors, buried beneath huge mounds of earth, shaped into pyramids, comprise an awesomely impressive sight to the west of Chang'an. One of the best-preserved tombs is that of the Emperor Mao Ling.

Metallurgical expertise grew as well. China already had a long history in the production of bronze implements, but by 500 BC cast iron was manufactured through the use of very high temperatures. Cast iron was used in China, therefore, some 1,800 years before its appearance in other civilizations. The iron industry was so important in the Han period that it was nationalized in 119 BC and consisted of forty-nine state foundries.

One of the great archaeological legacies of the Han period is the number of tombs that have been discovered. In the last centuries BC people with any pretensions to rank were buried in shaft tombs, which were gradually superseded by stone or brick chambers underneath mounds, or chambers carved out of cliff sides. Since the beliefs of the time fostered a desire for immortality, the tombs resembled houses and an enormous variety of household goods were laid to rest with the deceased for his or her afterlife. Valuable pottery and bronze or lacquered containers were often deposited in the tombs, but gradually these were replaced by much cheaper pottery model equivalents. The Han emperors were entombed in chambers underneath vast artificial hills, probably raised by convict labour. Nine tombs of the Western Han emperors lie on the north bank of the Wei, some 25 miles (40 km) west of Chang'an, surrounded by smaller tombs of nobles and generals, including that of Huo Qubing, an eminent general born in 140 BC. One of the most impressive of the imperial tombs is that of Mao Ling, the Martial Emperor, who came to the throne in 140 BC and ruled for fifty-four years. He desperately tried to avoid his burial by attempting to make himself immortal. He put a bronze statue in a high tower to catch pure dew in a bowl, which he drank with powdered jade. However, the potion proved ineffective and he died in his seventieth year. Jade funerary suits, made up of thousands of jade pieces threaded with gold, were the ultimate status symbol for the dead.

AD
1

One of the most celebrated burials of the early Han period is the shaft tomb at Mawangdui, in which was buried the Marquis of Dai (who was the prime minister of the kingdom of Changsha), his son and his wife. She was wrapped in twenty layers of garments and lay in the innermost of four decorated coffins. When discovered earlier this century, her skin was still elastic and her internal organs were perfectly preserved. Death had occurred at about the age of fifty between 168 and 145 BC. Accompanying this grand lady was an incredible assortment of grave goods, including a silk banner depicting the person's journey to the afterworld, a remarkable collection of lacquerware, 162 wooden tomb figures dressed in silk, a prodigious amount of foodstuffs and over 300 bamboo slips which itemized the name, size and quantity of each funerary object.

Wealthy though Han China undoubtedly was, it could not continue to support endless wars of expansion on the very limits of its territory. Gradual unrest was clearly exploited by a powerful faction, and this created the conditions for the usurper, Wang Mang, to seize power in AD 9. Chang'an must have been heavily damaged in the fighting at the end of Wang Mang's rule. When the Han dynasty was restored in AD 23, the capital was moved to the east, to the lower reaches of the Yellow River. Excavations at the Xuanpingmen Gate at Chang'an show that the walls of the gate had been burned to a red colour and that parts had collapsed, burying coins of the Han dynasty and the Wang Mang period. Yet Chang'an remained an important city and eventually recovered to play a significant role in the later history of China.

Less than 1 mile (1½ km) from the mound of Mao Ling lies the tomb of his general, Huo Qubing. He was fighting nomads at the age of eighteen and died when he was twenty-four. Sixteen remarkable stone sculptures have been found at his tomb, including a horse trampling a nomad, a tiger, a boar, an elephant, an ox – and a fish, illustrated here.

AD
1

The Americas

MONTE ALBAN, MEXICO

Monte Alban was built by the Zapotecs, a sophisticated indigenous people who flourished in the fertile valley of Oaxaca.

The state of Oaxaca lies in southern Mexico. In 1521, when the Aztecs were routed by the Spanish conquistador Hernán Cortés, the conqueror of Mexico chose part of this region for his own estate, because of its dense population and potential wealth. Although Oaxaca is primarily mountainous, considerable numbers of people live in intermontane basins within the region, and the valley of Oaxaca, located at the centre of the state, has been and continues to be one of the most densely occupied areas of Mesoamerica. For some 2,500 years the inhabitants of this valley have spoken one of a family of languages known as Zapotec. They are tone languages, where the meaning of a word is frequently determined by the pitch of the voice. Ancient Zapotecan does not seem to have been written very often; spoken, however, it possesses a musical character that prompted one French traveller to describe it as the Italian of the Americas. Descendants of the Zapotecs still inhabit the region today, although their culture has been much altered by the Spanish conquest. Nevertheless, despite Spanish domination, the lyrical tones of Zapotecan can still be heard in some homes, a distant echo of the times when the whole valley was unified under the control of the political and ceremonial capital, Monte Alban.

The growth of Zapotec power is reflected in the history of Monte Alban, which is usually divided into three separate phases. By 500 BC (during Monte Alban I) the site was first occupied, and at the start of Monte Alban II in 100 BC the area of settlement had expanded to more than $1\frac{1}{2}$ square miles (4 sq. km). During this period the valley was probably occupied by a number of independent Zapotec states which were linked by trade and intermarriage. These gradually came under the control of Monte Alban, which emerged as the capital of an empire. The zenith of Monte Alban was reached during phase III, which lasted from about AD 200 to 750. The ruling élite of the city at this time were either dominated by priests or were priests themselves, worshipping gods of fertility and agriculture and consolidating the unity of the valley of Oaxaca. The foundations of the empire were probably laid in the preceding periods. By around AD 900 the empire of Monte Alban had collapsed and the site itself was in decline.

The rulers of Monte Alban constructed their city on a group of limestone and sandstone hills, rising some 1,320 feet (400 m) above the valley floor. Elevation was clearly a desirable aspect of residence. When the major hill of Monte Alban itself was colonized, the inhabitants did not spread out over the flat plain below but preferred to seek

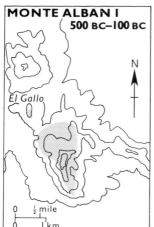

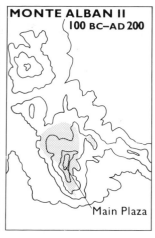
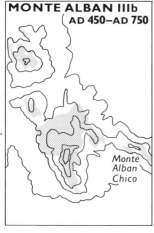

| MONTE ALBAN I 500 BC–100 BC | MONTE ALBAN II 100 BC–AD 200 | MONTE ALBAN IIIa AD 200–AD 450 | MONTE ALBAN IIIb AD 450–AD 750 |

The development of the city of Monte Alban took place over 1,000 years. The site was first occupied around 500 BC (during Monte Alban I), with buildings concentrated mainly on the prinicipal hill, and also on El Gallo. Around AD 1 the principal hill would still have seen the greatest settlement concentration.

Dominating the largest hill at Monte Alban is a rectangular, flattened space called the Main Plaza. This area was fringed with temple and residential platforms and formed the principal ceremonial focus of the Zapotec settlement. By AD 500 the settlement had spread to the hill at Atzompa and the ridge of Monte Alban Chico.

locations on the summits and flanks of adjoining hills. Extending east from Monte Alban proper is a long, rugged ridge known as Monte Alban Chico, while to the north of the main hill are two smaller summits, known as El Gallo and Atzompa. All these ranges were at some stage deliberately terraced and then inhabited, as well as a small area in the north-west of the principal hill.

AD 1

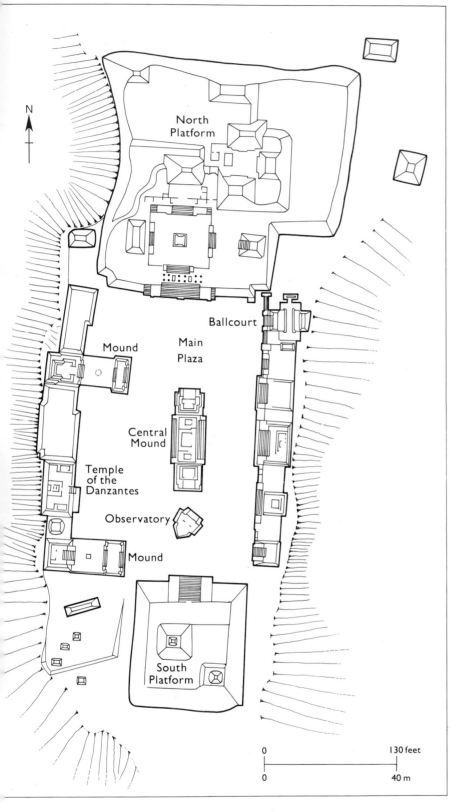

N

North
Platform

Ballcourt

Mound

Main
Plaza

Central
Mound

Temple
of the
Danzantes

Observatory

Mound

South
Platform

0		130 feet
0		40 m

AD
1

Plan of the Main Plaza at Monte Alban. It was surrounded by an impressive, enclosing collection of eight temple-pyramids, with additional stone mounds running down its central axis. Particular structures to note are the Temple of the Danzantes, the Ballcourt and the observatory.

Dominating the largest hill at Monte Alban was a rectangular, flattened space referred to as the Main Plaza. This was the political and ceremonial centre of the city and measured some 990 feet (300 m) from north to south and 330 feet (100 m) from east to west. It was surrounded on all sides by a range of public buildings, generally in the form of square or rectangular stone mounds, which were climbed by impressive flights of steps from the Plaza. On top of the mounds were various buildings or additional smaller mounds. Down the central spine of the Plaza were more stone mounds, all on the same alignment as the Plaza, except for an arrow-shaped structure at the southern end which pointed towards the south-west. Some of these mounds have been interpreted by archaeologists as temple-pyramids, others as palaces. The sloping faces of the pyramids were achieved by plastering over the indentations caused by construction in stone. The temples on their summits usually consisted of a single-storey adobe building of two rooms, possibly covered by a thatched roof. Not all of the architecture on the Plaza was religious in character, however. An early structure buried beneath a later mound consisted of a gallery of

This building in the middle of the Main Plaza supports the central altar of Monte Alban. It has principal staircases on both its east and west sides.

This building stands in the south-east corner of the Main Plaza. Behind it, on the upper part of the adjacent mound, on the east side of the Plaza, is the 'Palace'.

carved stone slabs, each bearing a human figure in a dance-like pose. Closer examination of the figures revealed distorted limbs, sexual mutilation and blood, possibly suggesting that these figures might have been chiefs or kings killed by the early rulers of Monte Alban. Clearly some of the peoples who were ruled from Monte Alban had been controlled by force rather than persuasion. Dating also from the earliest period (Monte Alban I) were stone pillars or stelae displaying signs which probably indicate dates, either from a ritual calendar of 260 days or from a 365-day calendar which was geared to the agricultural cycle.

It was during Monte Alban II, which covered the year AD 1, that the Plaza took on its final shape. Its construction must have required considerable amounts of labour, since deep cavities were filled and rock outcrops were levelled. Some effort was spared by incorporating rock outcrops into the edifices at the northern and southern ends of the square. The population size of the city at this time was probably around 15,000, although it may have shrunk towards the end of the period, when the outlying hills were temporarily deserted. Undoubtedly, the Plaza reached its maximum development during phase III. The North and South Platforms, the two largest constructions in the city, dominated the Plaza from either end. The difficult access on to the South Platform has persuaded some to interpret it as a temple, while

AD 1

These powerful stone carvings, from the Temple of the
Danzantes on the west side of the Main Plaza, were once
thought to represent dancers. Closer examination
suggests that they may indicate the corpses of prisoners.
The symbols, or glyphs, in front of the prisoner's
mouths may give their names.

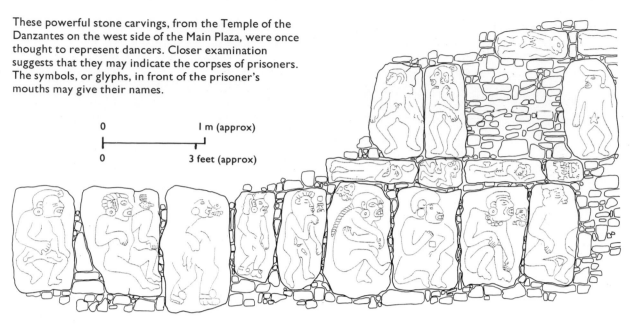

the North Platform, with its broad staircase,
columned halls and sunken patio, seems to invite
the visitor. On the north-east of the North
Platform is a very secluded group of stone mounds
and it has been suggested that these were the
residence of the rulers of Monte Alban, while the
principal plaza of the North Platform constituted
an audience hall for visiting dignitaries.

Two other structures on the Plaza can be
identified with certainty. At the northern end of
the eastern side stood the Ballcourt, a rectangular
playing area surrounded by smooth, sloping side
walls. The ball game was probably watched from
surrounding temple platforms. Little is known
about the rules of the game, but it involved passing
a hard, rubber ball from player to player by
bouncing it with the hips. It is probable that
protective knee-pads and helmets were worn, so
there must have been physical contact and perhaps
fatalities from the contests. The second structure
capable of definitive interpretation is the
observatory, constructed in the decades before AD 1
and located in the southern half of the Plaza. Proof
of its function comes from the unusual arrowhead-
like shape of the building and its unique alignment
compared with the other structures on the Plaza.
The door on the front of the building seems to have
been aligned to a point on the horizon where the
bright star Capella would have had its first rising in
the dawn sky on the very day that the sun reached
its first zenith point over Monte Alban.
Corroborative evidence is claimed in an additional
significant alignment between the front stairs of
the observatory and a ritual pillar in one of the
mounds on the east side of the Plaza. Crossed-stick

symbols found on the observatory have also been
interpreted as sighting devices. An ancillary
function for the building has been suggested by the
carved slabs with signs or glyphs on them that
adorn the structure. Since they portray human
beings upside down, the traditional pose of the
conquered, it has been argued that these carvings
are records of victories, with the glyphs giving
names of towns and the dates of their capture.

The interpretation of the Plaza at Monte Alban,
and indeed of the whole city, is fraught with
difficulty given the lack of extensive excavation
and of documentary sources detailing how different
parts of the settlement functioned. Meticulous
surface surveys of the physical remains of the city
have resulted in some controversial theories about
Monte Alban. Certain archaeologists have
suggested that the Plaza did not function as a
marketplace or indeed even as a public place. All
the surrounding buildings faced into it, presenting
massive, vertical rear walls to the residential
districts of the city on the slopes below. Access
from the districts into the Plaza was restricted
through narrow passageways, while the major road
system of the city does not seem to serve the Plaza.
The Plaza, therefore, may well have been reserved
for the privileged rituals of Monte Alban's rulers
and priests.

Detailed surveys of the flanks of the hill below
the Plaza and of the adjoining summits produced
evidence for some 2,073 terraces in an area of
about $2\frac{1}{2}$ square miles (6.5 sq. km). The inhabitants
of Monte Alban had to level terraces in the sloping
hillsides in order to build their houses, workshops
and public places. On residential terraces several

AD
1

contiguous, rectangular rooms were usually arranged around patios, while other terraces supported public places dominated by mound structures adjacent to major roads. The terraces varied considerably in size, with some just over 16 by 33 feet (5 by 10 m) and others measuring hundreds of feet. Through careful mapping archaeologists were able to suggest that the whole of the city could be divided into fifteen divisions or districts, including the Main Plaza, each dominated by a cluster of mounds perhaps representing the places where marketing, administration and the performance of religious rites were undertaken for each district. Collections of surface material from the terraces indicated differences between each district. For example, district 2 contained a relatively large number of mound groups that appear to have been elaborate residences occupied by the élite. Confirmation of this hypothesis came from the discovery of prestige materials on the terraces, such as marine shells, obsidian and exotic minerals, including serpentine, onyx, and jade. In district 3 a particularly large terrace seems to have been reserved for food production, since on its surface were found quantities of pounders, mortars and pestles. District 4, to the east of the Plaza, contained two elaborate residences, a ballcourt and an open civic area. The principal marketplace at Monte Alban probably lay in district 7, where a large open space lay in the path of a major road, and the surrounding terraces produced ample evidence of ground stone tools, such as *manos*, *metates* (respectively upper and lower quern stones), mortars and pestles. Despite the presence of scatters of waste material from production processes, especially from the working of status commodities such as obsidian, the number of craft industries and the evidence of pottery manufacture at the site are negligible, despite its large size.

In AD 1 the dead of Monte Alban were buried in rectangular, stone-lined tombs, as demonstrated during excavations on the north-west perimeter of the site, just within the defensive walls. The burial chamber was aligned approximately E–W, with a simple ante-chamber at its eastern end. The ante-chamber was separated from the grave by a rectangular threshold stone, flanked by two thin stone slabs. At one time the entrance to the chamber had been sealed by a large, oval stone, while it is possible that the grave was once covered with horizontal stone slabs and then backfilled with rubble. Three old men were laid to rest in this tomb, not simultaneously but one after the other, and perhaps separated by a number of years, so that the second and third interments disturbed the earlier bones in the tomb. The grave goods with the three men amounted to some thirteen pottery

vessels and seven blades of green obsidian, the latter probably placed with the second individual.

In AD 1 the inhabitants of Monte Alban lived in a city where most artefacts were imported as finished items. Metal objects were not used, since metal was worked on a large scale only after AD 900 in Mesoamerica, so stone-working was taken to elaborate lengths, and there must have been a whole range of items made from organic materials such as leather or feathers which has not survived. A particularly developed skill among the Zapotec potters was the production of elaborate funerary urns to accompany the dead. In reality they were really ceramic sculptures, ranging in height from several inches to as much as 5 feet (1.5 m). They were made from hard-baked, fine-grained, light-grey clay and took the form of a cylindrical vessel which had a figure on the front and was open at the rear of the vessel to the top. It seems likely that many of the figures represented deities, but what was placed in the containers is still a mystery. Not all urns depicted deities, however. Some provide us with glimpses of more mundane Zapotec life, showing acrobats, jugglers, ball players, merchants, priests, warriors, farmers and even porters, while others are pure caricatures, detailing toothless grins, bulging paunches and cleft palates with obvious delight. Zapotec stone-workers excelled in their use of hard stones, especially in the manufacture of human figurines from jade. One of the most spectacular pieces of jade workmanship dates from Monte Alban II and was found as an offering under the floor of the Plaza. An exquisite jade mask of the bat god, it is composed of twenty-five pieces of jade, carefully made to fit together, with eyes of teeth and shell; three slate pendants hang from its chin.

Reconstructing the lives of the Zapotec inhabitants of Monte Alban around AD 1 is not an easy task, given that we possess only the material remains of the city, its Plaza and subsidiary squares, its terraces scattered with various kinds of debris, its defensive walls and a number of signs or glyphs that indicate dates, names or places. It is a difficult jigsaw puzzle with many of the pieces missing. Regarding religious matters, at least, some headway can be made. The figurines and sculpted pottery allow us to recognize the forms of fifteen deities that are known from later periods. It comes as no surprise to learn that there is a predominance of gods associated with fertility and agriculture. The most prominent is Cocijo, god of lightning and rain, while the importance of maize is indicated by a number of associated deities that form the so-called 'Maize Complex' (included in this complex are representations of the bat and monkey). Worship of the heavenly bodies was also of great

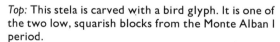

Top: This stela is carved with a bird glyph. It is one of the two low, squarish blocks from the Monte Alban I period.

Above: This is the larger of the two structures, separated by an open court, in the south-west corner of the Main Plaza. A pyramid of two platforms can be seen here, each with its own flight of broad steps; the top is surmounted by the remains of a temple.

This is the north-east corner of the pyramid shown in the previous photograph, part of System M. The upper two terraces correspond to the upper platform on which the temple remains (not visible) are situated; the remaining lower terraces correspond to the lower platform.

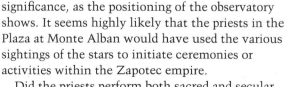

significance, as the positioning of the observatory shows. It seems highly likely that the priests in the Plaza at Monte Alban would have used the various sightings of the stars to initiate ceremonies or activities within the Zapotec empire.

Did the priests perform both sacred and secular duties as the rulers of Monte Alban? Or did they simply advise the ruling Zapotec dynasty at the site? That question cannot be answered with any certainty, but it does appear that the ruling élite of

Monte Alban lived in a series of sophisticated residences indicated by the mounds which lie around and adjacent to the Main Plaza. From here they went to worship or officiate at the temples in the Plaza, and from there they no doubt gave their orders and blessings to the warriors to capture the reluctant cities who refused to become part of the Zapotec empire. By AD 1 the whole of the valley of Oaxaca must have been subjugated and under the control of Monte Alban.

CONCLUSION

The cities and their empires that are the subject of this chapter were clearly heterogeneous, not least in terms of their overall area. The regions controlled by the Western Han emperors from their capital at Chang'an formed the largest of them all, dwarfing, by comparison, the biggest empire of the Mediterranean basin, the Roman empire. And the Roman empire in turn dwarfed the territories belonging to Petra, Meroe and Monte Alban. There were great differences too in the origins of each empire. The Han kingdom inherited the territories of successive Chinese dynasties, in particular the Shang, the Chou and especially the Qin. The Qin emperors were the first successful rulers to unite all China, constructing the Great Wall as a defence and permanent reminder of their achievement. The Han emperors owed the great extent of their territory to a violent revolution that overthrew the last Qin monarch in the closing decades of the third century BC. The new capital at Chang'an was laid out as a result of the uprising, while the former capital was destroyed. The gestation of the Roman empire was both lengthy and difficult by comparison. The pre-eminence of Rome resulted from the slow growth of that city in late prehistoric Italy, until its emerging military power gave it control over most of the peninsula by the last century BC. Its transformation into an imperial power came about through a series of wars, initially fought for defensive reasons but ultimately victorious and expansive, against hostile powers such as the Carthaginians and the various Celtic peoples. The defeat of enemies often resulted in the destruction of their armed forces and the retention of their lands.

In the case of the smaller empires, their origins are more difficult to discern. The rise of Meroe over several centuries and the ability of the Meroites to conquer their enemies depended on control of the upper reaches of the Nile and the Island of Meroe. Such a situation gave them the opportunity to harness the natural fertility of the soil, replenished by annual inundations, and to utilize the rich iron-ore deposits. It also left them distanced and relatively safe from any aggression by hostile northern neighbours, from the Egypt of the Ptolemies or of Augustus. Ability to trade directly with the Red Sea ports and the emerging civilization on the Ethiopian plateau provided the necessary commercial openings for economic growth. The rise of the Nabatean capital at Petra, however, owed a great deal to its favourable position on trading routes that linked Arabia with the Mediterranean coast and Egypt with the western end of the Silk Road. Occupying such an important location, and being the main entrepot that received Chinese silks, some conceivably coming from the Han capital at Chang'an, the merchants of Petra were able to accumulate considerable wealth, part of which they invested in creating a series of outstanding rock-cut monuments.

The emergence of Monte Alban as an imperial centre in the Oaxaca valley cannot be charted with any certainty. Carvings in stone of mutilated bodies from an early monument on the Plaza suggest that military prowess may have been an initial mechanism of expansion, but the ceremonial nature of much of the architecture on the Plaza also argues that a ruling priesthood, perhaps controlling the circulation of prestige traded items from the Gulf coast, may have been the sustaining factor.

We can also perceive distinctions in the nature of the cities. Pompeii in AD 1 was obviously a lively, commercial city. Its layout was centred on the forum with its surrounding range of religious and civic public buildings. Its baths, shops, theatres, workshops, fine houses and, last but not least, its graffiti, both amorous and political, attest to a thriving urban community with a good deal of individual liberty for the majority of its citizens in the areas of politics, commerce and pleasure. While the forum is large and the grid pattern of the streets demonstrates the authority of the city fathers and their ability to plan the overall layout of the city, most of the internal area is reserved for the houses, markets and shops of the citizenry. In contrast, the major part of the vast extent of Chang'an, surrounded by its walls of rammed earth and dissected by an orthogonal arrangement of wide avenues, was taken up by imperial compounds, each surrounded by its own wall of rammed earth and containing palaces and other buildings arranged around spacious courtyards. Very little *space was allowed for the houses of any citizens privileged enough to be able to live within the walled circuit of Chang'an.*

The distribution of temples, shops, houses and streets in Petra, despite its exceptional location on either side of a wadi surrounded by towering cliffs, suggests that its layout had been largely dictated by the same kind of requirements that were responsible for the city of Pompeii: town-planning with the needs of commerce firmly in mind. Monte Alban, on the other hand, with its ceremonial Plaza lined with palaces and temples and its fourteen districts lying on the flanks of the hill and adjacent summits, does not indicate strong commercial origins in its layout. It has been suggested that the site was a 'disembedded' capital, perhaps akin to modern Washington, DC, a centre of power where embassies from the regions of the empire, represented by the fourteen districts at the site, would take up residence. Our knowledge of Meroe is insufficient to come to any definitive conclusion. A 'Royal City' of palaces and temples surrounded by the town proper indicates a carefully demarcated religious and secular focus, but its exact relationship to the town must wait upon further excavation. Speculation suggests that the model for the city would be closer to that of Pompeii than, say, Monte Alban.

Architectural origins of the cities were markedly different. That of Monte Alban was clearly the result of the gradual refinement of Zapotecan tradition, while the buildings within Chang'an probably replicated the traditional one-storey designs of previous Chinese dynasties. Even so, there was room for innovation, as the multi-storeyed model houses from the Han period demonstrate. The architecture of Pompeii drew heavily on the inspiration of earlier Greek buildings. All of the Pompeian architects must have been aware of the styles and plans of Greek temples at neighbouring Paestum and on the island of Sicily. Even if they had never travelled to Greece, typical Greek domestic features such as the peristyle were incorporated into Roman houses in the city. The buildings of Meroe and Petra represented derivative but exotic amalgams of styles constructed in extraordinary locations. The temples on the Island of Meroe and much of their decorative carving were a unique blend of African

and classical Egyptian influences, while the buildings of Petra were a mixture of Egyptian, Roman, Arabian and Nabatean ingredients.

Dissimilarities in the origins and physical character of the cities were reflected in political and economic differences in the societies which produced them. Chang'an was the capital of an emperor who ruled with absolute authority over a vast dominion. It was planned to impress visiting dignitaries as a political and religious complex, not to act as a commercial centre or protected residence for a large number of inhabitants. Pompeii, on the other hand, was the product of a society that had just exchanged a republican system of government for an imperial one. As such it reflected its origins as an almost quasi-autonomous city state, with the city administration allowed much freedom of choice and action. As a result, the city acted as a commercial, administrative and residential centre. Monte Alban, by contrast, with its Plaza screened from the residential terraces below, was a political and ceremonial capital, the possible location for embassies from conquered territories. With its absence of coinage and metals it did not have a significant commercial focus, nor was it a place for the general population to live. Meroe and Petra, as cities dependent to different degrees on trade, probably resembled Pompeii in nature more than Chang'an or Monte Alban. Capital cities usually display impressive architecture and often monumental tombs for their dead. The rock-cut tombs at Petra are well known and so too are the steep pyramids east of Meroe, which are matched in form if exceeded in size by the enormously impressive earthen pyramids of the Han emperors some 25 miles (40 km) west of Chang'an.

The monumental remains from these cities have long outlasted the empires they were intended to glorify. The complex social, cultural and political processes that have produced some of the world's most powerful empires, unifying disparate peoples with an ideological and imperial identity, have proved difficult to sustain in perpetuity. The cyclical rise and fall of great powers occurs with the inevitable regularity of the changing seasons. Some winters may be colder than others, some summers longer, but the transition from one to the other is unavoidable. Pompeii, of course, was

overwhelmed by a volcanic catastrophe. Meroe fell prey to economic difficulties and to invaders from the east. Petra was absorbed by the growth of the Roman empire, while Chang'an was attacked shortly after AD 1 and went into decline with the transfer of the Han capital further to the east in AD 23. Only Monte Alban survived for most of the first millennium, although it too, around AD 900, was in decline, eventually being overrun by the Mixtecs and the war-like Aztecs.

By AD 1000 new cultures were flourishing in some very novel places. The violent diaspora of the followers of Muhammad led to some remarkable cultural transplants, perhaps the most brilliant being that in southern Spain. Trade between the states of eastern and western Asia allowed ports like Siraf to flourish in a hostile environment. South of the Sahara, away from the influences of the Mediterranean and Islamic worlds, African communities constructed a long-lived town at Jenne-jeno, while, in the American south-west the ancestors of the Pueblo Indians developed some outstanding masonry techniques in their cliff and canyon dwellings. And, on one of the earth's most isolated places, Easter Island in the South Pacific, descendants of colonists who had made a landfall several hundred years previously, were busily carving and erecting an unique larger-than-life collection of stone statues, the meaning of which would eventually puzzle people the world over.

CHAPTER 4

NEW DIRECT

AD 1000

IONS

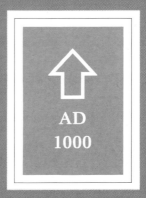

AD
1000

INTRODUCTION

The five locations described in Chapter 4 contain a minute sample of the monuments of the world in the year AD 1000. Nevertheless, the people who constructed them were all, in one sense or another, following 'new directions'. They were innovative achievers and demonstrated new levels of sophistication for human communities in some novel places. They broke the links with their particular pasts and the results were both surprising and stimulating. The themes for this chapter are, therefore, innovation and the potential fragility of an apparently successful cultural adaptation in a hostile natural environment.

The locations described in this chapter were chosen because each one, through its own success, has so surprised subsequent generations that attempts have been made either to ignore their achievements or to seek external causes for their flourishing. Crude suggestions, for instance, have been offered in order to argue that the sophisticated masonry techniques demonstrated by the Anasazi Indians of Chaco Canyon were inspired by contact with more developed societies in Central America. In a similar vein, the Incas are sometimes proclaimed as the inspiration for the expertise of the Easter Islanders, perhaps sailing from the east to bring to the island distinctive and advanced techniques of stone sculpture and megalithic architecture. Less obviously, there have been those who sought to explain some aspects of the success of Jenne-jeno in terms of contacts from the north, denying that it could be a purely African town. Likewise doubts were expressed, until the results of a hinterland survey dissipated them, about the Sirafis' ability to feed themselves from their own fields. In a more invidious manner the triumph of Christian Spain over the Moors, and the Christian conquest of such fabulous cities as Seville, Granada and Cordoba, served to destroy not just the Muslim faith but also the rich Islamic culture of Andalucia, eventually replacing it with a much inferior product.

The most obvious 'new direction' was that followed by the Easter Islanders. Some time between AD 300 and 400 families crowded into slight but seaworthy boats to make the long and hazardous journey eastwards from the Central or East Polynesian islands. Once they had arrived, they must have realized that a return journey over such a distance was extremely hazardous and, with the human, animal and plant resources they had brought with them, they started to cultivate, to hunt, to organize and to grow as a community. Centuries later, isolated but successful, they began quarrying and erecting those remarkable statues, probably as personifications of their ancestors, unlike anything in Polynesia or, indeed, the wider world.

Elsewhere 'new directions' of a different kind were taking place. The merchants of Siraf on the northern shores of the Persian Gulf had managed to carve out for themselves an important role as middlemen in a network of trading routes that brought exotic items such as fine pottery from the east coast of China and ivory from Zanzibar to the Buyid rulers in Baghdad. They grew rich on such trade and their wealth could provide them with elegant houses and cool baths – essential for daily life in such an arid, hot environment. Commerce and discomfort were uneasy partners in another trading town, Jenne-jeno at the southern end of the inland Niger delta in present-day Mali. If you were prepared to put up with the heat and the risk of insect-borne diseases, there were riches to be had in exchanging gold and ivory for salt, glass and ceramics brought across the Sahara on the backs of camels. In faraway Spain the tide of Islamic conquest that had lapped around the shores of the Mediterranean had reached its high-water mark. In southern Spain it produced a brilliant civilization, devoted to culture rather than conquest, and saw the construction of the palace of Medina Azahara, a royal residence fit for a most cultured caliph. Finally, in the dramatic setting of the Chaco Canyon in New Mexico, indigenous Indians were building Great Houses, complex multi-storey collections of storerooms, houses and meeting-places, and linking them together with a network of roads. Architecturally they were without parallel, and Pueblo Bonito was perhaps the finest example.

In one way or another societies in these locations followed new directions with radically different results. Yet like the empires from the previous chapter, they were similar in at least one respect, demonstrating, as they do, the often

AD
1000

cyclical nature of growth, climax and decay in complex societies. Such societies are usually controlled by clear authority structures and exhibit division and diversification of the citizen-body into a variety of social, economic, political and religious classes. Perhaps because their innovations were often carried out in remote or hostile environments, they were more precariously rooted than other communities. It is certainly true that societies flourishing in these locations around AD 1000 had become impoverished or had disappeared by AD 1500. Even the resourceful Easter Islanders could not escape. Their over-exploitation of the tiny island had destroyed too much woodland. There was simply no timber left that was long enough to enable them to construct vessels on which they could set sail in the desperate hope of finding undiscovered islands.

AD
1000

Europe

MEDINA AZAHARA, SPAIN

The walled city of Medina Azahara stands in the parched sierras of southern Spain, on the Guadalquivir River. Built a few miles to the west of Cordoba, Medina Azahara reflects the full flowering of Islamic culture.

AD 1000

By AD 1000 the followers of the prophet Muhammad had been in Spain for almost 300 years. Islamic culture had flourished in the fertile soils of Andalucia, and at Cordoba, the capital of Moorish Spain, a magnificent and bustling city grew up on the banks of the Guadalquivir. Half a million citizens, including Jews and Christians, lived in a city of 3,000 mosques, 300 public baths and over 80,000 shops. It was an established centre of learning where every encouragement was given to literature, science, medicine and philosophy. Cordoba was the most civilized city west of Constantinople, but it owed its success to a new direction: it drew its inspiration from centres of Islamic learning in Arabia and the Middle East.

In order to escape the stifling heat and congestion of the capital, and to receive foreign embassies in more tranquil surroundings, the caliph of Cordoba, Abd al-Rahman III, had begun building in AD 936 an enormous palace-city a few miles to the west of Cordoba. The site chosen was on the lower flanks of the Sierra Morena, from where views of the capital, and beyond to the snow-capped summits of the Sierra Nevada, could be enjoyed. He called it Medina Azahara, after al-Zahara, his favourite wife. By AD 1000 this remarkable creation had reached new heights of architectural elegance.

Medina Azahara was enclosed within an enormous rectangle, measuring nearly 1 mile (1.5 km) from east to west and nearly $\frac{1}{2}$ mile (750 m) from north to south, occupying an area of about 296 acres (120 ha). It was surrounded by a monumental double wall, formed by inner and outer walls, each 16 feet (5 m) wide, with a central passage of the same width. Its construction on the lowest hills of the Sierra Morena meant that the city was laid out over three great stepped terraces.

On the highest stood the palace of the caliph, built some 53 feet (16 m) above the lowest level of the city. It was a rectangular building, formed by three blocks, and incorporated a range of reception rooms, bedrooms and bathrooms. The reception rooms were richly furnished with tapestries, carpets and cushions, while most of the palace was paved with patterns of red tiles and yellowish stone. Access between rooms was often through graceful horseshoe arches, whose columns and capitals carried intricate carvings. Bathrooms were built of white marble and were connected to small dressing-rooms. Complex patterns of decorative interlinking foliage covered the walls. The total absence of focal points in their design relaxed the eye and soothed the mind.

On the middle terrace, to the west of the palace, lay a residential quarter of 400 houses where various court officials lived, including ministers, generals, administrative officials, members of the royal family, poets and assorted freemen. The administrative offices were situated to the south of the palace, while to the immediate east were buildings which probably incorporated the vizier's or prime minister's offices, the headquarters of the military and the principal rooms of the diplomatic service. Beyond these, and further to the east, stood three magnificent reception rooms where official audiences with the caliph were held. The western one, like all the large buildings in Medina Azahara, consists of five parallel aisles, the middle three separated only by a continuous line of horseshoe arches, the outer two screened by the addition of three doors in each side. In front of this building lay the superbly appointed royal guest-house,

Above: The graceful horseshoe-shaped arches of the royal reception room form three continuous lines, dividing the elegant interior of the building into five parallel aisles. An ornate design of interlinking foliage has been applied to the walls.

Below: A view down from the middle terrace showing to the right the remains of a fortified wall which separated Medina's middle terrace from the lowest level. Much of the flat, brown expanse in the photograph beyond the fortification wall once contained those buildings of the lowest terrace, such as the zoological gardens and military barracks.

AD
1000

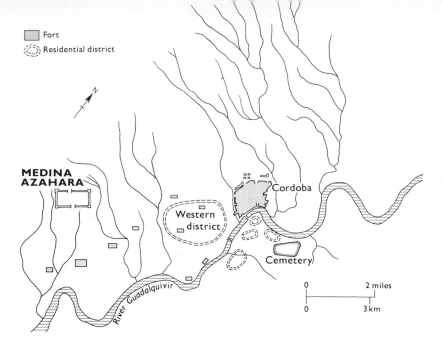

MEDINA
AZAHARA

Cordoba

Western
district

Cemetery

River Guadalquivir

0   2 miles
0   3 km

A map of Cordoba, showing Medina Azahara a few miles to the west. Cordoba passed into Islamic hands during the conquest of the eighth century, and enjoyed outstanding prosperity in the tenth century.

---

which was separated by a large pool from the visitors' waiting-room, the southern-most structure on the middle terrace. Water, conveyed to Medina Azahara by an aqueduct, and displayed to its inhabitants through countless pools, cascades and fountains, was both a source of relief in the heat of the summer and a mirror of delight, with its numerous reflections of the architectural wonders of the city.

There is little left now to remind the visitor of the splendid reflections once created by the imaginative use of water-filled pools.

The middle terrace at Medina Azahara was separated from the lowest level by an imposing wall, fortified by towers. Just to the south of this wall the first building in the city was erected in AD 941. This was the mosque, which again had at its core five aisles and was the only structure to be oriented towards the east and Mecca. The remaining areas of the great expanse of the lowest level were taken up with the barracks for the cavalry and the military, a quarter for shops, businesses and markets, and elaborately planned zoological gardens, where the brilliance of the flowers rivalled the beauty of the beasts. Beyond all these, the perimeter wall was broken by the principal gate, through which all visitors to the caliph would enter.

Medina Azahara took twenty-five years to build and was completed around AD 961. The project was an enormous undertaking and work was supervised throughout by chief architects and master masons. Massive blocks of limestone from local quarries were the principal building material. Every day 6,000 were used, brought by 1,500 pack animals and the caliph's 400 camels. The 4,000 sky-blue marble columns were fashioned from stone excavated from particular quarries in the Sierra Morena, while marble for the pink columns was obtained from a quarry in the Sierra de Cabra, some 44 miles (70 km) south of the capital. In prestigious buildings in Medina Azahara, such as the mosque, the two colours were deployed alternately to wonderful effect. Other columns were brought from distant ancient cities such as Carthage and Constantinople to emphasize the importance and connections of the caliph. Just as admirable as the water distribution above ground was its collection below ground in a network of large drains. These collected the run-off from courtyards and fountains, as well as the waste from sewers and kitchens, and eventually joined in one long canal, which traversed the plain for several miles before emptying into the Guadalquivir.

The flowering of Medina Azahara was all too brief, however. Problems of succession in AD 1010 brought civil war and eventually led to the end of the caliphate. Rebel Berber mercenaries, retreating from Cordoba, took refuge in the palace-city, where they looted, destroyed and finally set fire to some of the buildings. In succeeding centuries the site was pillaged and used as a quarry for new structures erected by subsequent Moorish dynasties. The incomparable Giralda, the minaret of the mosque in Seville, was begun in 1148 and incorporated over 120 capitals from the ruin of Medina Azahara. By 1236 Cordoba itself had fallen to the Christians and as a result Andalucia began to turn away from its dazzling oriental origins.

In the years around AD 1000, however, Arab Spain was at its most brilliant. It had developed in the stable conditions provided by the rule of caliph Abd al-Rahman III. When the caliph was in residence at Medina Azahara every effort was made to overawe visiting dignitaries. On one occasion, to create a suitable impression, the caliph lined the road from Cordoba to Medina Azahara with a double row of soldiers, whose drawn swords formed an arcade under which the ambassadors were led. At periodic intervals along the principal road inside the palace-city, finely dressed individuals were seated on exquisitely fashioned chairs and the cowering visitors fell before each one, thinking they were in the presence of the caliph himself. Each time they were corrected with the words, 'Raise your heads. This is but a servant of his servants.' At last they entered a plain courtyard, whose floor was covered with sand. At the centre sat a figure, coarsely dressed, head bowed. In front of him was a copy of the Koran, a sword and a fire. 'This is the Caliph,' the ambassadors were told, whereupon they threw themselves on the ground before him. Before they could speak he said to them, 'God has commanded us to force you to submit to this.' He pointed at the Koran. 'If you refuse, we shall compel you with this.' He lifted the sword. 'And if we kill you, then you will go thither!' He gestured to the fire. The terrified ambassadors retreated without uttering a word, and shortly after signed a peace treaty, agreeing to the conditions the caliph had imposed. When people of different religious beliefs did not oppose Islam, however, they were allowed to build their own places of worship. Part of the greatness of Moorish Spain was the harmonious co-existence of Muslim, Christian and Jewish communities under Arab rule. Racial differences were to pose far more of a threat to Moorish Spain than religious divisions. The population was hetcrogencous, formed by contingents of Arabs, Berbers, Visigoths, Romans, Iberians and Jews.

Although Moorish civilization in Spain produced heavily populated cities furnished with public buildings and sophisticated architecture, these cities still displayed the original tribal divisions of Arab society. The Islamic city did not have those organized features that were characteristic of Roman city-planning, namely the grid-iron plan, the central square and the regularity in size of the residential blocks. At the heart of the Islamic city was a market formed by a web of narrow, winding alleys flanked by rows of countless shops. The artisans tended to concentrate in groups so that a particular alley might be lined with shops that sold the same kind of article. Such a system prevented unfair price differences for the same commodity.

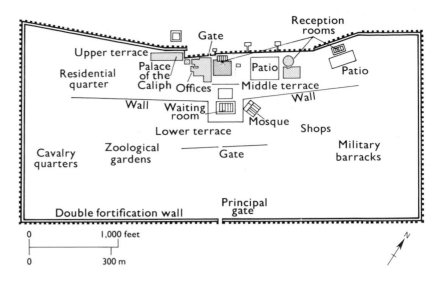

The palace-city was constructed on three south-facing terraces. The highest held the palace of the Caliph, while the mosque was on the lowest.

The market usually surrounded the mosque, and slightly wider streets led from the market to the city walls. Between the market and the walls were the residential quarters, which grew in a haphazard fashion without any preconceived plan, reflecting both tribal differences within the city and the varying fortunes of individal families. Houses were lit by means of internal courtyards, and their exterior walls were often windowless, ensuring that

The mosque was the first building to be constructed on this site and the only one to be oriented towards the east, and therefore Mecca.

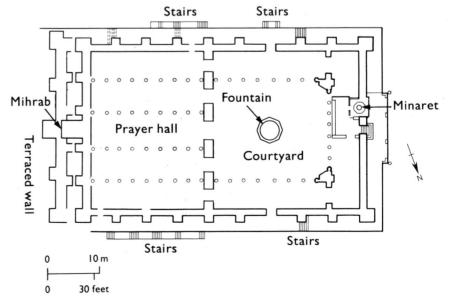

In the most prestigious buildings, different-coloured marbles were juxtaposed on alternate columns to achieve a colourful effect, and to show that money had not been spared.

family life could continue hidden from the prying eyes of the public.

Enormous sums of money were spent on public architecture. During the time of Abd al-Rahman III one-third of state income was reserved for public buildings, and a great many mosques, markets, hospitals, universities, baths, inns, bridges and fountains were constructed for the benefit of the people. In particular, great attention was paid to the provision of public and private water supplies. The Arabs improved not only life in the cities but

also work in the fields. Along some of the rivers they built huge, wooden water-wheels, which were turned by the current. Around the outside the wheels had compartments which carried water up from the river and then deposited it in raised channels which delivered it to the surrounding gardens and fields. The agricultural year was probably governed by a solar calendar, compiled in Cordoba in the tenth century. By predicting the positions of the sun and major constellations each month, it was used to foresee changes in the

AD
1000

weather, indicate how domestic and wild animals would behave from month to month, and pinpoint the times for planting and harvesting. Through such a device astronomical information and agricultural activity were inextricably linked; many ancient cultivating peoples regarded the heavenly bodies as the active and productive powers, with the earth as the receptive beneficiary. Cultivation of the soil was inevitably bound up with curiosity about the stars.

The intellectual curiosity of Moorish Spain ranged far and wide. The Arabs wrote copiously on history, science, philosophy, jurisprudence, religion, mathematics and medicine. The introduction of linen and cotton paper gave a significant impetus to the literary movement. The most important library was the royal library at Cordoba. It was expanded by Abd al-Rahman III and especially developed by al-Hakam II when he came to the throne in AD 961. He amalgamated the three libraries of the caliph into one enormous

institution containing about 600,000 volumes. Many ancient texts in Greek and Latin were translated into Arabic in Spain, and from there the knowledge of their contents spread into Europe. In this way Moorish culture become a bridge between the classical and medieval worlds. In AD 982 a physician to Hisham II at Cordoba wrote a book on medicine based mainly on the Arabic translation of the *Materia Medica* of Dioscorides. Another physician who practised at Medina Azahara compiled a medical encyclopedia called *Kitab al-Tasrif*. The three parts dealing with surgery are the most important and the work was translated into several European languages, serving as a guide to surgeons in northern Europe.

The Moors were also keen geographers and their mariners seem to have explored the coast of west Africa before the year AD 1000. Indeed, it is claimed by some that it was an Arabic chart that showed Vasco da Gamma the sea route around the Cape of Good Hope to India.

Moorish jewellers achieved a level of perfection in Islamic Spain. The pair of Hispano-Moresque gold earrings, decorated with filigree rosettes, dates from AD 1000. Similarly dated is the silver-gilt bracelet with filigree decoration. Such jewellery would have been regularly worn at Medina Azahara.

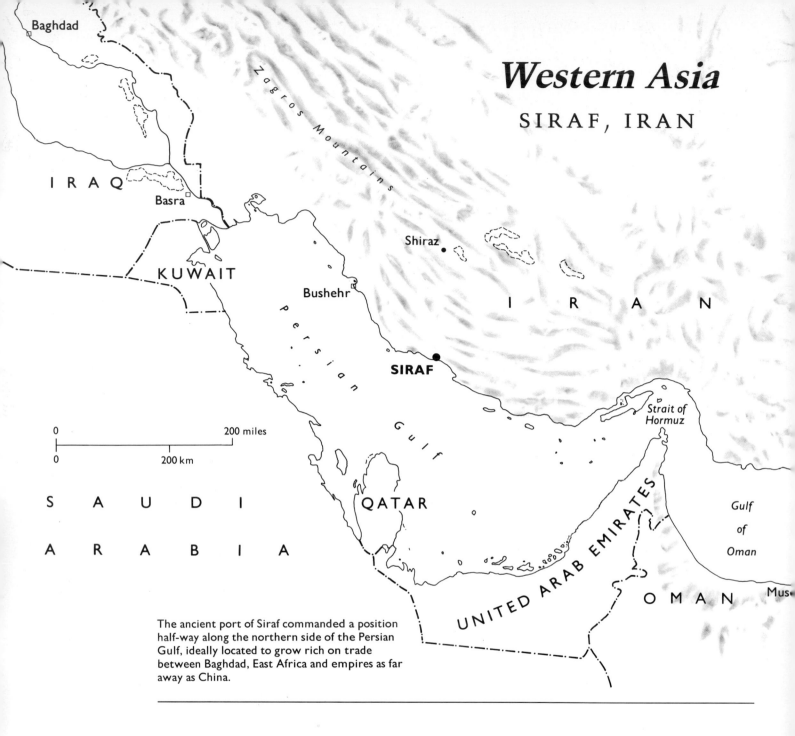

Western Asia
SIRAF, IRAN

The ancient port of Siraf commanded a position half-way along the northern side of the Persian Gulf, ideally located to grow rich on trade between Baghdad, East Africa and empires as far away as China.

The modern oil tankers that make their ponderous voyages up and down the Persian Gulf routinely pass by the sleepy village of Tahiri, which lies on the Iranian side of the Gulf, some 138 miles (220 km) from the nearest large town, Bushehr, to the north-west, and about 280 miles (450 km) from the Strait of Hormuz.

Yet it was not always so quiet, for modern Tahiri is partially constructed on the buried remains of ancient Siraf, and in the two centuries before AD 1000 Siraf was one of the most prosperous ports in the Persian Gulf and one of the greatest entrepots in western Asia. The merchants of Siraf were key players in a network of trading

links between the cities of the Middle East and China. Islamic Siraf extended along the shore for 2½ miles (4 km), from one arm of Tahiri Bay to the other. The sheltered anchorage allowed ships to remain offshore while their cargoes were transferred to warehouses by smaller craft. Curtain walls and forts protected the city from the east and west, while the northern mountains were so formidable that no artificial defences were necessary. A defensive wall was not constructed on the seaward side until the tenth century. The total area within the walls amounted to some 618 acres (250 ha), which included at least 272 acres (110 ha) of densely packed buildings within the western half

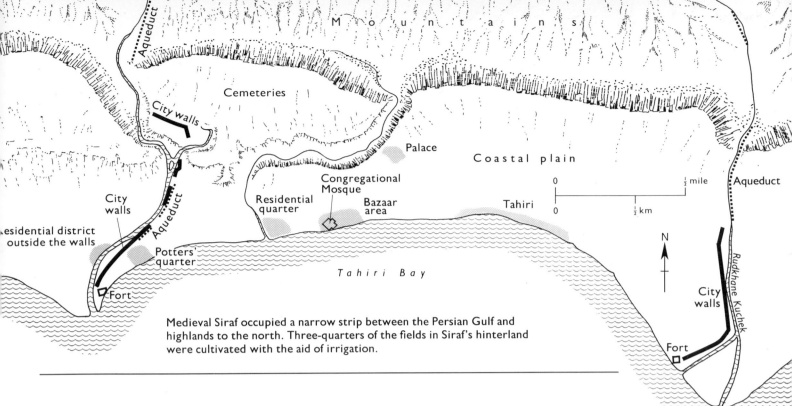

Medieval Siraf occupied a narrow strip between the Persian Gulf and highlands to the north. Three-quarters of the fields in Siraf's hinterland were cultivated with the aid of irrigation.

of the city. Here narrow streets separated the large Congregational Mosque, the bazaar and the residential and industrial quarters. On the sloping flanks of the mountains probably stood the extensive residences of the wealthiest merchants (as yet unexplored), admirably placed to take advantage of any slight breeze that blew. Behind these, and higher still, sprawled the city cemeteries. There were few permanent structures in the eastern half of the city. In all probability this area contained garden plots or insubstantial palm-frond huts of a considerable working population.

The earliest reference to Siraf occurs in the writing of Ibn al-Faqih (active around AD 850), who noted that Sirafi ships traded with India. A contemporary of his, Suleiman the Merchant, recorded that Middle Eastern goods bound for China were first sent from Basra to Siraf, from where they were dispatched by way of Muscat and Quilon, an important port on the Malabar coast off southern India. In about AD 900 Abu Zaid, himself a merchant of Siraf, noted that Sirafi merchants visited Jidda on the Red Sea and the Zanzibar coast. He also commented on the fact that Chinese coins were still circulating in Siraf, although the volume of trade between the Persian Gulf and China had decreased after the massacre of foreign merchants in Canton in AD 878.

The fullest account of the city was written by the geographer Istakhri shortly before AD 950. He described Siraf as second in importance to, and almost as large as, Shiraz. Despite its position on the hottest part of the coast and the scarcity of drinking water, fruit and vegetables, all of which

had to be imported from the plain of Jam in the hinterland north of Siraf, the city was prosperous and possessed imposing buildings. Multi-storey houses were constructed of stone and of timber imported from East Africa. The merchandise which passed through Siraf included aloes, ambergris, camphor, gemstones, bamboo, ivory, ebony, paper, sandalwood and other perfumes, drugs and spices. The city was an important market for pearls and among its own products were linen napkins and veils. However, by the time that Muqaddasi wrote a description of Siraf in the late tenth century, the beginning of what proved to be a steady decline had begun. The city was still a bustling entrepot with rich merchants living in elegant houses, but a severe earthquake had damaged the city in AD 977 and some of its citizens had moved elsewhere.

The physical remains of the city were investigated in a series of excavations conducted between 1966 and 1974, and revealed a wealth of information on different aspects of the city, such as its defences, water supply, mosques, bazaar, houses, industries and cemeteries. These details allow us to build up a picture of Siraf in the year AD 1000. The Islamic city was vulnerable to attack along the coastal plain and from the sea. The approaches by land, therefore, were barred by curtain walls which ran parallel with the watercourses. In the east the bank of the Rudkhane Kuchek was reinforced with a curtain wall which protected the eastern approaches. The wall itself survived only as a foundation of boulders and mud about 3 feet 3 inches (1 m) in width. It was reinforced with at least four semicircular towers. At

AD 1000

On the site of ancient Siraf now stands the modern village of Tahiri, dominated by the fort of the local sheik. Around its base lie the village houses, while behind rise the mountains of the interior.

The Congregational Mosque stood near the shore and it was to this main mosque that many of the city's faithful would flock in large numbers. Within its courtyard archaeologists have uncovered the remains of an earlier fortification from the Sassanian period, a pre-Islamic Persian dynasty.

AD
1000

The excavated remains of all periods of the
Congregational Mosque are illustrated in the lower half,
while the upper half offers a tentative reconstruction of
how the Mosque probably looked around AD 1000.
Islamic Siraf grew rich after the foundation of Baghdad
in AD 762, but was in decline by the twelfth century.

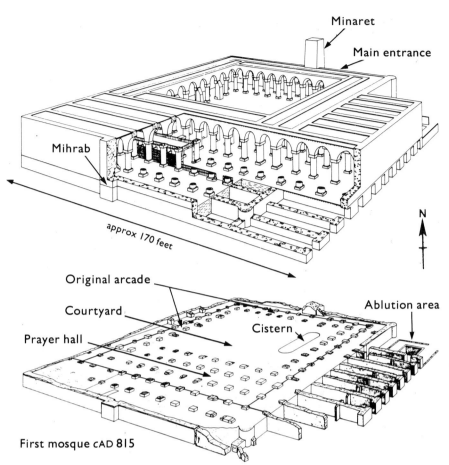

Minaret

Main entrance

Mihrab

approx 170 feet

N

Original arcade

Courtyard

Prayer hall

Cistern

Ablution area

First mosque cAD 815

its southern end it terminated in a small fort, 69
feet square (21 m sq.), with towers at its angles.
The west wall of Siraf was considerably sturdier.
It extended for about 1 mile (1.5 km) from the tip
of the coastal promontory to a vantage point
high up above the gorge, with an uninterrupted
view of the route from Jam. The outer face of the
wall was reinforced at irregular intervals with
semicircular buttresses. At its southern end it
joined on to an irregular compound which
contained a bath-house or hammam, a probable
arsenal and a building that may have been a
barracks. It therefore seems likely that small
garrisons were stationed at both terminations of the
land walls as they approached the sea. It is clear
that a sea wall did not form an integral part of the
initial design for the city's defences. A curtain wall
was located running between buildings near the
Congregational Mosque, however. The most likely
historical context for its construction would appear
to be the outbreak of hostilities between the
Omanis and the Buyid dynasty of Baghdad which
lasted from AD 943 to 973.

The faithful of Siraf were served by at least
eleven mosques distributed throughout the city.
The largest and most important was the
Congregational Mosque, situated in a central
position close to the shore. The building was
oriented towards Mecca and was surrounded on
the north, east and possibly the west sides by the
city's bazaar. To the south, beyond the qibla wall,
lay the waters of the Gulf. By AD 1000 the
Congregational Mosque comprised three elements:
an extensive rectangular platform some 7 feet (2 m)
in height which supported the floor of the
structure; and a lateral extension and some
external ablution facilities, both added to the
south-east side of the original building. The first
mosque, a rectangular edifice some 168 feet (51 m)
deep by 145 feet (44 m) wide, was probably
completed as early as AD 815. It comprised a
courtyard surrounded on three sides by a single
arcade, with a prayer hall three bays deep. The
principal access to the mosque lay in the north-east
wall, next to the minaret. The mihrab was sited in
the middle of the south-western wall, facing Mecca.
Not long afterwards, and no doubt in response to
the increasing population, the mosque was
redesigned and enlarged. A new arcade was inserted

on all four sides of the courtyard, the prayer hall
was extended by one bay and the extension and
ablution facilities on the south-east side were
added. In addition there were at least ten smaller
mosques in the western half of the city, with two
in the suburb to the west of the city walls; some of
these were private places of prayer attached to the
houses of the wealthy. The smaller mosques, like
all of the excavated structures at Siraf, were
constructed of rubble bonded with mortar or mortar
and mud. These mosques were small in comparison
with the Congregational Mosque, ranging in size
from about 17 feet square (5 m sq.) to 33 feet square
(10 m sq.). Most were rectangular or square in plan
and were divided by transverse arcades. No ceilings
have survived but it is assumed that most had flat
roofs made of poles.

The bustling centre of Siraf was, of course, the
bazaar, which occupied an area of some 12½ to 25
acres (5 to 10 ha) north and east of the
Congregational Mosque. Indeed, the contrast
between the clamour of the crowded, narrow
streets outside and the relative silence of the prayer
hall inside must have been quite marked. Abutting

AD
1000

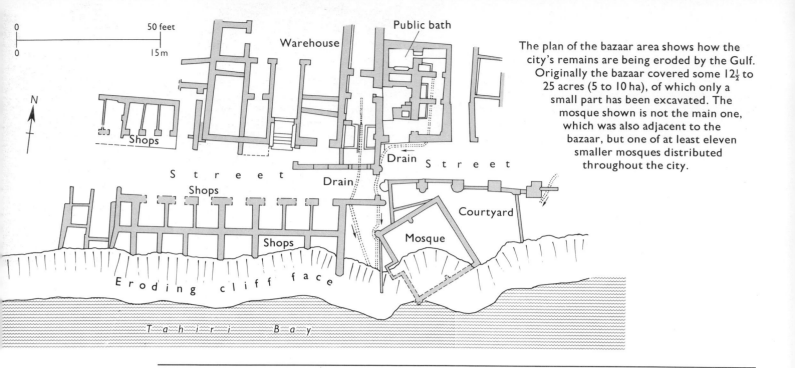

50 feet

15m

N

Warehouse

Public bath

Shops

Street

Shops

Drain

Drain Street

Mosque

Courtyard

Shops

Eroding cliff face

Tahiri Bay

The plan of the bazaar area shows how the city's remains are being eroded by the Gulf. Originally the bazaar covered some $12\frac{1}{2}$ to 25 acres (5 to 10 ha), of which only a small part has been excavated. The mosque shown is not the main one, which was also adjacent to the bazaar, but one of at least eleven smaller mosques distributed throughout the city.

AD 1000

upon the mosque, for example, were twenty self-contained one-room shops, each with an entrance on to the street. Some of their functions could be identified. One contained a large oven and operated as a bakery; in another the broken fragments and rough-outs from the manufacture of stone vessels were located; while in a third a series of miniature furnaces of unknown function were discovered. Certain industries were allocated to particular sections of the bazaar. Crucibles, slag and metal droplets in the area north of the Congregational Mosque indicate that this was where the citizens of Siraf came to haggle over the price of a copper or bronze artefact.

East of the Congregational Mosque some of the single-roomed shops had low platforms of mortared rubble outside their entrances, almost certainly display areas where a craftsman could arrange his wares or even work outside his premises. There were also larger commercial enterprises, consisting of buildings with rooms on all sides which enclosed an internal courtyard. It is quite likely that these comprised a complex of shops, workshops and accommodation and that the public could either enter shops from the street or walk into the central courtyard to view other merchandise. When the artisans and merchants finally decided to shut up shop, they could always hurry along to the hammam to relax. They had to be quick, though, to make sure of a place, since the building was quite small, measuring just 20 by 30 feet (6 by 9 m). It was entered from the street and had only six rooms. From the entrance hall patrons went into the changing-room and then made their way through a sequence of cold, warm and hot rooms. A

workman stoked the furnace from a sunken boiler-house which supplied hot air to the underfloor heating systems in the hammam.

Siraf was a place of exchange and not a major exporter. Of its own products linen and perhaps a type of edible clay were the principal items. The clay was green and supposed to taste like radishes (earth-eating provided some of the tribes of the interior with minerals that were lacking from their diet). The list given by Istakhri of merchandise at Siraf does not include the vast quantity of Chinese ceramics that were imported and exported from the city. Their wide distribution around the shores of the Gulf, and in coastal areas from Sri Lanka to East Africa, shows that they were widely sought after. Stoneware bowls, ewers and jars with appliqué ornament made in the kilns of Ch'ang Sha (Hunan) occur at Siraf. Later in the ninth century Sirafi merchants began to import white- and green-glazed bowls, which were superseded in the tenth century by bowls of translucent white porcelain.

These exquisite oriental ceramics were being used on the tables of the wealthy, in spacious and well-planned houses belonging to rich merchants. Such houses generally occupied elevated positions on the highest and coolest parts of the escarpments. An enormous complex north-east of the Congregational Mosque spread over an area of at least 500 by 250 feet (150 by 75 m) and was enclosed by its own perimeter wall. It is likely to have been the residence of a very wealthy merchant or even the palace of the governor himself. Less extravagant but still comfortable was the residential quarter west of the Congregational Mosque that included five houses separated by a gridded street plan. Although each house was different, all possessed entrances which gave access on to internal courtyards surrounded by rectangular rooms. There were certainly second storeys to these structures, although the lack of windows found during the excavations suggests that, on the ground floor anyway, exterior walls were largely blank, with rooms lit by doorways from the courtyards. Such an arrangement provided privacy, of course, and at the same time sought to exclude noise, dust and the worst of the summer heat. Despite the elaborate stucco ornament, incorporating inscriptions from the Koran, that was applied to the walls of these houses, they completely lacked any main drainage or public supply of water. Sewage was directed into stone-lined pits in the side streets, while drinking water was drawn from private wells or was brought in in large water pots from outside.

The water pots were manufactured in the potters' quarter at the western edge of Siraf, close to the shore and inside the city walls. It consisted of complexes of workshops, kilns, drying-sheds, clay-preparation areas and a cistern. Their peripheral location was well chosen. The risks of fire and pollution were less of a problem on the edge of town. Raw materials from the hinterland could reach the workshops without having to traverse the crowded city streets and finished products could be loaded on to small boats at the water's edge and transferred easily to larger vessels anchored in the bay.

When an inhabitant of Siraf died he or she was buried in one of the cemeteries that were situated at the edge of the city, usually on high ground which was too steep or inaccessible to accommodate buildings. The great majority were buried in rock-cut graves, each intended to receive a single inhumation. Most of the graves were aligned N–S, although some were set in an E–W direction, while the orientation of others was governed by the limited rock surface available. Many of the rectangular rock-cut graves had ledges or offsets which supported a row of stone slabs that covered the body. Above the slabs the grave was backfilled with earth and rubble; plinths of mortared rubble, plaster-covered domes, inscribed stone or stucco grave-covers marked the grave above ground. Some of the graves were accompanied by wells and small enclosures, which may have contained areas reserved for individual families. The most distinctive cemetery at Siraf was a group of monumental tombs on a spur overlooking the western end of the city. By AD 1000 as many as forty such buildings housing collective burials may have occupied this hill. Individual graves, a few of which had stone or

The entrances to the houses of the wealthy were formed of mud brick and pisé. The walls were then plastered and representations of architectural motifs, such as friezes, were added.

stucco covers with inscriptions from the Koran, surrounded them.

The walls of Siraf enclosed an area of more than 618 acres (250 ha) and it is clear that the city possessed a population both numerous and wealthy. The size and prosperity of the city were particularly striking in the context of the local environment, where limited rainfall and searing heat produced seemingly inhospitable terrain, especially for agriculture. Extensive surveys in the hinterland north of the city have demonstrated, however, the presence of medieval fields, and it is calculated that within a $3\frac{3}{4}$-mile (6-km) radius some 1,730 acres (700 ha) were potentially cultivable. About 75 per cent of these fields were associated with some form of irrigation. The greater

A view into one of the middle-class homes in the residential quarter west of the Congregational Mosque. The courtyard is surrounded on all sides by rooms.

The remains of the potters' quarter comprised several circular kiln-bases, perforated internally with horizontal rows of holes. These presumably supported holders for layers of unfired vessels as they were stacked in the kiln.

The comfortable houses in the residential quarter all had rooms arranged around a central courtyard. They were separated from each other by narrow lanes. Sewage was tipped into stone-lined pits in these side streets.

manpower of the Sirafis enabled the installation and maintenance of irrigation systems, whereas the present inhabitants of Tahiri are still largely reliant on the unpredictable returns from dry farming. Even so, the fields of Siraf were not sufficient to provide for all the populace and produce was imported from the valley of Jam and the plain of Galehdar along paved caravan routes.

The decline of the great city of Siraf was a protracted one, brought about by a variety of factors. Mention has already been made of the earthquake of AD 977 which caused so much damage. More important, though, was the fact that its fortunes were inextricably linked with those of

the Buyid dynasty, based in Baghdad. Siraf had grown rich only after the foundation of Baghdad in AD 762, because this had stimulated trade and led to considerable demands for Chinese, Indian and East African goods in the markets of the Middle East. The fall of the Buyids in the middle of the eleventh century, and particularly the fall of the last Buyid governor of Shiraz, opened the way for an opportunistic emir to establish the island of Kish as a rival entrepot, and indeed to capture Siraf itself. The Congregational Mosque underwent what was to be a final refurbishment in the twelfth century and the last inhabitant of medieval Siraf to have a carved grave-cover died in AD 1144.

AD
1000

Africa

JENNE-JENO, MALI

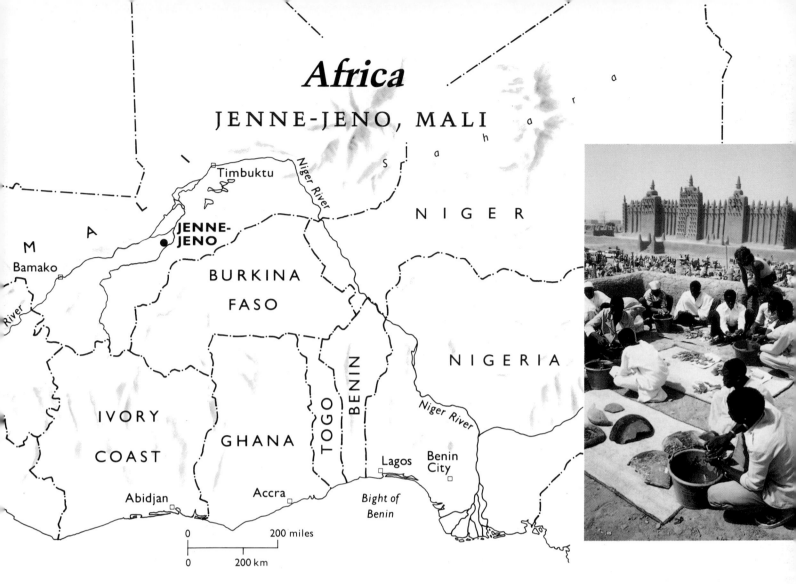

According to one Arab chronicler, over 7,000 villages once occupied the area around Jenne-jeno, on a floodplain to the south of Timbuktu. Settlement began around 250 BC and by AD 1000 Jenne-jeno enjoyed great prosperity, trading in iron, gold and copper until its decline in the thirteenth century when, under Muslim influence, the site was moved to Jenne. Rooftops in modern Jenne provided space for archaeological relics to be sorted.

By the year AD 1000 the far north west corner of Africa had been settled by various Muslim dynasties for over three centuries. The Straits of Gibraltar were crossed in 711 as Muslim armies began the conquest of the Iberian peninsula. Muslim penetration in the opposite direction, to the south, was more difficult. An effective barrier was formed by the huge expanse of the Sahara. On the far side of the desert the sandy wastes eventually gave way to the tall grasses of the savanna. Here the waters of the Niger flowed around a great bend before beginning their long journey south to the Atlantic Ocean. Knowledge of these grasslands and the tropical forests beyond filtered northwards across the desert, spread by merchants plying the trans-Saharan trade routes. Vital commodities such as salt, and luxury objects such as glass and ceramics, were carried south by

camels to indigenous settlements in these areas; slaves, ivory and gold were brought back in return.

One such settlement was located at Jenne-jeno (or Old Jenne). The site occupied a large mound that today rises up to 23 feet (7 m) above the floodplain of the inland Niger delta, some 2 miles (3 km) south-east of the present-day town of Jenne. Only a few acacia trees and a clump or two of mangoes now grow on the deserted surface of the ancient town. The inland delta is a large alluvial basin, which at first glance stands comparison with the great floodplains of Mesopotamia and Egypt. In all three, an arid countryside is bisected by a life-giving ribbon of water whose annual floodings deposit rich alluvial sediments, which in turn support lush seasonal vegetation. However, the amount of alluvial deposition is less in the Niger delta, and the local topography is more varied.

AD 1000

Excavators at the site of Jenne-jeno carefully collect up surface indications of settlement, such as iron slag and pottery sherds. Even on a site that has not been occupied for 700 years, the distribution of such surface material often provides clues to what might lie beneath.

The teardrop-shaped mound of Jenne-jeno measures roughly ½ mile (800 m) along its longer, N–S axis by roughly ⅓ mile (550 m) E–W. The surface area of the site is approximately 82 acres (33 ha). At its zenith, from AD 700 to 1100, the town also probably included the 22-acre (9-ha) mound of Hambarketolo, which lies immediately to the north and was connected to Jenne-jeno by an earthen dyke. Just west of Jenne-jeno is a seasonal channel called the Senuba, which retains water throughout the dry season. In addition, north and east of the site are two large ponds which may have been created by the removal of considerable amounts of clay for the manufacture of mud bricks. Although settlement at Jenne-jeno began as early as 250 BC, it was around AD 1000 that the town reached its greatest extent. By that date a town wall, constructed of solid courses of cylindrical mud bricks, surrounded the town. In places the wall was over 12 feet (3.6 m) in width and traces of what may have been a deliberate mud coating of the external wall faces were discovered. The town wall was erected on a level of prepared clay, within which at one point an upright pot had been placed containing the remains of an infant. A gold earring

dating to slightly before AD 1000, the only gold object found at Jenne-jeno, was recovered from below the northern section of the town wall. At the north-east side of the site there was probably a brick and rubble gate some 60 feet (18 m) wide.

The surface of the mound is covered with a thick blanket of potsherds, mud bricks, iron lumps and slag, suggesting intensive occupation, both residential and industrial in character. Ten areas have been explored by excavation. These demonstrate that houses were both circular and rectangular and were built of either rectangular or cylindrical mud bricks. The majority of the dead of Jenne-jeno seem to have been buried in the south-eastern part of the town. However, it is dangerous to generalize about such a large site when so little of it has been excavated. The results from the small excavation in the northern part of the town allow us a brief glimpse of urban life in the centuries either side of the year AD 1000.

The remains of three buildings were located in the excavated area, one on top of the other and all built and destroyed within a relatively short period. The earliest was a rectangular structure of cylindrical mud bricks. The lack of pottery and

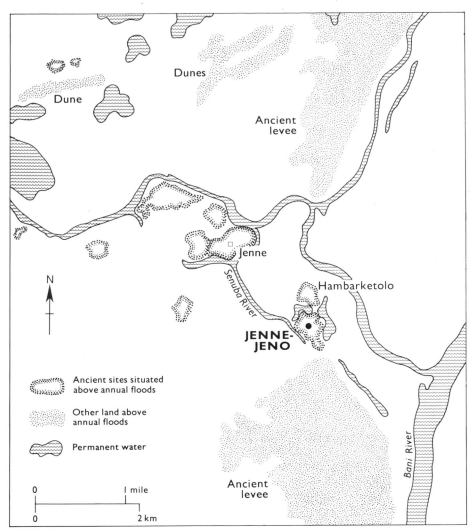

Dune

Dunes

Ancient levee

Jenne

Hambarketolo

JENNE-JENO

Senuba River

Bani River

Ancient levee

N

Ancient sites situated above annual floods

Other land above annual floods

Permanent water

0   1 mile

0   2 km

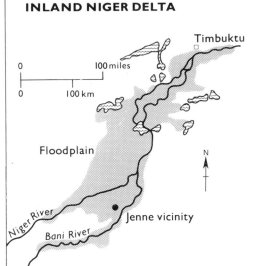

INLAND NIGER DELTA

Timbuktu

0   100 miles

0   100 km

Floodplain

N

Niger River

Jenne vicinity

Bani River

The ancient site of Jenne-jeno, by the Bani River, occupies a large mound that rises up to 23 feet (7 m) above the floodplain of the Niger delta. This inland delta is crossed by rivers and annual flooding deposits rich alluvial sediments, which support lush seasonal vegetation.

animal bone from inside the house led the excavators to suggest a non-domestic function. This was then superseded by a circular structure, about 20 feet (6 m) in diameter and built of irregular, cylindrical mud bricks. Again there were few pieces of domestic pottery or animal bones in the interior of the building. There was, however, a collection of very unusual pottery on the floor. Some of the sherds were decorated with representations in relief, including a headless human figure, a snake and an anteater. Particularly significant was the discovery of a terracotta statuette which shows a figure in a kneeling position with its legs forming part of the rectangular base. Some kind of covering from the waist to the knees is indicated by a series of incised parallel lines. The arms are crossed over the chest, with the hands resting on the shoulders. A large torque hangs around its neck, while a number of incisions on the wrist and lower arm probably signify bracelets. It seems that soon after this figure was placed on the floor, the walls were deliberately collapsed inwards and another rectangular building

This particular and unusual fragment of pottery is adorned with what seems to be an intentionally headless figure. The figure probably had a religious or mythic function.

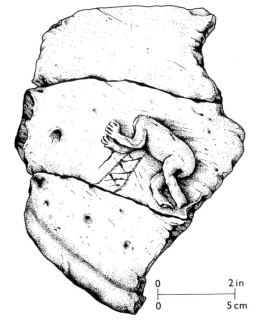

0   2 in

0   5 cm

AD 1000

The modern town of Jenne juts out into the surrounding floodplain.

was erected over its levelled walls. The buildings encountered in the other excavations in the town indicate that the earliest inhabitants of Jenne-jeno lived in round houses constructed from poles covered with straw or rush mats daubed with clay. Shortly before AD 1000 cylindrical sun-dried mud bricks were introduced at the site and both rectangular and circular structures co-existed for a considerable length of time. Indeed, round mud-brick houses are still built in the Jenne hinterland today.

Life in modern Jenne seems to provide an explanation for the statuettes. In the early 1900s a colonial official noted that many of the doorways into the houses at Jenne incorporated small altars. On these altars there was frequently placed a statuette in the likeness of an important ancestor. At these shrines sacrifices could be made to the deceased. It seems plausible that practices in the Jenne of the 1900s reflected an unbroken tradition that linked the inhabitants of the town then with those of 900 years earlier.

Some pieces of the Jenne-jeno jigsaw will always be missing. We will never know the names of the communities who lived at Jenne-jeno or those of the peoples who fished and farmed in the delta. It is apparent, however, from the distribution of present-day communities that a multiplicity of ethnic groups co-exist in the area and they probably did so in the past. These contemporary peoples, each occupying a particular environment, are joined together by the inter-group exchange of products, services and labour that is vital to their individual needs. Such a system of interacting

communities may well have existed in the past, so it is possible that the inhabitants of Jenne-jeno in AD 1000 were drawn from several different groups.

Archaeological surveys carried out in the area west of Jenne-jeno have produced evidence for a number of settlements and burial mounds that mirror the great length of occupation at the town. In particular, pottery collected from the surface of many of the sites has shown that the apogee of Jenne-jeno around AD 1000 is matched in its hinterland by the greatest number of settlements of any period. One Arab chronicler reported that there were once 7,077 villages in the territory of Jenne-jeno, and so close were they that messages could be transmitted by crying out from village to village. Such a statement may well be a memory of this period of prosperity. That prosperity may have been related to increased agricultural surpluses generated by the highest levels of the floodwaters, which were reached around AD 1000. With the rise of the waters, lengthier periods of inundation may have encouraged multiple yields of rice and sorghum. The humid period that brought more extensive flooding probably ended between AD 1200 and 1300 and was followed by an increasingly drier climate.

Analysis of the surface remains from sites shows that around AD 1000 the most common type of house was circular in ground plan and constructed of cylindrical mud bricks. Rectangular houses were fewer and may have developed as a result of architectural ideas spreading from the north. Burials were encountered at several sites and show a preference for the eastern side of

AD
1000

A round mud-brick house, excavated to its floor, which probably once sheltered a wife and her children; the husband's other families would live in connecting dwellings. In this atmospheric reconstruction, braziers burn in the actual ancient hearths.

This is a superb example of a clay statuette, approximately 10 inches (25 cm) high, from Jenne-jeno, with the sensuous quality of its three-dimensional moulding, the elaborately decorative bracelets and necklaces, and the dagger strapped to the figure's left arm. More than one such statue has been found, and it is possible that they were fashioned in the likeness of dead individuals and revered as ancestors.

AD
1000

settlements. The customary rite of burial was to place the deceased in a foetal position in an upright funerary jar in a pit in the ground. The mouth of the jar was then covered by an inverted pot or lid. Additional burials, presumably of other family members, were later placed in the urns in some cases. Many of the settlements were covered with concentrations of iron slag, indicating the presence of widespread iron production. The forging of iron implements must have been carried out at many centres and this is especially significant given the lack of high-grade iron ore in the delta. It strongly suggests that there was considerable trade in iron ore and that the delta must have been more wooded to supply timber for the smithing process.

The surveys showed not only that there were a considerable number of sites in the Jenne-jeno region around AD 1000 but also that they varied in size from small to large. The different sizes suggest that the larger sites may have been administrative centres, perhaps controlling a stable pattern of co-existence in this varied environment and providing the necessary conditions for different ethnic groups to exchange goods and services. Certainly the number of sites occupied at this period argues that the population must have been considerably higher than it is today. And the similarity of artefacts collected from the surfaces of the mounds also indicates that they participated in the same networks of trade and exchange.

Jenne-jeno developed into a town without any demonstrable stimulus from the Mediterranean or Muslim world. It was a purely African development. Its citizens may have been drawn from various ethnic groups in the delta and its leaders may have controlled the regional exchange of goods and services in this area, but its activities extended beyond the delta. The amount of iron slag on the surface at Jenne-jeno suggests that already smelted iron was being imported to the site and forged into implements; there is no suitable source of iron ore for smelting in the delta. However, nineteenth-century accounts of the region refer to imports of bloomery iron from some 31 miles (50 km) to the south-west being exchanged for salt in Jenne-jeno. It seems plausible that this trade is of considerable antiquity. Salt is a prerequisite for human life and in tropical parts of the world it must be taken in mineral form. The savanna communities probably depended on salt being brought from the few major rock-salt deposits in the Sahara. Another Saharan commodity being traded south into Jenne-jeno was probably copper. The trade in both salt and copper perhaps developed in the early centuries AD, when both were brought south to the Niger Bend, from where they would be shipped southward and upstream to Jenne-jeno, at the extreme southern end of the navigable delta. Water transport for such heavy commodities was far more cost-effective than using pack animals or human head-porters. Once there, these precious items could be exchanged for staples such as rice or dried fish, or more permanent materials such as iron or even gold from the gold fields to the south of Jenne-jeno.

In the year AD 1000, therefore, Jenne-jeno must have been a thriving town, full of farmers, fishermen, craftsmen, merchants and families, with perhaps a population close to 10,000. Yet by AD 1468 it had been abandoned. Almost certainly the cause of its dramatic decline lay in the thirteenth century, when the area came under Muslim influence (the king of Jenne-jeno was converted to Islam in AD 1240). It is possible that commercial control now passed into the hands of Muslim merchants based at a new town, Jenne, founded only 2 miles (3 km) to the north-west of the old site. Such a small shift in location was not undertaken for any practical reason, but was probably motivated by religious considerations: the new location would be unpolluted by pagan practices. The Muslims simply took over a successful exchange network that had been found centuries earlier by the peoples of the savanna. As a result one of the most sophisticated settlements of the indigeneous communities of sub-Saharan Africa was abandoned and finally almost forgotten.

Miniature model camels and cattle, made out of clay, are still a common sight in Jenne today. This meant that broken pieces of similar clay models from ancient Jenne-jeno could be immediately identified as toys by workmen on the excavation team.

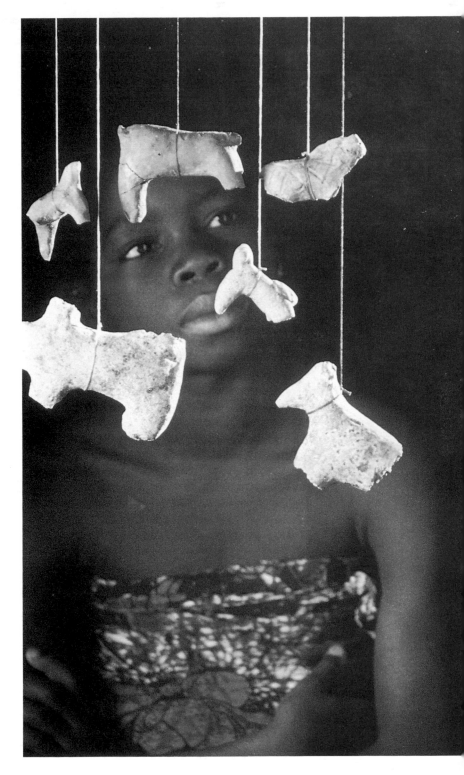

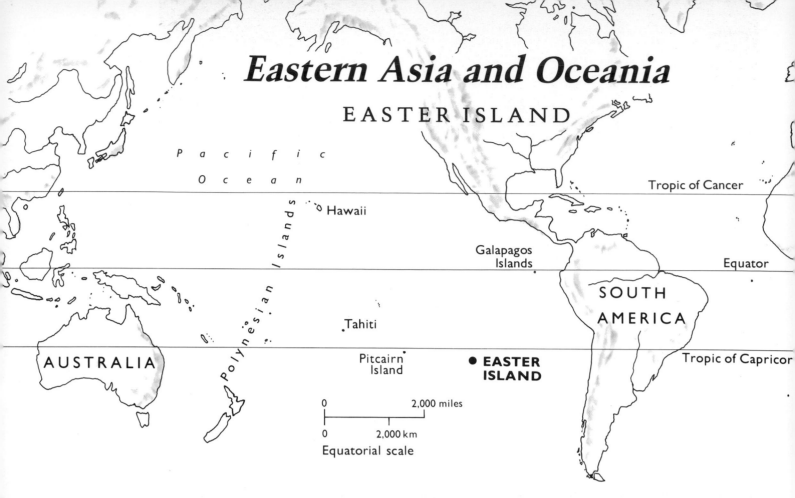

Eastern Asia and Oceania

EASTER ISLAND

Tropic of Cancer

Pacific Ocean

○ Hawaii

Polynesian Islands

Galapagos Islands

Equator

.Tahiti

SOUTH AMERICA

AUSTRALIA

Pitcairn Island

● **EASTER ISLAND**

Tropic of Capricor

| 0 | | 2,000 miles |
| 0 | | 2,000 km |

Equatorial scale

An isolated volcanic outcrop, Easter Island lies just south of the Tropic of Capricorn on a line running between Australia and South America. Set nearer to the South American mainland than to the islands of Polynesia, it was nevertheless colonized by Polynesian explorers, possibly as many as 700 years before this period.

AD 1000

Easter Island is one of the remotest islands on earth, as is recognized by the islanders' own name for their home, Te Pito o te Henua, which can be roughly translated as 'land's end'. It is an isolated volcanic outcrop separated to the east by some 2,314 miles (3,703 km) from the nearest significant landmass, South America. To the west an equally impressive 1,137 miles (1,819 km) of ocean swells between it and Pitcairn Island. By any stretch of the imagination Easter Island is a tiny landfall surrounded by a huge and extensive sea. And yet perhaps as early as AD 300 a small party of men and women set sail from one of the Central or East Polynesian islands in search of new land. Weeks later, and no doubt beginning to despair of any hint of landfall, the first volcanic peaks of Easter Island pierced the horizon. It must have been an incredible moment, the prehistoric equivalent of stepping out on to the surface of the moon, although, of course, it was a much greater achievement since these courageous navigators could not have known that Easter Island existed at all. No doubt one of their very first acts on reaching

these untrodden shores was to offer up a sacrifice and prayers to the gods and ancestors who had guided them safely to their destination. The geographic isolation of Easter Island meant that a return trip was unlikely. They had come to stay, and by AD 700 they had laid the new directions of a society that produced some extraordinary and unique ritual monuments.

Easter Island is not a typical tropical or subtropical Polynesian Island. Several geological, oceanographic and climatic conditions make the island relatively marginal when compared with its distant neighbours to the west. The island was formed by the coalescing flows of three principal volcanoes, whose peaks are situated in the angles of this triangular-shaped landmass. The land surface amounts only to some 62 square miles (160 sq. km), most of it rising through undulating hills to the higher volcanic cones. There are no permanent streams and most water sinks directly into the porous volcanic soils. Rainfall is moderate, with the average between 4 feet (1.25 m) and 5 feet (1.5 m) per annum; this is sufficient for several

Above: A line of seven stone statues stare out into the Pacific from the north coast of Easter Island, at a site known as Anakena. The Dutch sailors who rediscovered this remote landfall in the early eighteenth century must have stared with disbelief at such monuments.

Below: On the southern tip of the island, petroglyphs of the birdman cult mark a spot where the annual contest of the Easter Islanders to obtain the first eggs of the sooty tern, nesting on an offshore island, may well have begun.

AD
1000

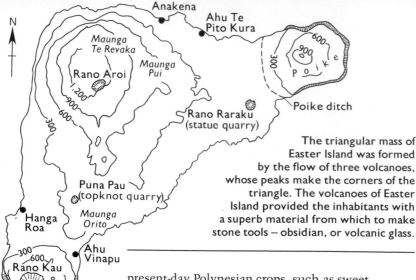

The triangular mass of Easter Island was formed by the flow of three volcanoes, whose peaks make the corners of the triangle. The volcanoes of Easter Island provided the inhabitants with a superb material from which to make stone tools – obsidian, or volcanic glass.

present-day Polynesian crops, such as sweet potatoes, yams, bananas and sugar cane, although droughts are not uncommon. Since the island lacks year-round watercourses, the original inhabitants were unable to develop irrigation agriculture. Instead, their water supplies were met by two crater lakes and rainfall was collected in prepared stone basins. Easter Island lies just outside the tropics and is swept by cold-water currents from the Antarctic. The absence of fringing coral reefs prevented the formation of lagoons and limited the variety and quantity of available fishing. The average annual temperature is about 72°F (22°C) and the island is buffeted by trade winds.

The island that the first human beings set foot upon, therefore, was clearly no paradise. The local fauna was very restricted. There were no indigenous land mammals, few insects and the only reptiles present were two species of small lizard. A variety of migratory sea birds existed on the island, but not a great number of marine mammals or turtles. It is unlikely that the land surface was much more forested than it is today. If the first settlers brought different species of plants and animals to their new home, not many survived the adaptation process. Only chickens were successfully carried to Easter Island, along with the rat. If dogs and pigs were brought ashore, they did not adapt, and neither did such tropical East Polynesian plants as coconut and breadfruit. From the beginning, therefore, the subsistence possibilities for the inhabitants were limited.

The immigrants to Easter Island brought with them not only material possessions, agricultural expertise and architectural knowledge; they also imported more intangible elements such as ideas about family life, community relationships, ritual practices and religious beliefs. These were ideas they had grown up with in their former island homes in Central or East Polynesia and some of them were adopted on Easter Island. The principal community organization appears to have been

based on the identification of a related group of people headed by a common male ancestor. Such a group formed a lineage which was led by a chief or *ariki*, who often possessed both ritual and secular powers. Not all lineages were equal in status. The chief of the most important lineage was believed to be a direct descendant of the gods. Each lineage had an *ahu* or temple located near the coast which served as a focus for rituals, some of which probably involved funerary and mortuary practices. The *ahu* consisted of rectangular stone platforms and many were topped by an entirely novel Easter Island creation: hundreds of stone statues, quarried from a location known as Rano Raraku and hauled several laborious miles before being erected upright on the *ahu* platforms. It was these incredible monolithic statues, their facial characteristics stylized in stone, that so astonished the first Dutch explorers who rediscovered the island on Easter Sunday 1722.

By AD 1000 the population of Easter Island was approaching its maximum of about 10,000 people, and the great phase of statue quarrying, transport and erection was well under way. The population was divided into several social and economic categories. The majority were farmers, of course, while there were a growing number of craftsmen, priests and warriors. The pattern of settlements across the landscape mirrored the social organization of the lineage. Most *ahu*, some supporting statues, were built near the shore, and from there these silent stone images watched over and protected the lands of their community. Each community, or lineage, possessed a broad strip of land that ran from the coast towards the centre of the island. Inland from the *ahu* stood several elliptical buildings which housed the chief and highest-ranking individuals in the lineage, as well as the priests who officiated at the *ahu*. A particularly large boat-shaped structure in this group may have functioned as a kind of secular community hall. Further inland were the dispersed houses, ovens, chicken sheds and garden enclosures where the majority of the lineage lived. In this well-ordered society, therefore, the spatial patterning of a community's buildings reflected the social position of individual members within a group. Easter Islanders knew who they were by where they were.

The most remarkable remains on Easter Island were not, of course, those created for the living but those quarried, carved, hauled and erected in honour of the dead. The most widely accepted interpretation of the more than 600 stone statues is that they represented chiefs or other deceased high-ranking individuals. Finished statues ranged in height from 6 feet 6 inches to 32 feet 4 inches (2 to

AD 1000

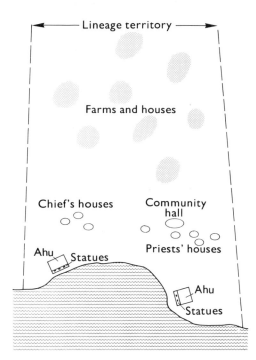

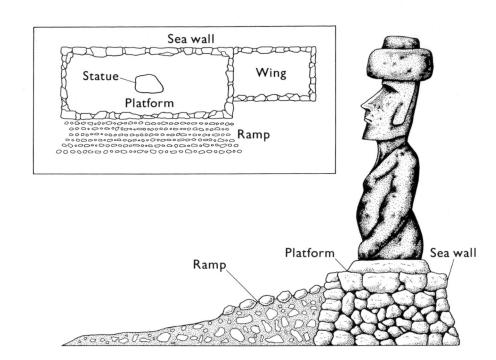

Above left: Each lineage or community of related individuals possessed a territory that included a coastal strip with land running back into the interior of the island. By AD 1000 the population had reached its peak of 10,000 inhabitants on this tiny island.

Above right: The sacred sites, or *ahu*, surmounted by a single statue were erected facing the sea.

10 m), with the average estimated at about 13 feet (4 m). The largest ever erected is that at Ahu Te Pito Kura, which has been calculated to weigh 81 tons. The facial characteristics of these megalithic ancestors appear to have become more stylized over the centuries. In addition, the problems of transport are clearly reflected in the distribution of the statues, with the largest being closest to the quarry at Rano Raraku, where volcanic tuff was used as the material for most of the images.

The classic form of the statues is usually a male human figure from the hips upwards, with the arms held tightly at the sides. The hands are turned in to meet each other on the lower abdomen. The head is an elongated rectangle, with a straight or slightly concave nose and thin, compressed lips. Noses are prominent, with broad nostrils. Foreheads are convex, while some earlobes are carved to appear perforated and hang far down the sides of the face. The backs of some statues bear detailed designs which appear to represent some form of tattooing. When the statues finally reached their chosen *ahu* destination and were erected, coral or red scoria rock was inserted into the eye sockets.

Ever since the statues were discovered there have been attempts to fathom two important technical questions: how they were carved and how they were transported. The quarry at Rano Raraku has provided certain answers. At least some of the statues were carved from the rock in a horizontal position, the back of the statue being the last area to be freed from the bedrock. Experiments have suggested that dampening the rock prior to carving would have assisted the work of stone masons who relied on stone picks in their work. Once freed from the bedrock, the statues were manoeuvred on to the slopes of the quarry, where they were set upright and their backs were finished. Over seventy statues still stand on the lower slopes, both inside and outside the quarry, where they were undergoing this finishing process. Once the statues were complete, the long task of hauling them to their final resting-place, the *ahu*, was begun. Again, experiments this century indicate that the statues were placed horizontally on a frame or sledge and then dragged by up to about 150 people along specially prepared roads to their destination. Clearly there were failures. The largest statue on an *ahu*, measuring some 32 feet 10 inches (10 m) in length, was transported successfully to its site but fell and broke before it was completely erected.

This remarkable feat of civil engineering by a Stone Age society was, in certain cases, taken even

AD
1000

further, with stone topknots being placed on the heads of some of the statues. These topknots could weight up to 10.8 tons and were carved from a red scoria at another quarry on Puna Pau, located near Hanga Roa. Some have claimed that the topknots were indications of hair styles in the Easter Island population, while others suggest that just as not all chiefs were equal in life, so not all ancestors were of the same status in death. The additional red scoria topknots, of which there are fewer than seventy surviving, may indicate that some *ahu* were more important than others.

Not all of the approximately 300 *ahu* on Easter Island supported statues. However, those that did consisted of raised platforms of rubble contained by façades of fitted stones. Sometimes the close fitting of these stone façades was exceptionally fine, as in the case of Ahu Vinapu, tempting many casual observers to make superficial comparisons with Inca stonework, some of the finest example of which can be seen at Cuzco, the Inca capital in Peru. There is no evidence, however, to support the controversial theory that some of the inhabitants reached Easter Island from coastal Peru. Usually, on the landward side of the *ahu* there was a stone-paved, sloping ramp which led up to the platform, and a rectangular court or plaza bounded on three sides by an earthen embankment. The number of statues erected on an *ahu* could range from one to a maximum of fifteen. There is considerable evidence for detailed planning in the construction of these complex structures. The façades of some *ahu* may have been aligned with some particular astronomical orientation, such as the rising or setting sun at the solstices and equinoxes.

In the year AD 1000, then, some of the separate lineage communities of Easter Island had a well-developed subsistence base. Although limited in variety, it was sufficiently productive in terms of quantity to support many hundreds of able-bodied adults while they devoted their time to the laborious tasks of carving and erecting stone statues. They were governed by a range of Polynesian gods, whose representatives on their island were the chiefs and the ancestors of former chiefs represented in the monolithic sculptures.

Left: Once cut free from the bedrock, statues were moved to the slopes outside the quarry and set upright so the backs could be carved.

Right: Statues from a platform at Anakena. Each wears one of the red stone topknots that were symbols of added power.

The number of statues appears to have grown steadily over the years as more were commenced by groups of people supported by individual lineages. Settlements were formed as lineages multiplied, and material possessions included a range of stone, obsidian and bone artefacts, such as adzes, scrapers, fishhooks and needles. The priests had even begun to develop a form of writing, the rongorongo script, which may have been used to record sacred chants and the genealogies of chiefs. Any tendencies for rivalries between communities found an outlet in increasing efforts to produce bigger statues, more elaborate *ahu*, and grander feasts and ceremonies.

Yet the island could not support an ever-expanding population and the centuries after AD 1000 were ones of increasing social stress. Forest clearance resulted in widespread erosion, and as the forests were decimated, the amount of available timber decreased. This in turn ensured that canoes were smaller and the resulting catches of fish less. Competition between groups could not now be expressed in the traditional way of *ahu* construction, since the food surplus to support the workforce had disappeared and the timber for

transporting statues was no longer to be found. A new cult emerged in which competition took the form of an annual contest to obtain the first egg of the sooty tern from its nesting place on an offshore island at Orongo, on the southern tip of the island. The chief whose servant managed to return first with the egg was granted great sanctity and effective control over most of the islanders. More often than not, however, such authority led to revolts and reprisals, which gradually escalated into endemic warfare. In the centuries before European contact small communities attacked their neighbours, taking their lands, enslaving them and perhaps toppling the statues of their ancestors. As signs of the times, some islanders retreated to live in defended caves and even fortified their stone houses against human predators. By the early eighteenth century the warrior class had gained control of the island. When the Dutchmen arrived in 1722, Easter Island society was at war with itself. The benign protection of the megalithic ancestors had vanished. Their impoverished and neglected descendants faced their first encounter with the outside world divided and alone.

This is the seaward face of a basalt wall from Ahu Vinapu. The close-fitting megalithic masonry has invited superficial comparisons with Inca architecture.

AD
1000

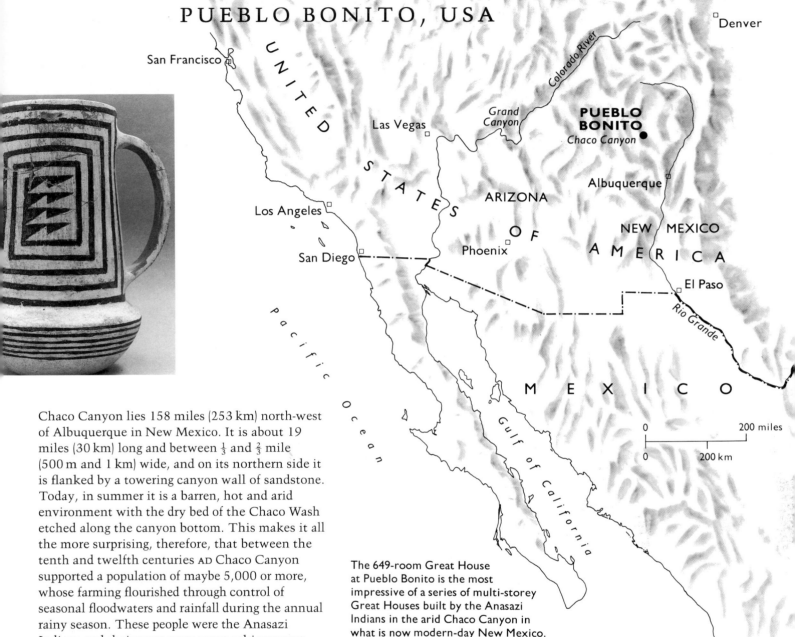

The Americas

PUEBLO BONITO, USA

Chaco Canyon lies 158 miles (253 km) north-west of Albuquerque in New Mexico. It is about 19 miles (30 km) long and between $\frac{1}{3}$ and $\frac{2}{3}$ mile (500 m and 1 km) wide, and on its northern side it is flanked by a towering canyon wall of sandstone. Today, in summer it is a barren, hot and arid environment with the dry bed of the Chaco Wash etched along the canyon bottom. This makes it all the more surprising, therefore, that between the tenth and twelfth centuries AD Chaco Canyon supported a population of maybe 5,000 or more, whose farming flourished through control of seasonal floodwaters and rainfall during the annual rainy season. These people were the Anasazi Indians and their most permanent achievement was the construction of a series of masonry pueblos, or Great Houses, which displayed such architectural sophistication that it immediately set them apart from earlier building traditions. Pueblo Bonito (literally 'pretty town'), with its multi-storeyed houses and massive curving walls, is the most outstanding example in the canyon.

The Great House at Pueblo Bonito extended over $3\frac{3}{4}$ acres (1.5 ha) and at the peak of its development it contained 649 rooms. These were arranged in a semicircle and overlooked an enclosed courtyard, containing numerous ritual meeting-places known as *kivas*. The complex was built in several phases between AD 900 and 1100 and was almost certainly an important centre in the Anasazi world. It has been possible to use tree-ring dating on the pine trunks used in the roofs of the buildings, which had survived in the very dry conditions, so we have an idea of the dates of these different phases.

The 649-room Great House at Pueblo Bonito is the most impressive of a series of multi-storey Great Houses built by the Anasazi Indians in the arid Chaco Canyon in what is now modern-day New Mexico.

Inset: A black-on-white Anasazi pitcher, about 8 inches (20 cm) high, illustrates a vessel popular around AD 1000, when Anasazi society was at its peak. The geometric pattern can be traced back to an earlier design produced as a result of working with coiled basketry.

AD 1000

The huge semicircular D-shape of the Pueblo, which housed over 1,200 inhabitants, is most easily appreciated from the air. The large, circular depressions are the remains of *kivas* – half-buried ceremonial rooms which were reached with the use of ladders.

By AD 1000 the first Pueblo Bonito, or Old Bonito, had probably been in use for nearly a century. It comprised a crescent arrangement of rooms built end-to-end in the shadow of the north canyon wall, amid huge blocks of sandstone that had fallen from the cliff. Only a minority of the rooms seem to have been permanently lived in, however; the majority were either for seasonal occupation or for storage. All walls were constructed of irregularly shaped sandstone slabs set in beds of mud mortar. Irrespective of size, the rooms of Old Bonito were usually floored with trampled mud and roofed with whatever timbers were available. Cottonwood, pine, pinyon or juniper logs – their ends gnawed beaver-like with stone axes – appear to have been used indiscriminately. The flat wooden ceilings were often covered with a mixture of brush, reeds, grass and cornstalks. Shortage of timber clearly left the builders of Old Bonito with structural problems. Weak beams and those that were not adequately seated in wall masonry needed supporting posts. Nearly every room, no matter how small, had one or more timber props. Rooms were numbered in the original excavation report and room 323, one of four large living-rooms, measures approximately 13 by 26 feet (4 by 8 m). A single, slab-lined fireplace

was the sole source of heating, while five pots buried rim-deep at the southern end of the room provided storage. The living-room had entrances in all four walls, each at an unusual height. The sill on the north-east wall, which gave access to a neighbouring room, was some 5 feet (1.5 m) above the floor, and probably required a wooden-post step or ladder for use. All doors at Old Bonito were small, with sill heights varying from several inches to over 6 feet (2 m). Some rooms had more than one storey, communication between storeys being achieved through rectangular hatchways.

The curving exterior wall of Old Bonito had no doors, an absence which was to be repeated in all subsequent phases of the site. Entrance to the rooms was therefore from the courtyard, through doors in the concave wall, or through hatchways in the roofs. In the courtyard stood a number of *kivas*, circular rooms dug into the ground and roofed over. These functioned as meeting-places for the men of the settlement and probably the surrounding region. The west wall of one of the *kivas* of Old Bonito lay partly underneath the later room south of room 211. The walls of this *kiva* were over 10 feet (3 m) in depth and sloped inwards at the bottom to provide a circular floor some 23 feet (7 m) in diameter, which was reached by a

AD
1000

Above: The site is overlooked by the north wall of Chaco Canyon, and in turn looks out over the floor of the canyon, which is bisected by the Chaco Wash.

Below: A reconstruction of Pueblo Bonito as it might have looked during its final phase. Note that the tallest part of the complex was originally part of Old Bonito and *kivas* are illustrated that are no longer visible on the surface.

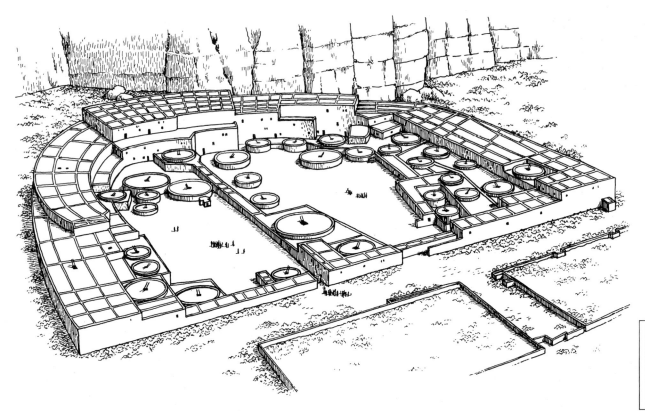

AD
1000

Masonry techniques involved using sandstone slabs set in mud mortar. Lintels were timber, as were upper floors which were made of pine and covered with a mud plaster.

the Chaco complex. The Great Houses are all characterized by their large size, averaging 216 rooms, and their multi-storey architecture. Walls were mortared and faced with a veneer of coursed ashlar, often in alternating bands of thick and thin stones, forming various patterns. These were then covered with adobe plaster or matting. They had plazas enclosed by a line of rooms or a wall, and most plazas contained a larger or *Great Kiva*, with further examples associated with the residential areas, making a ratio of one *kiva* to every twenty-nine rooms. *Kivas* were entered either through a recessed masonry stairway on the side of the structure or by means of a ladder. Great Houses also acted as centres of trade. A variety of exotic and ritual items has been found in them, including cylindrical vessels or vases, incense burners, copper bells, shell trumpets, macaw skeletons and articles of shell, wood or basketry inlaid with mica or turquoise. The limited number of rooms that were used for permanent residence and, in comparison,

Circular *kivas* provided the focus for male kin ceremonies at Pueblo Bonito. Around the bottom of the wall ran a sandstone bench coated with white plaster.

AD 1000

ladder. Around the wall ran a sandstone bench that had been coated with white plaster, while the circular wall was adorned with four pilasters. The inhabitants of Old Bonito and its seasonal visitors threw their rubbish beyond the *kivas*. The resulting dumps slowly grew in size until they needed retaining walls, which were added by the later dwellers of the site. The rubbish tips had reached a height of more than 6 feet 6 inches (2 m) when the Great House was radically transformed. After AD 1000 several more phases of development occurred, producing the final form of this remarkable settlement.

Pueblo Bonito was not the only planned Great House in Chaco Canyon. There were at least nine similar sites on the north side. Although such a position made these sites more liable to flooding from rain water run-off from the cliffs, their southern orientation afforded them more hours of sun, making winters slightly more bearable for the inhabitants. In addition, their location seems to have been governed by the need for good sightlines to the signalling stations that became a feature of

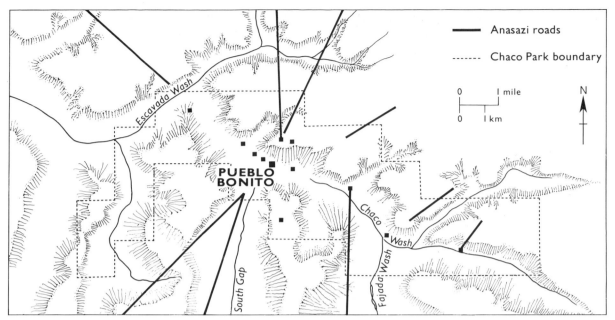

the great storage capacity and indications of considerable numbers of seasonal occupants argue for a predominantly storage and ceremonial function for the Great Houses.

As well as the Great Houses there were a large number of small houses in Chaco Canyon which appear to have grown without any formal planning on both sides of the canyon. They tend to average about sixteen single-storey rooms and face south-east. The standard of masonry is much less sophisticated here than in the Great Houses. The *kivas* are small, with a *kiva*-to-room ratio of 1:6½, and luxury items such as copper bells and inlays are generally absent. In AD 1000, therefore, the Chaco Canyon was densely populated by farmers who lived in Great Houses and small houses, and who indulged in long-distance trade in order to acquire coveted materials. Furthermore, the influence of the Chaco Anasazi Indians was not limited by the canyon walls. The canyon itself was the centre of a much larger region, covering as much as 115,830 square miles (300,000 sq. km), which contained outlying sites exhibiting similar architectural traits to those in the canyon and linked to the Chaco Great Houses by a system of signalling stations and roads.

At least 250 miles (400 km) of roads are known and this communication system constitutes one of the most remarkable aspects of the Chaco complex, particularly as the Anasazi had neither wheeled vehicles nor beasts of burden. The roads keep a straight course at all times, taking no account of topographic relief. Changes in direction are achieved not by means of a gentle curve but through a sharp, angular turn. When major

Above: The vast network of roads that radiated from the Great Houses is one of the most remarkable features of the Chaco complex.

Below: A cross-section through part of a typical Great House structure.

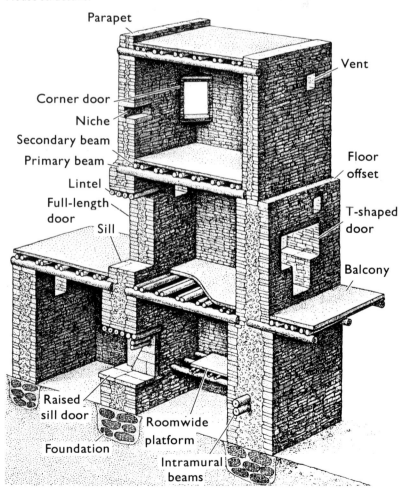

This view looks north across the Chaco Wash, with the four-storey high walls of Pueblo Bonito nestling below the north canyon wall. Ramps and stairways cut into the canyon rock led up to a system of roads which radiated out at least some 62 miles (100 km) from Chaco Canyon.

obstacles are encountered, such as the steep side of a canyon wall, then ramps or stairways carved out of the rock continue the line of the road. The roadways can be up to 30 feet (9 m) wide in the vicinity of the canyon. Some are cut through bedrock or soil to a depth of 5 feet (1.5 m), while surface routes may be lined with masonry borders. With some of these roads radiating out from Chaco Canyon for a distance of 62 miles (100 km), the impression is one of great regional organization.

Around AD 1000 the farmers in Chaco Canyon went to great lengths to ensure the success of three distinct crops: corn, squash and beans. All three had been introduced to the south-west thousands of years earlier from Mexico. The earliest squash provided edible seeds and fruit, and a thick rind that could be used for containers and tools. The beans included pinto beans, red kidney beans and navy beans. Given the uncertainty of the rainfall, however, and the unpredictable levels of the Chaco Wash, elaborate constructions for conserving rainwater run-off from the canyon walls were built. Numerous dams and canals controlled the flow of water to earth-bordered gardens. One of the better-preserved irrigation complexes lies at Rincon-4 North. Here a dam diverted run-off into a canal that fed a large pool immediately above the gardens. The purpose of the pool was to slow down the water and ensure its distribution to all areas of the gardens. In addition to agricultural produce, diet was enhanced through gathering and hunting. Various plants, fruits and nuts were collected, including agave, cactus fruits, wild onion, wild potato, juniper berry and goosefoot. Meat was obtained by hunting game animals such as mule deer, pronghorn antelope and bighorn sheep, or trapping smaller animals such as jackrabbits, cottontail rabbits, squirrels and voles.

The physical layout of the small houses and Great Houses in Chaco Canyon, and especially the ratios of rooms-to-*kivas*, has led to much speculation about whether it is possible to interpret the architectural arrangements in terms of individual clans. According to such a hypothesis, a small house might be the residence of a few clans, with each one occupying some of the rooms and using one particular *kiva*. In the Great Houses a greater numbers of clans would perhaps seasonally congregate at the site, each again with their own special *kiva* but also with a so-called *Great Kiva* to provide the forum for inter-clan ceremonies. An unresolved question concerns the nature of any astronomical observations undertaken by the Chaco Anasazi at Pueblo Bonito. It is well known that traditional farming peoples throughout the world tend to be concerned with such matters. They are critical to the timing of planting and harvesting, especially in environments, like Chaco, where the growing season is short and rainfall unpredictable. It has been suggested that two third-storey corner windows at Pueblo Bonito were perhaps used to record the sunrise at the winter solstice. In addition, claims have been made for a solar observatory on top of nearby Fajada Butte. Spiral patterns carved into the rock catch shafts of sunlight that are directed between stones on to the carvings. The changing positions of these shafts of sunlight do mark the solstices and equinoxes, but

AD
1000

there is no agreement over whether the stone settings are contemporary with the Great Houses.

The small houses and Great Houses of Chaco Canyon around AD 1000 indicate a flourishing society whose leaders were exercising authority in both the secular and the sacred spheres of daily life. The Anasazi communities were less developed, however, than the state-level societies that existed to the south in Mesoamerica. In particular, the Anasazi did not have systems of writing or notation, and nor did they build extensive urban centres. Nevertheless, there are some who have argued that the origin of the extraordinary sites in the Chaco Canyon, so unlike anything else in North America, must have owed something to the activities of traders from Mesoamerican states. These traders may have brought macaws, copper bells and shell inlay to the Anasazi in return for turquoise. A consequence of trading contact would have been the introduction of novel architectural ideas. On the other hand, many of the Anasazi developments seem like logical consequences of earlier cultural traits. A preferable explanation, substantiated by evidence of a slightly improved climate for agriculture after AD 900, is that increased reliance on agriculture at the expense of hunting and gathering led to a much more settled existence and the emergence of Great Houses and small houses in Chaco Canyon.

The duration of this settled existence, was, however, relatively short. By AD 1150 many of the small houses and Great Houses in Chaco Canyon had been abandoned or suffered severe depopulation. Abandonment of settlements is a common phenomenon among contemporary Pueblo peoples. Despite the preference for movement, some explanation is required for the disintegration of the regional system centred on Chaco Canyon. Several possibilities have been suggested, including warfare, disease or the curtailment of trading contacts with Mesoamerica. Perhaps the most convincing is the verified change in the rainfall pattern after AD 1150, which proved less favourable to intensive agriculture. The economic balance shifted slightly towards hunting and gathering as a result, but in this most marginal of environments it was enough of a shift to encourage the Chaco Anasazi to revert to a more mobile life style, leaving behind one of the most outstanding architectural achievements of prehistoric North America.

Soon after AD 1300, drought or the threat of Navajo or Apache invasion forced the abandonment of Pueblo Bonito. Today's Pecos and Hopi Peublo peoples are descended from the Anasazi.

CONCLUSION

All of the communities in Chapter 4 were flourishing by AD 1000 and then declined in the following centuries. Given the disparity in the types of societies represented, it is instructive to wonder why such growth was truncated so rapidly. Among the Easter Islanders the story appears to be relatively straightforward. Here was a remote island colonized by the first human beings some time around AD 300. From the beginning the small area of the island must have been apparent to the new settlers. As the population grew, more and more land was brought under cultivation and related families began to form lineages or clans headed by leaders or chiefs. Pressure on land became more intense and the chiefs began to mark their territories by erecting huge stone statues to stand guard over the fields of the lineage. The farmers were persuaded that it was in their interests to undertake such feats of quarrying, carving and transport by the appeal of the chiefs to the ancestors represented by the statues. If the populace carried out the work and gave tribute to the chief, then they would be protected from the malevolent designs of their ancestors and also from the hostile claims of their neighbours. Over-exploitation continued, however, resulting after AD 1000 in increasing signs of open conflict, and by the time the Dutchmen arrived, Easter Island society was clearly in decline.

For the Indians of Pueblo Bonito and the Chaco Canyon the secret of their mysterious and sudden architectural achievements must be linked to an understanding of how a network of sites developed over such a huge area outside the canyon, joined by a system of roads and signalling stations, and what held the system together. We are not as yet in a position to answer these questions, but it may be that the exchange of ritually important items, such as macaws, and the need to amass surplus stores of food to relieve some communities in times of hardship played a significant role. Coupled with these factors was the necessity for groups of Anasazi men to come together for ceremonial purposes at kivas at various times of the year. Chaco Canyon, therefore, could have been a sacred centre, perhaps a place of pilgrimage, a place where surplus commodities were stored under the watchful eyes of chiefs, ritual leaders and a few selected followers – a place not for ordinary habitation but for extraordinary clan gatherings at critical times in the calendar. The fragility of the extensive exchange system could have been disrupted by any number of factors, including disease, climatic change, warfare or the termination of the supply of a vital commodity.

At Jenne-jeno the picture seems a little clearer. The site had been occupied for centuries but by AD 1000 was reaching its zenith. The natural fertility of freshly inundated soils at the southern end of the inland Niger delta, in addition to the enormous resources to be had from fishing and hunting, meant that a considerable population could be supported in one region. Proximity to the gold-fields to the south and the terminus of the trans-Saharan camel trains to the north meant that a considerable volume of trade developed at the site, with exchanges of ceramics and salt from the north for gold and iron products from the south. Jenne-jeno was a walled African town and owed none of its development to external influences. Its demise, however, was linked to external causes. By the thirteenth century the area had come under the influence of Islam and pagan Jenne-jeno was soon abandoned in preference for a new Jenne only 2 miles (3 km) to the north-west.

Trade was indisputably the cause of the remarkable rise in the fortunes of Siraf. The foundation of Baghdad in the eighth century AD led to an enormous demand for Indian, East African and Chinese goods in the markets of the Middle East. The sailors of Siraf were admirably placed to control this trade as it moved up the Gulf, and as their fleets and vessels grew larger, they undertook longer voyages themselves, bringing back the wares so coveted by the civilized Islamic states to the north and west. The almost total reliance of the Sirafis on trade, however, proved to be their downfall. With the collapse of the Buyid dynasty in the eleventh century, the bubble burst and the foundation of a rival entrepot on the island of Kish proved to be the beginning of the end.

The flowering of Moorish Spain in the tenth century was a more complex affair. It was certainly based on the agricultural productivity of the soils of Andalucia and on the innovations in farming and irrigation that the Muslims introduced. It also

AD
1000

owed much to the independence of the Caliphate of Cordoba from the Islamic rulers of Baghdad. It seems to have been a particularly eclectic society, open to all sorts of foreign influences, typified by its attitude to Jews and Christians, who were allowed to follow their own faiths provided that they did not insult Allah. In such a society, with a free exchange of radically different viewpoints, the arts and sciences developed enormously, with the foundation of libraries and the translation of the works of classical authors. Yet racial not religious tensions lay just below the surface and erupted in AD 1010, bringing death and destruction to Cordoba and its exquisite palace-city of Medina Azahara. Moorish Spain was a brilliant flower while it lasted but its tangled roots brought its life to a premature end.

As these 'new directions' turned one by one into dead ends, the seeds of a new world order were being sown. Ever since the days of the Roman empire, and probably before, transport of people and goods by sea had been more efficient than carriage overland. Developments in sea-craft and navigation now increasingly made long-distance voyages a possibility. Technical expertise was not the determining factor, however, for long voyages of exploration. The correct political and social stimuli were needed to act as a springboard. Arab sailors had already followed the coasts of East and West Africa for considerable distances, while the Chinese had sailed westwards around India to the Middle East. Yet the Chinese were inspired more by curiosity than by conquest, coming from a vast country capable of supplying all its own needs from within its own borders. For an overcrowded Europe the perspective was entirely different. Discoveries of new countries meant additional material resources, slaves and a vastly increased territory. By AD 1500 the first seeds had already germinated. Columbus had discovered the Americas almost a decade earlier. Both the flowers and the weeds of European colonization were about to spread.

AD
1000

CHAPTER 5

CITIES OF THE

AD 1500

WORLD

EUROPE
London, England

WESTERN ASIA
Moscow, Russia

AFRICA
Great Zimbabwe, Zimbabwe

EASTERN ASIA AND OCEANIA
Peking, China

THE AMERICAS
Cuzco, Peru

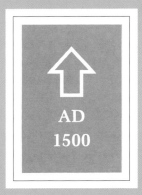

AD
1500

INTRODUCTION

In the year AD 1500 the world was on the verge of witnessing, on a scale never before experienced, the export of one culture (western European) to many different parts of the earth. This would initiate a process that would eventually lead to the disruption of many local cultures, the occasional obliteration of some indigenous peoples and the subsequent installation of a foreign and European-inspired way of life. At this juncture it is important to contrast some major settlement sites in order to appreciate how various heavily populated centres or cities had evolved or been planned prior to European contact. Clearly one of our reference points in this study is the late medieval city of London, the result of nearly 1,500 years of organic growth from the Roman period, and typical of many western European cities. Of the other four sites, Moscow offers the closest parallel, developing under the guidance of Grand Princes who tried to emulate the grandeur of European cities. Completely different were the cities of Peking (Beijing) and Cuzco. These two originated largely as the result of formal planning which was undertaken for political and religious, rather than commercial, reasons. They have a strong case for being included here since they were the capitals of two of the world's largest empires in AD 1500. Lastly, but by no means least, the 'Athens of Africa', Great Zimbabwe, can scarcely be ignored. Its lack of obvious overall planning suggests that some other, as yet hidden, philosophy lies behind its layout. We shall see that these cities were the products of their own political, social and economic contexts and that each gives us an insight into the particular society that created it.

Many people throughout the world live in cities, and the majority of those who do not are familiar with the appearance of the modern city. Asked to describe a city we might list several characteristic features and functions: large population; numerous religious and civic public buildings; centre of communications; seat of local or central government; diversified economic structure, typified by a range of factories, shops and markets; financial centre; and so on. Many of us would add some rather more disagreeable attributes, such as

traffic congestion, pollution and a high incidence of crime. We are so accustomed to daily life in our crowded cities that it is difficult to imagine what their pre-industrial predecessors were like. Walking along the congested streets of London it takes a considerable leap of the imagination to envisage them without cars, houses without electric light and buildings low- instead of high-rise. The sounds and smells of late medieval London are even more difficult to conjure up, although we would doubtless find some of the latter not exactly appetizing. More strange are cities like Cuzco, the Inca capital, where the streets were not designed to accommodate wheeled vehicles and now seem narrow and cramped. Where the planning of streets is not determined primarily by the need to facilitate communication, then other factors may be more significant. The grid pattern of wide avenues in the Ming capital of Peking owed its origin to traditional Chinese beliefs concerning the importance of the cardinal directions and their respective associations with good and bad influences.

The link that we often make between defence and the ancient city is sometimes not quite so straightforward. City walls or strongholds such as the Tower of London certainly had military purposes, but other seemingly defensive edifices were constructed to show status. The walls of the Kremlin in Moscow were to some extent symbolic, while the Inca fortress of Sacsahuaman above Cuzco probably never functioned as a defensive stronghold until the Spanish arrived. We are more confounded when faced with a site such as Great Zimbabwe, clearly the most important centre in its territory. As such it would have performed the role of 'city' for its inhabitants but it does not display some of the more formal aspects of layout, such as a regular street pattern and planned defences, familiar to us from other contemporary cities of the world.

There is little agreement among scholars over the definition of the term 'city'. Too often in the past cultural, national or individual prejudices have produced a definition that was too tightly drawn and excluded some obvious candidates when applied to wider geographical areas. For instance, many students of the ancient cities of the Near East have suggested that written records should be

AD
1500

a requirement, but this would mean that the capital of the Inca empire, Cuzco, the greatest empire of the Americas, would not have been classed as a city. It seems clear that no complex definition, involving lists of characteristics, can apply to all the manifestations of the 'city'. The nearest we can get to an all-encompassing description is simply to say that a city is a large settlement, a concentration of people located close together for residential and protective purposes. As a rule of thumb 'large' is taken to mean at least 5,000 people. We can judge just how well that description fits, and how different cities of AD 1500 were, by comparing Peking under the Ming dynasty, the London of Henry VII, the Inca capital at Cuzco, Great Zimbabwe and Moscow.

AD
1500

Europe
LONDON, ENGLAND

Like most capital cities, medieval London was by a river, with easy access to the sea and widespread and valuable links with both northern Europe and the rich Mediterranean world. Animal hides from Ireland, glass from Venice and timber from Bergen in Norway were just some of the commodities unloaded alongside the Thames.

AD
1500

By the year 1500 London was a thriving capital city of some 70,000 citizens. It owed its commercial success largely to its position on the north bank of the Thames. From there the products of the kingdom, principally its high-quality cloth, could be loaded on to ships which sailed down-river towards the trading towns of northern Europe or the more wealthy entrepots of the Mediterranean world. It was a bustling city of narrow and often dirty alleys, where numerous shops and houses competed for a space on the street frontage and lively markets crowded on to the riverfront. The spires of over 100 parish churches broke the skyline above the three-storeyed properties. The citizens and their buildings were contained within the circuit of medieval city walls, which ended to the south-east in the formidable fortress and palace of the Tower of London. Suburbs had been built across London Bridge, at Southwark on the south side of the river, and between the western walls and Westminster, the seat of government. By the year

1500 the first Tudor king, Henry VII, had been on the throne for fifteen years.

The Tower of London in the south-eastern corner of the walled city, was the principal fortification of medieval London, and was virtually completed by the forceful Edward I. In the ten years after 1275, while waging victorious campaigns against the Welsh, which resulted in some daunting royal castles in Snowdonia, he spent vast sums of money encircling the Tower of London with a concentric system of walls. He paid particular attention to the riverside defences and the entrance across the moat in the south-west corner. The Tower of London covered some 18 acres (7.5 ha) in final form. It dominated the city of London and was an impregnable fortress, given the depths of its defences, which were concentrically designed. However, its garrison sometimes proved less reliable. On at least two occasions, in 1381 during the Peasants' Revolt and in 1460 during the War of the Roses, the garrison preferred to surrender rather than fight on.

Above: Aerial view of the Tower of London showing the regular pattern of its concentric defences. The older Norman square keep, or White Tower (*inset*), which stands at the centre of the fortification, was begun in 1078 under the Norman conquerors. It took over 20 years to build and comprised two floors above a vaulted basement.

The two other castles on the western edge of the city, Baynard's Castle and Montfichet's Tower, are likely to have been earth-and-timber fortifications of the motte-and-bailey type. Both were abandoned by 1275, when the land on which they stood was granted to the Blackfriars. This settlement of the Blackfriars resulted in an extension of the city wall to the banks of the River Fleet. The name Baynard's Castle survived in the area and was given to another prominent house, rebuilt in 1428, which became the residence of Richard, Duke of Gloucester, later to become Richard III. By 1500 the castle was square and had a wall with towers on the riverfront, and an internal courtyard and walled garden.

Except for the extension to accommodate the Blackfriars, the medieval city wall ran along the line of its Roman predecessor. The wall itself was defended by an expansive ditch (re-excavated at

the time of King John) which reached a breadth of some 82 to 100 feet (25 to 30 m). In addition, bastions or towers were attached to the walls and provided extra protection. The eastern series of bastions, from the Tower to the head of the River Walbrook, probably dates from the late Roman period, while its western relatives, some thirteen in number, are likely to date from the medieval period. Several major gates punctuated the walled circuit. A rebuilding of Cripplegate in 1491, possibly in brick, shows that it comprised a low arch flanked by two octagonal towers. The gates not only acted as defensive barriers but also controlled access to the markets within the city. The streets now called Bishopsgate, Aldersgate and Aldgate widened immediately outside the gates so that tradesmen and carters could queue to pay tolls. The gates were sometimes let for non-military purposes: two permanent prisons were

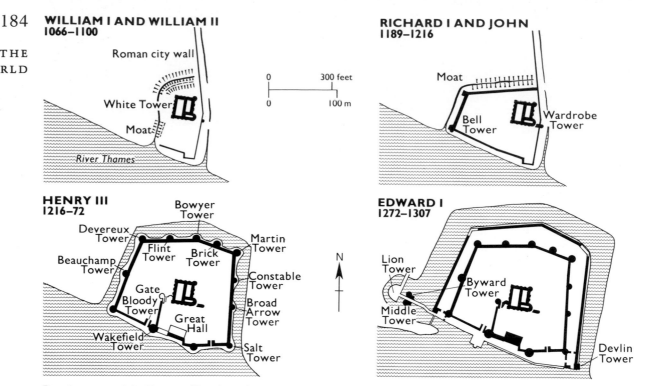

Development of the Tower of London, the city's main fortification, illustrates how the original Norman nucleus grew into the great fortress seen today. Edward I's design – the last main development for the tower – incorporated the latest ideas of concentric defence, an inner circuit of walls inside an outer defensible perimeter.

situated at Ludgate and Newgate. In 1471 Kentish rebels attacked the city and were repulsed at Aldgate. This prompted renovation of parts of the city walls: some of the upper portions were repaired in brick and occasional brick arches reinforced the rear, perhaps to provide additional strength against bombardment by cannon or to carry a widened wall-walk. As suburbs expanded beyond the walls after 1500, the medieval defences to the city became increasingly irrelevant.

Out on the river, trade became busier and vessels larger. London Bridge, begun in 1176, comprised nineteen arches and a drawbridge and was some 907 feet (275 m) long. By 1500, however, the drawbridge no longer functioned and large shipping was confined down-river. The bridge supported a community in its own right, including a chapel and, by 1358, 138 shops. The construction of the bridge caused changes up-river: water salinity, velocity and levels were affected, and there was a higher level of pollution, since waste entering the river from the Fleet could no longer be easily washed out to sea.

On the waterfront in the western part of the city detailed evidence concerning the appearance of the riverside has come from the excavations at Trig Lane, where three adjacent medieval properties were examined. The occupiers of each had periodically laid out their own wharves,

complete with stairs to the foreshore, reclaiming land and erecting new wharves further out as and when required. This situation produced an indented and varied frontage, in contrast to the uniform Roman riverside wall. The excavations were significant given the excellent survival of the timber wharves or revetments in the waterlogged conditions. Many of the carpenters' joints had been preserved, providing an insight into medieval wood-working techniques. Furthermore, assembly marks on the timbers show that the revetments were prefabricated elsewhere and brought to the river for final assembly. Two principal types of revetment were discovered: front-braced structures, which were supported by diagonal timbers on the riverward side during the eleventh and twelfth centuries, and the back-braced frontages which replaced them and were an improvement since they offered an unimpeded vertical timber wall to the river. By 1440 the frontage had been transformed by the construction of a continuous stone wall. The wall sat on a raft of elm piles driven into the foreshore. The external face of the wall was constructed of ragstone ashlar blocks and the core comprised chalk rubble. A single gap in the centre of the wall allowed access to the river via stairs. As well as producing information on the waterfront, the Trig Lane excavations also indicated contemporary

AD
1500

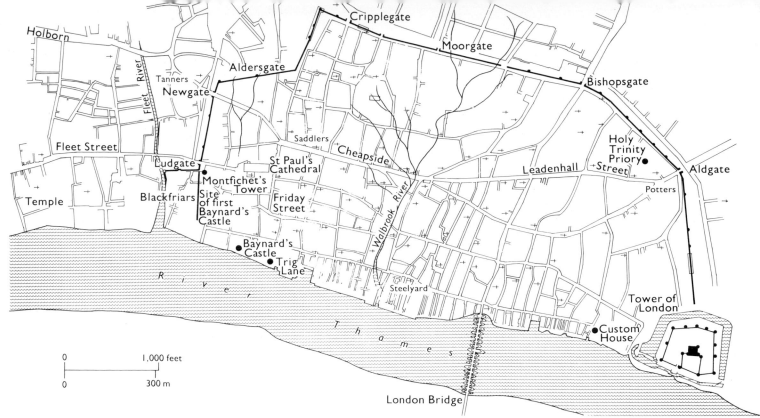

A plan of the late medieval city of London. Over 100 churches crowded within the strong fortification walls, which were lined with towers, but by AD 1500 the city had already started to spread beyond these boundaries. The position of the excavations at Trig Lane on the waterfront is marked.

methods of rubbish disposal, for it is clear that as the riverfront was reclaimed, the land behind was infilled with the refuse of the city.

There were a great number of ecclesiastical buildings in medieval London, including parish churches, priories and friaries. As far as we can tell, many parish churches had, by 1450, a standard plan of a nave and two aisles. Wooden pews provided seats for the faithful, although men and women sat separately, even when married. In pre-Reformation London the interiors of the churches were brightened by statues and painted images, and contained additional attractions in the form of holy relics. Among the objects collected by St Margaret's in New Fish Street were some truly miraculous survivals: pieces of the burning bush and of Moses' rod, a comb that belonged to St Dunstan and one of the teeth of St Bridget. The parish church performed civic as well as ecclesiastical functions and was often the centre of neighbourhood life. Groups of citizens, or fraternities, would become attached to a particular church. Their duties might involve the furtherance of their professions but could also include charitable works, such as helping the poor, sick or imprisoned. The priories of London, enclosed by their high precinct walls, were self-contained small towns with their own water supply, legislative centre (the chapterhouse),

bakehouse and infirmary. It is possible from excavated evidence to reconstruct the ground plan of the Augustinian priory of Holy Trinity, Aldgate, as it must have looked in AD 1500. Another major group of religious buildings comprised those constructed by the various orders of mendicant friars who established themselves in the capital from the late thirteenth century. They often preferred locations on the edges of cities, with access to the citizens but somewhat removed from the urban community. The Blackfriars' situation at the western edge of the city is a good example.

Houses in medieval London ranged from impressive courtyard houses, with halls as large as churches for the well-to-do, to one- or two-room cottages for the poor. The standard shape of property was long and thin and at right angles to the street, with the most important rooms fronting on to the street. Houses of the rich were likely to possess stone undercrofts supporting three storeys that progressively overhung the street. A contract of 1410 states that three houses were to be built in Friday Street. Each was to have a fully-fitted shop on the ground floor, while on the floor above was to be a hall, a larder and a kitchen, with, on the next floor, a privy, a principal chamber and a retiring-room. The poor made do with two rooms, comprising a hall and a bedroom. Public hygiene remained a constant problem. From the fourteenth

AD 1500

The timber revetment of c.1385 found at Trig Lane also included provision for a timber tank at the water's edge – possibly for keeping fish. The area behind the wall was infilled with household rubbish.

century, building contracts commonly specified the provision of a cesspit. When arrangements were made in 1370 to construct a range of eighteen shops, they were to be provided with ten stone-lined pits for the privies, eight of them to be shared between two shops and each to be over 10 feet (3 m) deep. The real Dick Whittington died in 1423, but during his life he performed several works of public benefit, which included the construction of 'Whittington's Longhouse', a public privy that was built out over the Thames. Two rows of sixty-four seats, one for men and one for women, overhung a gulley which was flushed by each tide.

A characteristic of most medieval cities in Europe was a tendency for certain trades to congregate in particular streets or quarters of the city, and London was no excepton. Roughly one-third of the lanes and less than one-third of the streets carried names that associated them with a specific trade or commercial activity. An Italian visitor to London in 1500 remarked: 'In one single street [Cheapside] leading to St Paul's, there are fifty-two goldsmiths' shops, so rich and full of silver vessels, great and small, that in all the shops in Milan, Rome, Venice and Florence put together, I do not think there would be found so many of the magnificence that are to be seen in London.' The Walbrook ward, for example, was associated with skinners; they had vintners, cordwainers and other craft groups as neighbours. Some trades which

often caused public hygiene problems, such as the butchers, fishmongers and tanners, were probably given locations where their activities would cause less offence. The tanners were attracted to the Fleet, on the western edge of the city, and were frequently in court for obstructing the stream with hides and stakes. Potentially dangerous commercial activities, such as potting, smithing, bronze-working or the production of lime, may have been forced out into the suburbs. The waterfront in London had clearly defined areas of specialization: for example, Billingsgate and Bridge wards for fish and wool; Dowgate and Steelyard for merchants of the Hanseatic League; Queenhithe for corn; and Fleet for coal. Pottery from Cheam and Kingston and from the Continent also arrived at London's wharves. By 1422 there were at least 111 different crafts in the capital and many of these had formed associations and built guildhalls. The guilds were able to regulate the practices of their members and also act as representatives of their trades with the city officials.

By the year 1500 the buildings of London were starting to spread beyond the city walls and into the surburbs. Already a large suburb had grown along the riverside between the Fleet and the palace at Westminster, occupied by prominent ecclesiastics and the law schools known as the Inns of Court. Other notable constructions included Eltham Palace, south-east of London, built by Edward IV in 1479, and the palace of the

AD
1500

Above: A wonderfully decorative miniature from an edition (*c.*1500) of the poems of Charles, Duke of Orleans, who was captured by the English and held prisoner in the Tower of London.

Right: Many of London's medieval churches contained exquisite glass windows such as this stained and painted glass depicting the forlorn figure of a lute-playing angel.

Archbishop of Canterbury at Lambeth, which was equipped with a brick-built gatehouse in 1490. Brickmakers are known from four eastern suburban parishes by the late fifteenth century. Across the river from Lambeth lay the palace and abbey of Westminster, where Parliament met. To the north-west of the city, the Bishop of Ely had, by AD 1290, acquired properties over a large area north of Holborn, where he built a town house for his successors.

The London and England of AD 1500 flourished in the twilight of the medieval world. Henry VII consulted Parliament irregularly and there was still no standing army or police force. English interests in France, stemming from the Norman Conquest and fought for at Agincourt, had been finally extinguished. On the other hand, there were rapid developments in the economic and religious fields. The wool and cloth trades had brought prosperity

to many people and by 1500 the population was starting to rise again after the ravages of the fourteenth-century plague known as the Black Death. The first printing-press had been invented and had resulted in growing literacy among the population at large. Gunpowder was beginning to have a significant effect on the development of weapons. The English Church was growing ever more anglicized in its attitudes towards Rome. The last decade of the fifteenth century witnessed some extraordinary voyages of exploration by Vasco da Gama for Portugal, Christopher Columbus for Spain and John Cabot for England. The boundaries of medieval Europe had been broken for good. In such a short space of time the area of the known world had expanded ten-fold. It was the task of that very English monarch, Henry VIII, to work with Parliament and begin asserting England's position in this new world.

AD
1500

By AD 1500 the warring principalities of Russia had been united under the leadership of the Grand Princes of Moscow, who were already claiming the inheritance of the old Byzantine empire.

AD 1500

Situated in the centre of Moscow, on top of a hill whose summit lies about 132 feet (40 m) above the level of the Moskva River, the Kremlin dominates the entire city. It has done so ever since Italian architects were summoned by Ivan III towards the end of the fifteenth century and given the task of redesigning and reconstructing its massive fortification walls. In AD 1500 the Kremlin was one of the most impressive medieval citadels in the world. Its battlemented walls enclosed a triangular-shaped area of land on which were erected a variety of palaces, churches and cathedrals, the latter lavishly decorated inside with exquisite frescoes and icons, while outside they were covered with bulbous cupolas clad in gold and silver. Seen from afar, reflecting the sunlight, they epitomize the exuberant polychrome decorative architecture which is essentially Russian. In AD 1500 the Kremlin was the core about which the scattered and feuding principalities of medieval Russia had become united under the leadership of the Grand Prince Ivan III and his grandson, Ivan IV, the first tsar. It was to develop into the all-powerful capital of tsarist Russia.

Two major historical developments had allowed Moscow to assert its authority and reach a position of dominance. The first concerned its relationships with the Mongols. Many of the Russian princes ruled only with the approval of the Khan of the Golden Horde, and even when they had been confirmed in office by him, some still had to make the arduous and lengthy journey to Mongolia to receive his personal sanction. The Mongols or Tartars proved to be ruthless overlords, and between 1236 and 1462 they ravaged Russian lands no fewer than forty-eight times. On some occasions their incursions were the result of revolts, at others they were simply punitive measures, and then again, sometimes they were invited in by one Russian prince to attack the holdings of another. Ultimately, when the power of the Golden Horde began to wane, the princes of Moscow were able to lead the liberation movement, thus paving the way for their future role as rulers.

The second development was Moscow's association with the Orthodox Church and Constantinople. In the first part of the fourteenth century one of the factors that assisted the emergence of Moscow was the decision of the Church authorities to transfer their highest-ranking ecclesiastic in Russia, the Metropolitan Peter, from

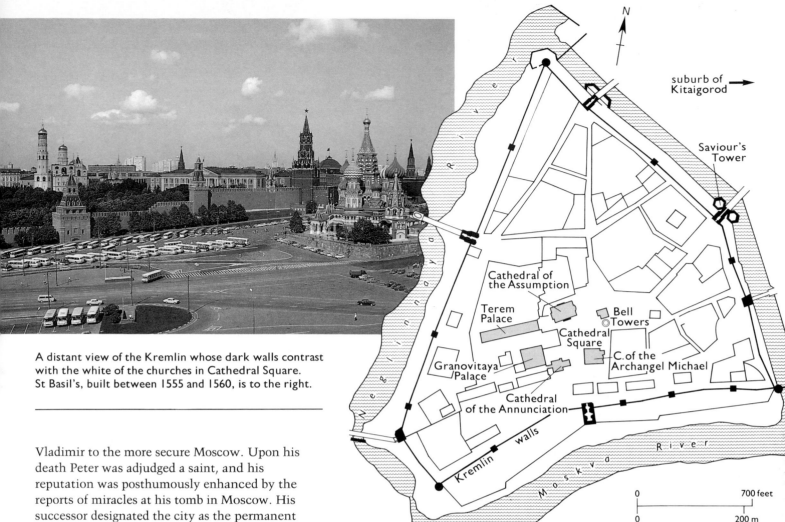

A distant view of the Kremlin whose dark walls contrast with the white of the churches in Cathedral Square. St Basil's, built between 1555 and 1560, is to the right.

A plan of the Kremlin as it was around AD 1533. The cathedrals and palaces near Cathedral Square formed the heart of the city.

Vladimir to the more secure Moscow. Upon his death Peter was adjudged a saint, and his reputation was posthumously enhanced by the reports of miracles at his tomb in Moscow. His successor designated the city as the permanent home of the Church in Russia, despite subsequent efforts to reinstate the Metropolitanate at Kiev. The significance of this move was reinforced when the Turks finally overran Constantinople in 1453, killing the last Byzantine emperor, Constantine IX. Ivan III saw his opportunity to make Moscow the major centre of the Orthodox Church and the 'Third Rome', after Rome and Constantinople. Taking steps towards this goal he married Zoe Palaeologina, the niece of Constantine IX. Ivan III patterned the court at the Kremlin on the Byzantine model, while Zoe brought with her the court customs of Byzantium, as well as priests, scholars, artists and architects from Italy, where she had been brought up. Ivan III even adopted the Byzantine imperial arms – the two-headed eagle – as Russia's own.

The brick walls of the Kremlin were largely constructed between 1485 and 1499 and replaced earlier timber and stone defences. The walls outlined an irregular triangle, nearly 1½ miles (2.5 km) in total length, and varied in height from 30 to 66 feet (9 to 20 m) and in thickness from 13 to 20 feet (4 to 6 m). Nineteen towers, all different in design though sharing basic architectural features, rose from the walls, which were pierced by five gates, no two of them alike. The technical knowledge and manufacture of bricks played a large part in the successful erection of the walls. Aristotele, a native of Bologna invited to oversee the works, established a brick-making plant near Moscow and also taught the Russians how to prepare the necessary mortar. The first walls and towers were built on the south side of the Kremlin, facing the river, since this direction was thought to be the most vulnerable to attack. Over the next fourteen years, the remaining perimeter was constructed. Each tower was composed of two principal parts: a massive square or circular base erected during the reign of Ivan III, and a superstructure added to it towards the end of the seventeenth century. All of the five gates were likewise composed of two basic elements: the main

AD 1500

Above: It was Ivan III who managed to bring together the scattered and feuding principalities of medieval Russia under his leadership. Ivan had married Zoe, niece of the last Byzantine emperor, and was determined that Moscow should become the 'Third Rome'. To make his city a religious and secular focus, Ivan ordered the building of a new and imposing edifice, the Kremlin.

Above right: Red Square, with the Lenin Mausoleum in front of the Kremlin's north-eastern fortification walls. The circular tower at the far end of the fortification walls marks the northern corner of the fortress.

tower with its superstructure, and a barbican tower in front, covering and protecting the entrance gates. Perhaps the most remarkable gate is that known as the Saviour's Tower, rising above the main entrance to the Kremlin and giving access to the citadel from Red Square. A small, two-storey barbican tower protects the gate-tower proper, which consists of three storeys: the gate passage itself, a second storey housing a covered gallery and a third storey with an open terrace protected by a battlemented parapet. A later steeple was added to the tower. The Saviour's Tower is marked by Russian and Latin inscriptions indicating the name of the architect and the date of construction: 'Built by Pietro Antonio Solario, the Medilanets [the Milanese] in 1491'.

AD
1500

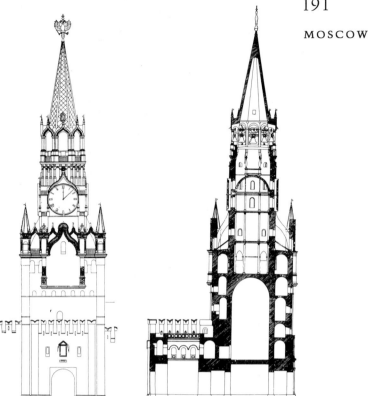

Above: One of the most ornate of the five Kremlin gates was Saviour's Tower, which gave access into the citadel from the area we know as Red Square. Originally a two-storey barbican protected a three-storey gate-tower proper, but later a steeple was added to the original tower.

Below left: In general the original walls and tower of the Kremlin surround later buildings, although to the right can be seen the famous 'onion' domes of Cathedral Square, where Ivan III insisted on using Russian architects rather than the Italian ones he had hired to design the Kremlin walls.

Inside the Kremlin, around Cathedral Square, a group of churches erected in the late fifteenth and early sixteenth centuries made this square the heart of the fortress. Three cathedrals faced the square itself, and there were other churches in other parts of the walled area, including the Church of the Saviour in the Wood, built in 1330 but no longer surviving. Although Ivan III entrusted certain large-scale construction work on the Kremlin to the Italians, when it came to the design of the churches, he was wary of Papal influence and insisted that Russian architects be consulted. The churches at Kiev, Novgorod and Vladimir were used as models. The Italians were given much more freedom in non-religious architecture, such as the Granovitaya Palace and the fortifications.

AD
1500

The Cathedral of the Assumption was the first of the cathedrals to be built in Cathedral Square. It was started in 1475 and finished in 1479, and its frescoes were completed by 1515. Modelled on the Cathedral of the Assumption in Vladimir, it was far from a precise copy. It was rectangular in shape, with entrances on all but the east side. Five apses were constructed at the eastern end of the building, while the structure was crowned with five helmet-shaped golden domes. The vaulting of the cathedral rests on six pillars, four of which – huge, circular columns – support the central cupola. The interior of the cathedral was a wonder to behold, so much so that when the Tsar and the bishops entered the building for the first time they are said to have exclaimed, 'We see heaven!' All of the interior surfaces of the church were covered in frescoes, with the entire west wall decorated with a scene of the Last Judgement. In addition a gilded partition separating the nave from the altar carried icons illustrating two themes: the universality of the Church and the unification of the Russian princedoms by Moscow. It was in this church that the tsars were crowned and the Metropolitans were buried.

The ornate Cathedral of the Annunciation was completed in 1490. Its exterior is rich in detail and a band of blind arcading echoes an architectural motif used in the nearby Cathedral of the Assumption.

The second, and smallest, of the three cathedrals in Cathedral Square to be built under Ivan III was the Cathedral of the Annunciation, completed by 1490. It was designed not by Italians but by architects from the Russian princedom of Pskov. It is almost square in plan and contains the central cubical element – five cupolas carried by the exterior walls and four internal columns – seen in the other churches. A novel element, however, was the introduction of taller arches and the use on the roof exterior of corbelled arches receding in tiered steps. This produced the impression that the towers of the cathedral were simply the tallest architectural elements in a roof that rose in several steps from the corners. The internal arrangements of the church were similar to others in the Kremlin. The floor was paved with mosaics of jasper and agate, and the walls were covered with frescoes. The iconostasis framed holy icons and was itself richly adorned in gold and silver and incorporated precious stones and pearls; just the case of the image of the Annunciation alone is said to contain over $17\frac{1}{2}$ lb (8 kg) of pure gold. The icons and frescoes were executed by the most notable painters of the time, including Theophanes the Greek and Andrey Rublyov.

The Cathedral of the Archangel Michael completed the trilogy. It was originally built in wood in the middle of the thirteenth century, but in 1505 Ivan III's successor, Vassili III, commissioned an Italian named Alevisio to erect a new cathedral in its stead and this was finished by 1509. Although the interior of the new church conformed to characteristic Russian orthodox models, certain decorative features on the outside reflected its Italian inspiration. From the fourteenth century onwards the princes of Russia had been buried in the Cathedral of the Archangel Michael, and when the new cathedral was finished in 1509, Vassili III had their tombs removed and reinterred there. From the time of Ivan III until the period of Peter the Great all Russian sovereigns, with one exception, were buried in the Cathedral of the Archangel Michael. The new building was constructed of whitewashed brick resting on a stone foundation, with decorative elements in white stone. The rectangular plan of the church conformed to the Russo-Byzantine standard model, as do the five exterior towers, topped by one gold and four silver domes. Foreign architectural elements were introduced, however, including vertical pilasters on the outside walls, which carried Corinthian capitals decorated with volutes. The Italian architect also used two elaborate horizontal cornices to divide the exterior walls, and above the upper one he added Venetian-style scallops to adorn the gables. The interior was richly

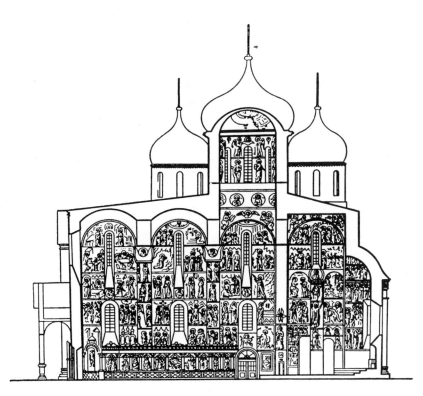

The first of the cathedrals to be constructed in Cathedral Square was that of the Assumption (*above left*), begun in 1475 and finished only four years later. The second to be built on the orders of Ivan III was that of the Annunciation (*above right*), completed by 1490. It was the smallest of the cathedrals in the square.

decorated, with six square pillars dividing the inside into three aisles.

By 1487 it became clear to Ivan III and his ambitious wife that the magnificence they had planned for the Kremlin, the 'Vatican' of the 'Third Rome', would not be complete without a splendid palace where native and foreign dignitaries could be entertained and impressed. Before the employment of Italian architects the Kremlin had been, for the most part, a collection of wooden buildings, including the royal palace. Now Marco Ruffo was commissioned to construct a stone palace on the west side of Cathedral Square. The resulting edifice was the Granovitaya Palace, or the Palace of the Facets, so called because of the rusticated stone facing on its eastern side. The most important room in the complex was the Great Hall on the first floor. The spaciousness of this chamber, which measured some 77 feet square (22 m sq.) and 30 feet (9 m) high, was greatly accentuated by the use of a single, central, massive pillar, which allowed four cross-vaults to span the entire room. The hall was used for the great formal receptions of foreign ambassadors, and the throne stood on the south side of the chamber. High up on the west wall of the hall, close to the ceiling, was a curtained opening through which other members of the royal family could view the proceedings below

without being seen. Ivan also decided that new living-quarters should be constructed for the sovereign, so in 1499 he asked the architect Alevisio to supervise another palace, to be built to the west of the Granovitaya Palace. The Royal living-quarters were housed in the new Terem Palace, a brick structure containing a series of small, vaulted rooms decorated with polychrome ornaments and images painted on gold and other-coloured backgrounds.

Outside the Kremlin lay the largely wooden city of Moscow, where the citizens carried on their daily lives. They were excluded from the citadel by the defensive works carried out by Ivan's son, Vassili III. He instructed Alevisio to dig a ditch along the east side of the Kremlin and, facing its banks with brick and stone, to create a moat. This separated the defences from Red Square. On the west side of the fortress the new ruler dammed the Neglinnaia River and, by a series of reservoirs, water was diverted to flow along the western wall. The Kremlin was thus entirely surrounded by water. In addition a second defensive wall with towers was built fronting the Moskva River.

Beyond the moats lay the suburbs of the city. The most important of these, known as Kitaigorod, was to the east of the Kremlin. It incorporated the square that later became Red Square (St Basil's

AD 1500

Cathedral at its southern end was erected between 1555 and 1560) and was the trading centre of Moscow. It was here that the wealthy traders and merchants and the few foreigners lived. The area was always full of people during the day, and the marketplace and streets leading to it were lined with shops. Each street specialized in a particular product, such as shoes, metalwork, horse-tackle or linen. From the early years of the settlement, this area was protected by a wooden stockade, which

---

To many people, St Basil's Cathedral outside the Kremlin walls, with its elaborate cluster of multi-coloured onion domes and ornate façade epitomizes Russian ecclesiastical architecture. Ivan the Terrible, grandson of Ivan III, commissioned the church to commemorate his army's seizure of a Tartar stronghold on 1 October 1552.

was replaced in the 1530s by a masonry wall. Beyond the trading quarter lay Bielgorod, the residential area for the privileged citizens, while in the outer ring of suburbs lay the wooden houses of the artisans and labourers. These were also defended by a wooden stockade, running along a line now used by the inner ring road for the modern city. In these outer suburbs the streets were for the most part crooked and winding, forming a veritable maze. The rain, the mud and the lack of sanitation must have made a walk along any of them an unpleasant experience. Most were unpaved, except in a few instances where a pavement of logs was constructed. The dwellings were almost all made of wood and some possessed large courts and outhouses. The single houses of the poor, however, were simply furnished with a table and a few chairs and appeared barren and uncomfortable to the few Europeans who ventured out from the trading district. The fact that Russians favoured wooden structures was not due to poverty or to lack of technical expertise in constructing in stone. In their cold climate, with its severe winters and wet springs and autumns, wooden structures held a distinct advantage: they were far more efficient at retaining heat, and their timber walls could 'breathe' and ventilate themselves, unlike stone structures.

In European diplomacy, Ivan III and Vassili III strove to gain international recognition for their status as rulers. In order to underline his equal standing with the kings of Europe, Ivan made increasing use of the word tsar. Derived from the Latin word '*caesar*' and previously applied by the Russians to the Byzantine emperor and the Tartar khan, it implied that the bearer was a fully independent sovereign and not the vassal or dependant of another prince. If there was one year which saw the emergence of imperial Russia under the absolute authority of the tsar, then it was 1480. In that year Ahmed, Khan of the Great Horde, the nomadic remnants of the Golden Horde, launched a large-scale Tartar invasion on Muscovite territory. The critical battle was more to do with confrontation than with actual conflict. Both sides faced each other across the Ugra River, south-west of Moscow. Ahmed's troops made one serious attempt to cross but were beaten back. A series of fruitless negotiations followed until Ahmed, despairing of his Lithuanian allies ever arriving, and mindful of the approach of winter, retreated quietly into the steppes. It was hardly a momentous victory for Ivan III, but later Russian writers were to agree that his prudence had saved Moscow from destruction and sealed his transformation from the Grand Prince of Moscow to the Tsar of Russia.

Africa
GREAT ZIMBABWE, ZIMBABWE

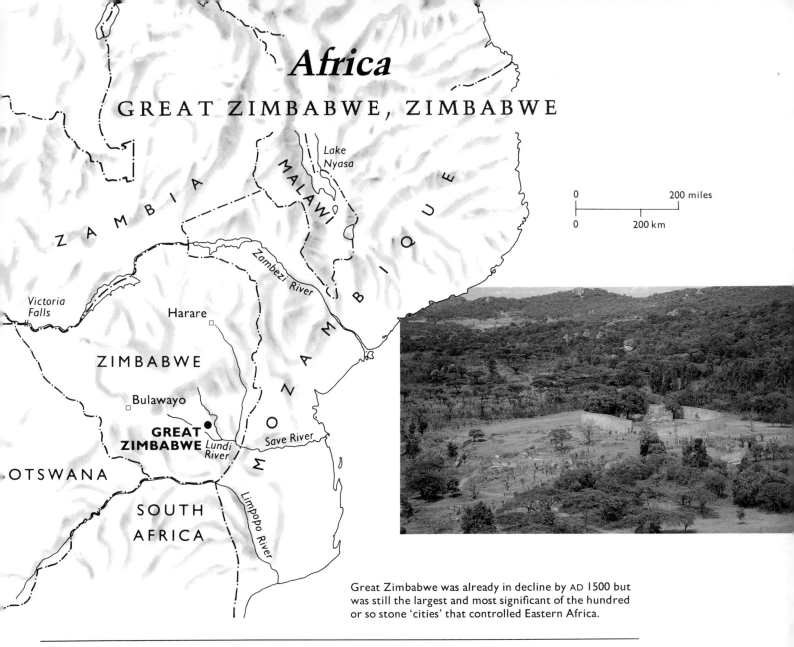

Great Zimbabwe was already in decline by AD 1500 but was still the largest and most significant of the hundred or so stone 'cities' that controlled Eastern Africa.

In AD 1500 the remarkable complex of structures now known as Great Zimbabwe, in the south of the country of that name, was in decline. Formerly it had been an important centre, controlling an area of about 1,000 square miles (2,500 sq. km) of upland regions to the north-west and lowlands to the south-east. But it still boasted the most sophisticated indigenous stone buildings in south and central Africa. Such was the character of the masonry that the many Europeans who described the ruins in subsequent centuries could not believe that they were the work of African peoples.

Great Zimbabwe (*zimbabwe* is a Shona word meaning 'venerated houses' and is generally used for chiefs' houses or graves) lies on the southern edge of the plateau that spreads between the Zambezi River in the north and the Limpopo in the south. Its ruins, great complexes of stone walls and

enclosures, are scattered over hill and valley in an area of some 99 acres (40 ha). The countryside around is a mixture of densely wooded valleys and uncultivated grasslands, pierced by bare granite outcrops. The site itself physically divides into two separate entities. There is a granite outcrop running E–W which forms the northern half, upon which were constructed a number of stone features and enclosures known collectively as the Hill Ruin. Below the Hill Ruin, in the valley to the south, lies another series of enclosures, the most famous of which is known as the Elliptical Building or Great Enclosure. The minor stone enclosures were all named after early explorers, such as the Posselt Ruin, and these names have sometimes been retained by modern writers for the sake of continuity and clarity. The stone enclosures seem the most important buildings at Great Zimbabwe,

AD 1500

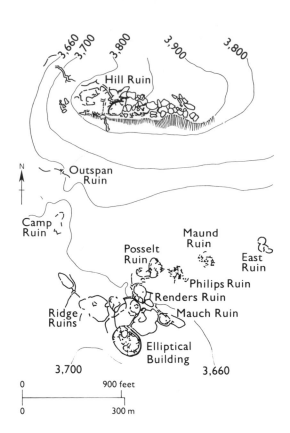

but they were not the only ones. Inside some of the stone enclosures, and in much of the area between the valley and the hill, were numerous circular structures, built with *daga* or mud, which housed most of the population of Great Zimbabwe.

The stone walls of Great Zimbabwe were constructed without mortar and from stone that was available locally. The most striking hills around the site are smooth domes of granite, from which thin slabs or rock periodically split and collect in screes at the foot of the outcrops. These slabs of equal thickness provided ideal material for the construction of walls in which the basic building sequence was to erect the massive walls to a full height at one point and then extend them to form the surrounds of an enclosure. The great thickness of the structures meant that the unfinished end-face of the walls could provide temporary steps and so obviate the need for scaffolding. All of the walls were curved and

---

Left: Great Zimbabwe is divided into two distinct parts. A granite outcrop, Hill Ruin, stretches along the highest part and below lies a series of enclosures.

AD
1500

A number of the high walls of Great Zimbabwe are topped by narrow stone monoliths that perhaps represent individual ancestors. Also present are small towers, thought to be symbolic grain silos which may have represented the wealth of the community.

changed direction slowly, with no sharp angles. The walls were pierced with simple doorways, no more than 4 feet (1.2 m) across. Some of the walls also ran up to and incorporated massive boulders in their construction. Certain architectural embellishments, such as domes and arches, were lacking. The stone walls did have one thing in common, however: they never supported roofs. They enclosed areas that were too large and irregular to have been roofed. The overall impression given by the layout of the site is the absence of formal planning, with enclosures built at different dates and to differing designs, producing no clear pattern. A greater contrast with the rigid plan of Ming Peking or the symbolic plan of Inca Cuzco could not be imagined.

In the interiors of all the enclosures at Great Zimbabwe are short lengths of stone walling. The complete excavation of the enclosure known as the Maund Ruin demonstrated that these discontinuous stone walls had been built up against ten circular *daga* structures, and radiated from them to form nine separate small courtyards. In the absence of any other suitable buildings within the enclosure, these ten *daga* structures must have been dwellings for the inhabitants.

That Great Zimbabwe developed over a number of centuries is indicated by the presence of three distinctive styles of masonry. The earliest was represented by stones laid in wavy courses that petered out after a short distance. The subsequent style produced the finest masonry. Walls were constructed from carefully sized and selected blocks which were dressed on site and then laid in very regular courses, which run continuously for considerable distances. Associated with this sophisticated walling are some of the more elaborate and idiosyncratic architectural features at

the site. Doorways developed curved sides which flanked high thresholds formed by curved steps. Inside most doorways stood a pair of semicircular bastions. These seem to suggest a defensive function but in practice only served to make entrances narrower and more tortuous. Some of the bastions had narrow vertical slots in their outer faces for holding upright slabs of granite, soapstone or schist. These had some symbolic, ceremonial or religious function since they were found not only in the bastions but also on moulded *daga* platforms inside enclosures and on the tops of the high, external walls. Some of the monoliths stood over 13 feet (4 m) high, and were decorated with geometric designs or carried carved representations of birds. Additional intriguing elements consisted of stepped platforms within the enclosures, probably for the display of objects, and numerous small stone turrets, erected both within enclosures and on the tops of external walls. It seems likely that many of these once supported stone monoliths, like the bastions. The third and last style of masonry at Great Zimbabwe was much poorer in quality. The walls were lower and built of irregular, undressed stones, with smaller stones wedged into the holes between the larger examples.

Two of the most important complexes of ruins at Great Zimbabwe are those forming the Hill Ruin and those in the valley which constitute the so-called Elliptical Building. The Hill Ruin consists of a number of enclosures spaced out along the cliff edge, interspersed with huge boulders. Most of these enclosures are built in the earliest style of masonry. The western end of the cliff terminates in the massive Western Enclosure, the largest on the

A plan of Maund Ruin, which shows the relationship between those stone walls which survive and the original *daga*, or mud huts, which do not.

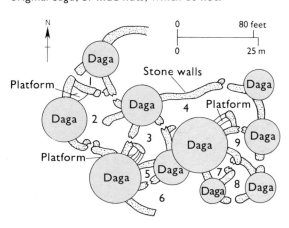

A plan of the Hill Ruin, showing the Western and Eastern Enclosures at either end of the complex and the more enigmatic features known as the Balcony and the Cave.

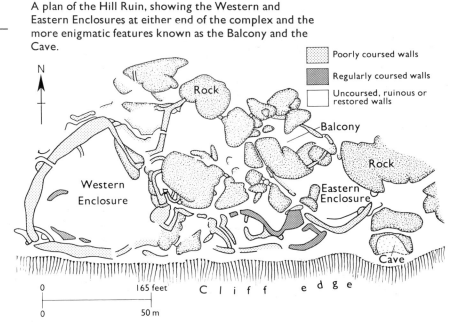

hill. Two curved walls, over 30 feet (9 m) high, capped by monoliths and turrets, enclose an irregular rock surface that was levelled off with *daga* brought up from the base of the hill. The Western Enclosure had room for about fourteen *daga* huts. At the other end of the ridge stood the Eastern Enclosure. Its southern wall was more regularly coursed than others on the hill and once carried a dentelle-patterned frieze – two courses of blocks laid at an angle to the wall face to form a continuous line of decorative triangular recesses. This enclosure seems to have been dedicated to ritual purposes as many stone monoliths were found in it. Adjacent to the Eastern Enclosure are two very enigmatic elements of the complex. A narrow passage leads to the north to the top of a large, flat boulder, from where extensive views can be had of the valley ruins. This viewing-platform has naturally attracted the name of the Balcony. Just below the Eastern Enclosure is a cave whose floor is littered with nodules of iron ore. Sounds in the cave are bounced off the walls and can be clearly heard in the valley below. It was once claimed that because of this property the cave might have been used as an oracle.

The apogee of design and construction was reached in the Elliptical Building. The outer wall of this enclosure, over 792 feet (240 m) long and, at its most monumental, over 16 feet (5 m) wide and nearly 33 feet (10 m) high, forms an irregular ellipse with a maximum diameter of nearly 300 feet (90 m). It probably contains more stone than all the

AD 1500

Above: The Conical Tower, set within the Elliptical Building, is a solid, circular tower decorated around the top with a dentelle-patterned frieze. The qualities of the stonemasons' work can be seen from the regularly laid, close-fitting courses.

Right: A plan of the Elliptical Building, or Great Enclosure. Note how the outer wall varies considerably in width. It is the largest contemporary structure to be found in sub-Saharan Africa.

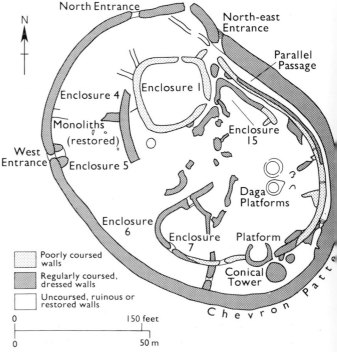

North Entrance
North-east Entrance
Parallel Passage
Enclosure 1
Enclosure 4
Enclosure 15
Monoliths (restored)
West Entrance
Enclosure 5
Daga Platforms
Enclosure 6
Enclosure 7
Platform
Conical Tower
Chevron Pattern

Poorly coursed walls
Regularly coursed, dressed walls
Uncoursed, ruinous or restored walls

0   150 feet
0   50 m

other enclosures of Great Zimbabwe put together. The wall increases in width from west to east and at its eastern end is capped by a frieze of two lines of chevron pattern and a number of monoliths. The outer wall encloses one complete walled enclosure known as Enclosure 1. The latter has a diameter of about 70 feet (21 m) and enough internal area for about five *daga* structures. Two outstanding features of the Elliptical Building are the Parallel Passage and the Conical Tower. The Passage was formed when the huge outer wall enclosed the north-eastern wall of an earlier enclosure. The Passage between the walls is both striking and narrow. It seems to have no obvious function other than, perhaps, to provide an elaborate, curving approach from the north-east entrance through the outer wall to the Conical Tower. The latter is a solid, circular tower, 18 feet (5.5 m) in diameter and over 30 feet (9 m) high, decorated around the top with a dentelle-patterned frieze. The slight batter or inward leaning given to many of the walls at Great Zimbabwe is also in evidence here, giving the tower the appearance of a truncated cone. The tower was undoubtedly the architectural focus of the Elliptical Building. Its importance to the inhabitants was recognized by the construction of the largest platform at Great Zimbabwe alongside the doorway that led from the inside of the enclosure to the tower.

Who were these inhabitants? The various excavations at Great Zimbabwe have shown that the people who constructed these extraordinary buildings, so unlike anything else in sub-Saharan Africa, were farmers who placed particular emphasis on cattle husbandry. They had also managed to build up a central position for themselves in extensive trade networks, some of which brought exotic items to Great Zimbabwe from the shores of the Indian Ocean. A great variety of objects has been found among the ruins and these bring into focus different aspects of the inhabitants' lives. Commonest among the imported ceramics on the site are sherds of Chinese celadon ware, a stoneware with a glaze in shades of green. Most of the celadon dates from the Ming dynasty (1368–1644). However, the absence of sherds of porcelain, which had taken the place of celadon on the coast by the sixteenth century, shows that by then Great Zimbabwe had lost its pre-eminent role as a trading nucleus.

Whatever activities took place within the enclosures, the preparation of grain and its cooking do not seem to have been among them, since few querns and little cooking pottery have been found. By contrast, iron-working and the production of copper or bronze wire ornaments were major activities, and some of the *daga* huts may have

One of the entrances through the outer wall of the Elliptical Building clearly illustrates the inward slope given to most of the walls at Great Zimbabwe. Relics found at this site include Arab pottery and porcelain from China. The arrival of the Portuguese in this area in the 1490s led to a shift of power and a decline in trade.

AD 1500

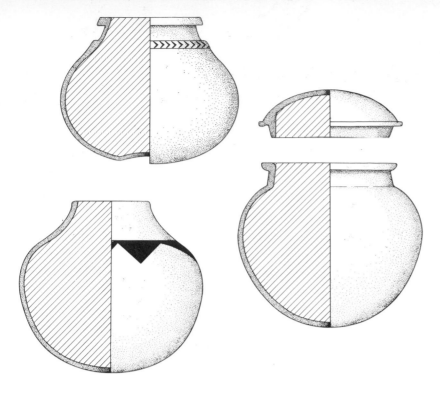

Although a great variety of imported goods have been found in Great Zimbabwe, there was also an active local pottery industry, shown by the discovery of simple round-bottomed bowls for domestic use.

AD 1500

The Great Enclosure or Elliptical Building is the most striking visible remain at Great Zimbabwe. The wall varies in width from east to west and is capped by a frieze. The building provided a ceremonial and defensive centre at Great Zimbabwe and from here the chief and his court controlled the export of Zimbabwean gold.

been reserved for metal-working. Gold was certainly worked at Great Zimbabwe. Like copper and bronze, it was drawn into wire and then coiled to form anklets and bracelets. It does not seem to have been any more valued than other metals, however. On a more mundane level, the presence of hundreds of spindle whorls indicates a flourishing textile industry based on cotton.

There is a category of objects whose function is more difficult to explain and must relate to the sacred role of Great Zimbabwe. Outcrops of a soft grey-green soapstone occur about 16 miles (25 km) from the site. This material was taken to Great Zimbabwe and carved into ritual implements. It is noteworthy that hardly any soapstone artefacts were found on any of the contemporary sites controlled by Great Zimbabwe. Paramount among the soapstone carvings are those of stylized birds, usually surmounting columns about 3 feet 3 inches (1 m) in height. These columns are matched by the monoliths previously mentioned, some of which were covered with bands of geometric carving. In the Shona religion the dead occupy an important position and it is essential to appease the ancestors regularly. It is possible that the monoliths represent individual ancestors. Other cult objects found within the ruins include a series of baked-clay animal figurines, most notably of cattle. Symbolism has similarly been invoked to explain the function of the Conical Tower. Although it is by far the largest single structure at Great Zimbabwe, there are other, much smaller, towers in the valley ruins and it has been suggested that the stone towers are symbols for grain bins. If this is so, the great size of the one in the Elliptical Building presumably indicates the scale of the largesse distributed by this most important chief.

The purely indigenous character of Great Zimbabwe can be demonstrated by placing this prehistoric centre in its regional surroundings. It obviously controlled a small territory and is one of the largest of at least 150 similar surviving ruins. Yet it was probably only one of perhaps ten autonomous or competing centres, each controlling a distinct zone of upland and lowland resources. The distribution of these *zimbabwe* above 3,300 feet (1,000 m) and beyond the line of maximum possible extension of tsetse fly from the lowlands is significant. Tsetse fly are carriers of trypanosomiasis, rapidly fatal to cattle, and cattle-herding is likely to have been a mainstay of the local economies. The *zimbabwe* in these ten autonomous territories were therefore not simply the product of long-distance trade but had integrated many different elements in their economies, including farming and cattle-herding, as well as gold-mining and foreign trade.

Eastern Asia and Oceania
PEKING, CHINA

THE GREAT WALL

PEKING

SHANXI

Chang'an

C H I N A

Yellow River

Yangtze River

Nanjing

Shanghai

KOREAN PENINSULA

Yellow Sea

JAPAN

East China Sea

HONG KONG

0   500 miles

0   500 km

Faced with the threat of the Mongol hordes in the north, the Ming dynasty moved its capital away from the heart of China, and the main agricultural areas. Peking was built in the far north-east and in so doing established what was then the most advanced civilization in the world.

It was under the Ming (the Chinese word for bright or brilliant) dynasty, which lasted from 1368 to 1644, that the capital of the Chinese empire was established by a native Chinese dynasty in the far north-east of the country at Peking. In AD 1500 the new capital was not yet a century old, but the hundreds of thousands of citizens who had worked on its construction had erected some of the most beautiful architecture in all of China. They laboured for an emperor who was known as the Son of Heaven. Unlike a western monarch, the emperor of the world's largest society led a cloistered life in the heart of the capital, in the palaces that are now known as the Forbidden City. By means of an ever-increasing throng of eunuch-advisers, the emperor made his wishes known to the people. These advisers could be much older than the emperor himself. Of the sixteen Ming emperors, only five passed their fortieth birthdays, and none did so during the

period from 1425 to 1521. In a society that was governed by the importance of precedents, the elderly advisers exercised a formidable influence on the young rulers.

In the century before AD 1500 the Ming dynasty had made significant advances. There were more printed books in China than the rest of the world put together. Chinese sailors had explored the coasts of India, Arabia and East Africa before the European voyages of discovery. The populace lived with a fairly low level of taxation. Yet two major problems came to dominate the direction of government in the latter half of the fifteenth century. Ever since the Mongols had ruled over China, and indeed long before, the difficulties of dealing with the country's hostile northern neighbours had been something of an obsession. Moving the capital north to Peking, which placed the most important city of the empire in a marginal location away from the main agricultural areas, was

AD 1500

partly a response to the need for greater imperial control of the northern frontier. The second problem concerned the decline in the importance of ministerial administration and the growth of advice provided by thousands of eunuchs. The lack of effective ministers of government meant that the emperor himself was responsible for making many decisions, a time-consuming procedure without any of the checks and balances provided by regular consultation with the organized civil service.

It was Emperor Yongle who initiated the process of transforming the existing city of Peking into the capital of China. In February 1403 he formally gave the city the status of Northern Capital to complement the existing capital at Nanjing. In 1404 10,000 households were moved from Shanxi to Peking to increase the metropolitan population. Between 1408 and 1409 a warden's office, a hostel for foreign envoys and a mint were constructed in the future capital. Work accelerated after 1416, when improvements were carried out on the moats, walls and bridges of the city and construction work started on the Emperor's residence, the Western Palace. By late 1417 most of the palace buildings were finished, but there was still work to do on the southern city wall. This had been completed under the preceding Yuan or Mongol dynasty, but had fallen into disrepair. It was replaced in 1420 by a new wall that ran a little to the south of its predecessor. The Bell Tower and the Altar of Heaven were also both completed in that year. The culmination of this massive undertaking was reached on 28 October 1420, when Peking was designated as the principal capital of the empire.

With the transformation of the city, the population increased greatly. The number of soldiers alone based at Peking was in excess of 250,000. They were divided into three training camps: infantry, cavalry and artillery. Overall, in the early fifteenth century there were about 2 million people in the city and its outlying province. This large number of inhabitants had to be fed and an immediate problem was to ensure an adequate supply of grain from the more productive rice-growing regions of the Yangtze delta. Under the Yuan dynasty a canal had been excavated between Peking and the lower Yangtze, although it had never functioned properly. Yongle decided to renovate and repair the northern section, using 300,000 conscripted labourers working for 100 days. In 1415 the southern section was reopened and 3,000 flat-bottomed barges were built to transport grain from the south to Peking. Yongle died in 1424 but the process he had begun was irreversible. The period of dual capitals, during which both Peking and Nanjing functioned as complementary administrative centres, ended in

1441, when all administration was concentrated in Peking.

In AD 1500 Peking comprised three rectangular walled enclosures. At the centre was the Forbidden City, which contained the imperial residences and audience chambers. Surrounding it was the Imperial City, which housed the offices of the eunuch-advisers, storehouses, workshops, gardens, parks and lakes. Just south of the Imperial City were the civil and military ministries, while the remainder of the Outer City houses the bulk of the populace. A fortification wall of rammed earth faced with brick surrounded the city. Nine gates pierced the outer wall, which ran some 4 miles (6.5 km) from east to west and 3½ miles (5.5 km) from north to south. The orientation of the city was designed to match the cardinal points of the compass, and the major internal streets followed those directions, producing a grid-iron pattern. Major palaces and houses faced south, to protect their occupants from evil, northern influences. More space was allocated to residential and commercial properties within the city walls than had been the case in preceding dynasties. South of

A bronze incense-burner beside the entrance to one of the audience halls. The technique of bronze-casting was a highly developed craft in ancient and medieval China.

AD
1500

the city lay the Temple of Heaven. Given that the majority of the buildings within the city were made of wood, they were frequently destroyed by fire, whether accidental or deliberate. Structures built to replace them tended to reproduce faithfully the earlier models.

The Forbidden City was entered from the south by way of the Wu Gate. This was the largest of all the palace gates and its dull-red walls, crowned with five towers, surrounded three sides of a square. Three arched entranceways gave access to an extensive courtyard through which ran a river known as the Golden Water, forming a wide curve in the shape of a bow. Five white marble bridges crossed the water and led to another ceremonial gate, also with three entranceways. The emperor used the central entrance, with the eastern gateway reserved for civilian officials and the western one for the military. Another large courtyard, some 660 feet (200 m) from east to west and seemingly even more spacious because of the low buildings on either side of it, was flanked on the north by the first of the three great audience halls, the Hall of Supreme Harmony.

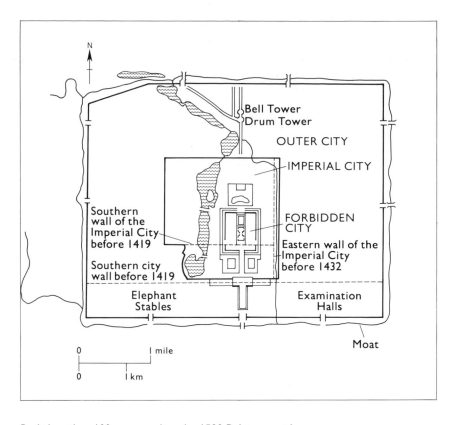

The rear of the huge Wu Gate, seen from within the Forbidden City. Wu Gate was separated from the Gate of Supreme Harmony by the 'Golden Water' river.

Built less than 100 years earlier, by 1500 Peking was the largest city on earth and comprised three rectangular walled enclosures with the emperor living at the centre in his Forbidden City.

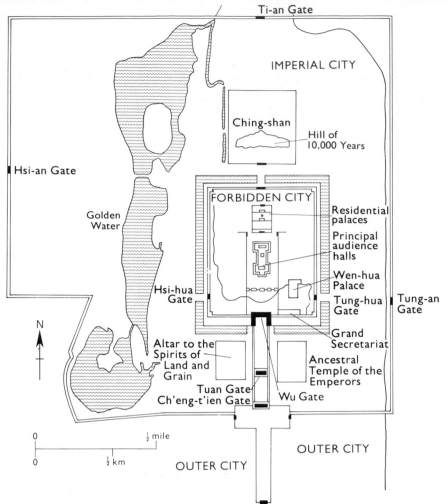

Outside the Forbidden City the Imperial City held the offices of the ever-growing numbers of eunuch-advisers, as well as the parks and lakes, while most of the populace lived in the Outer City.

The audience halls were constructed on top of a three-storeyed marble terrace known as the Dragon Pavement. The Hall of Supreme Harmony, constructed in the last decades of the Ming Dynasty, was a long, rectangular building measuring about 231 feet (70 m) from east to west by 132 feet (40 m) from north to south. The emperor came to this hall to receive the congratulations of officials on New Year's Day, the winter solstice and imperial birthdays. He sat on a throne inside the vast hall, shrouded from the lesser mortals by clouds of incense. Princes and nobility stood in the courtyard in eighteen rows according to rank and precedent, the civil officials on the east and the military on the west. Two diagonal lines of square paving-stones ran across the courtyard and were used as markers in arranging the different lines. As soon as the emperor had taken his seat, all of those waiting in attendance performed the Nine Prostrations, the principal act of the whole ceremony. Further to the

north, on the same terrace, lay the Hall of Middle Harmony. This was the smallest of the three halls and it was here that the emperor prepared messages to be read at the Temple of Ancestors. The third hall was the Hall of Protecting Harmony. Here the Emperor received princes of vassal states and also the scholars who had been awarded the highest degree in the state examinations for entry into the bureaucracy.

The northern half of the Forbidden City was largely taken up with the residential palaces of the emperor and empress, concubines and other members of the royal family. A second set of three palaces, on the same N–S axis as the audience halls, was built in the northern half by the Emperor Yongle in 1417. The most southerly of these, the Palace of Heavenly Purity, was burnt down and re-erected no less than three times. In the Ming period this palace was used as a residence by the last four emperors. The middle palace was known as the Hall of Vigorous Fertility and was where previous emperors' seals were stored and is thought to have been the throne-room of the empress. The residence of the empresses was the most northerly palace, the Palace of Earthly Tranquillity.

In the Imperial City, to the south-east of the Forbidden City, stood the Ancestral Temple of the Emperors. It was here that the spirit tablets, bearing the names of the deceased and thought to embody their spirits, of the dead emperors and empresses were kept, and offerings were made on various occasions by the current rulers to their ancestors. The temple complex was approached from the west through a grove of towering cedar trees. The emperor then turned to the north and entered a large, rectangular compound, whose architectural features replicated those in the Forbidden City. Six bridges crossed a stream before a ceremonial gate gave access into a huge courtyard. A rectangular oven decorated with glazed yellow tiles on the east side of the courtyard was used for burning paper and silk offerings. The ancestral tablets were held in three halls arranged on a N–S axis on the far side of the courtyard facing the emperor. South-west of the Forbidden City lay the Altar to the Spirits of Land and Grain. A number of small pavilions surrounded a terraced, square altar, the surface of which was covered with earth of five different colours: yellow in the centre, black in the north, green in the east, red in the south and white in the west. The Gods of Soil and of Harvest were worshipped here.

The western half of the Imperial City was reserved for an extraordinary collection of pavilions set around three artificial lakes. Yongle, when rebuilding Peking, had all three lakes dug out and created additional gardens and summer residences

AD
1500

The roofs and wooden eaves of the palaces in the Forbidden City were brightly painted. Fire was an ever-present hazard in any city formed of wooden buildings, and strategically placed gilded containers provided a ready supply of water in case of emergency.

in this area. In later years winter carnivals were held on the ice, when displays of skipping, skating and jumping were staged, on ice specially flattened by the application of hot irons. In the north part of the Imperial City a huge artificial mound, the Hill of 10,000 Years, was constructed from the earth taken out of the moat surrounding the Forbidden City. The mound was thrown up for geomantic reasons, to protect the imperial palaces against evil influences emanating from the north.

The Outer City contained most of the ordinary residences of Peking, as well as thousands of shops and workshops. Among the more specific structures were the Examination Halls that occupied the south-eastern sector of the city. They were contained in a vast compound bordered by high walls. Candidates from all over China came to sit the exams, which lasted for a number of days and nights, for entry to the civil service. Long rows of rectangular buildings contained nearly 8,500 cubicles, 6 feet 6 inches (2 m) square by 10 feet (3 m) high. The strain on candidates was enormous and not surprisingly some went mad or committed suicide in their attempts to succeed. In the south-western part of the Outer City the Elephant Stables were built in 1495. Elephants were delivered as tribute to the emperor in Peking from vassal states in Burma and Vietnam. The duties of the elephants included forming a ceremonial guard in front of the Wu Gate to the Forbidden City, and pulling a chariot carrying the emperor when he went to

worship at the Ancestral Temple of Heaven. The north-east quarter of the Outer City was dominated by two towers: the Drum Tower and the Bell Tower, both about 100 feet (30 m) high and constructed of bricks, stone and timber. The drum was beaten and the bell rung before daylight to summon all the government employees to assemble. The foundry that produced the bells was situated in the north-western part of the city. Flanking the main road to the southern gate of the Imperial City were the various ministries of the government, with military offices concentrated to the west and civilian ones to the east.

Houses in the capital often comprised rectangular, single-storey compounds, with buildings and halls arranged around one or more courtyards. Walls consisted of packed earth held in a timber frame, while wooden pillars on raised bases supported the tiled roofs. There were no dividing walls within the halls. Instead, screens could be moved to provide spaces for varying numbers of persons. The compound usually had a N–S orientation, according to the principles of *feng-shui*, with all windows and doors being on the south side, leaving the north wall blank. Such a layout was also eminently practical, ensuring that the house received as much of the low, winter sun as possible and was also sheltered from the north winds. Entry into the house was generally from the south and led past rooms of increasing importance until the parents' quarters were reached.

AD
1500

A prestigious construction outside the Outer City was the Temple of Heaven, built by the Emperor Yongle in 1420. The altar was enclosed by a double wall, the outer, square perimeter symbolizing the earth, and the inner, circular one representing the heavens. The altar itself comprised three superimposed terraces of white marble which represented, from the top, heaven, earth and man. Such religious buildings may have been influenced by Buddhist architecture. The Ming emperors may have devoted some time and attention in their private lives to Buddhism and Taoism, while in public they consciously promoted the teachings of Confucius; indeed the three creeds are not mutually exclusive. Ascent to the altar was by four marble stairways, at the cardinal points of the compass, in three flights of nine steps each. The emperor came to the Temple of Heaven twice a year to sacrifice a bull and to report to heaven on the state of the empire.

Once Yongle had decided to move the capital to Peking, he was faced with another problem: where he and his successors should be buried. It was critical that a suitable place be found since, although the emperor was regarded as the Son of

Four of the stone commanders on the Spirit Road wear the ornate court uniform of Ming generals. This one holds a baton in his right hand while his left hand rests on the hilt of a sword.

A superb example of the technical mastery of the late fifteenth-century Chinese porcelain industry. The decoration is executed in underglazed cobalt blue.

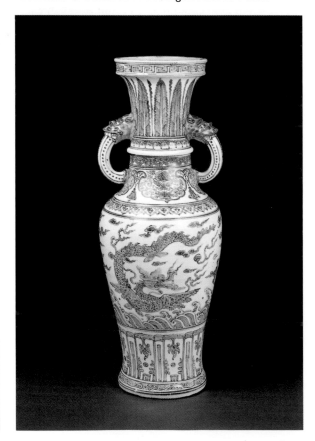

AD
1500

Heaven, he could communicate with the gods only through the spirits of the ancestors. It was vital to keep the ancestral spirits content, otherwise they would not co-operate. The spirit, however, could not survive without the body, hence the importance of the tomb. The valley chosen for the Ming tombs by the geomancers in 1409 lay some 28 miles (45 km) north-west of Peking. It was about 3 miles (5 km) long from north to south and 2 miles (3 km) wide. The mountains were highest in the north, lessening in height to the east and west. The cemetery was approached along a Spirit Road some 3,630 feet (1,100 m) in length. The road pointed to the north, but changed direction slightly just before reaching the tombs since it was believed that evil spirits travelled in straight lines and would therefore be confused by the sudden turn. The road was flanked by twenty-four stone animals and twelve stone men, symmetrically arranged in pairs opposite each other. Each animal was represented first sitting, then standing. According to Ming beliefs, this was to allow for the changing of the guard; at midnight the standing pair changed places with the two who had been resting. The statues of the men, however, were all standing, since it was forbidden to sit in the presence of the emperor.

Thirteen tombs were found in the chosen location, including that of Yongle. Each tomb complex consisted of two parts. First, a series of courtyards and halls where rituals and observances could be carried out to honour the spirit of the deceased. Beyond this lay the tomb proper, housed in an underground vault beneath a fortified mound or tumulus, where the body could be kept secure. The alignment of the tombs followed a N–S direction in accordance with the need to protect the spirits from evil, northern influences. The most prominent surviving buildings in each tomb complex are the stele pavilions that stood at the northern end of the courtyards, before the actual tomb mounds. Inside the pavilions, on a rectangular pedestal, stood the grave stele bearing the name of the deceased emperor and flattering epithets such as 'wise' or 'virtuous'. The tomb complex of Yongle was one of the grandest in the entire cemetery. In the middle courtyard stood the Hall of Heavenly Favours, one of the two largest structures in China before the introduction of western architecture. It was a large but simple rectangular building, erected on a white marble terrace and oriented E–W. Doors and windows were situated on the south side with only a small opening in the north wall. Only one tomb chamber, that of Wan-li, who died in 1620, has been excavated. It was built in stone and consisted of a main vaulted hall, which gave access to three burial chambers. The emperor was buried in this magnificent tomb with two women he was never fond of in life: his first empress and the mother of his eldest son and successor.

In AD 1500 Peking was a heavily populated city whose colourful one-storey buildings crowded within the confining fortification walls marked out by the Emperor Yongle some eighty years before and spilled over into the suburbs. Yet the very nature of the layout – the Forbidden City within the Imperial City within the Outer City – made it easy for the emperor and his family at the centre to become more and more isolated, protected from the civil service and the inhabitants of the Outer City by their eunuch-advisers. Unlike members of the civil service, these advisers did not have to pass any examinations. They controlled China's foreign relations and, in particular, the long-distance trade. Trade was not in the hands of individuals but was managed as part of the tribute system. Its forms were established by the Ministry of Rites and directed by the eunuchs. The failure of the state to

Stone camels formed part of the guard along the Spirit Road. No doubt it was thought that they would prove useful to the Emperor after death.

back any of the Chinese voyages of discovery earlier in the century produced an introspective bureaucracy that was keen to amass prestigious artefacts in huge storehouses around the capital; luxury items that were for the consumption of the privileged only. Above all, the direction of Chinese thinking was dominated by relations with the Mongol and Manchu tribes to the north. Sometimes these were peaceful and, in one of the few areas where private enterprise was allowed to develop, traders played a significant role in exchanging vast quantities of tea for Mongol horses, in constant demand by the Chinese cavalry. At other times hostilities broke out and the Ming state warred successfully against the Mongols, as it did in the decade between 1470 and 1480. It was during this period that the state strengthened part of the defensive walls that we know now as the Great Wall. Such concern, in the end, was not misplaced. The Great Wall could not stop the swirling clouds of yellow dust that swept down every year from the deserts beyond China to settle in a thin film over the capital. Nor could it prevent in 1644 an enemy from the north invading China to bring the brilliant Ming dynasty to an end.

AD
1500

The Americas
CUZCO, PERU

COLOMBIA

Quito
ECUADOR

Equator

Amazon River

B R A Z I L

PERU

Lima

CUZCO

La Paz

BOLIVIA

Pacific Ocean

CHILE

ARGENTINA

Santiago

Atlantic Ocean

0   500 miles

0   500 km

The Inca empire spread for over 2,500 miles (c.4,000 km) along the western coastline of South America, from the equator into what is now Chile and Argentina. An extraordinarily rapid growth occurred through the course of the fifteenth century with the capital city of Cuzco built high up in the original Inca heartland by Pachacuti Inca.

AD 1500

On 15 November 1533 a nervous and weary band of Spanish soldiers under the command of Francisco Pizarro entered the Inca capital of Cuzco unopposed. It was the culmination of an expedition that had left Seville in Spain almost three years earlier. The anticipated resistance of the Inca armies to defend the capital to the last had not materialized. The Inca warriors, accustomed to fighting on foot with clubs and bronze weapons, were at a great disadvantage when faced with Spanish cavalry armed with iron and steel swords. A momentous but inconclusive battle had been fought the night before in the hills outside the city. As a result the Incas must have decided that Cuzco could not be saved. As the Conquistadores rode through the narrow streets of the capital, the novel sound of iron horseshoes striking the paving-stones signalled the end of one

of the most remarkable empires of the Americas. For the success of the empire was inextricably linked to the continunation of the Inca ruling dynasty and with the well-being of their capital. Lying high up in the Andes at an altitude of 11,055 feet (3,350 m) above sea level, Cuzco was the centre of a vast territory under Inca control that stretched from the equator in the north, down the western coast of South America and into what is now Chile and north-west Argentina. The Inca alone had been able to unify under a successful administration the peoples of three very different geographical zones: the coastal desert strip, the high Andes and the Amazon basin beyond. The difficulties of the terrain were overcome by an extremely efficient road network that linked the four corners of the empire to Cuzco.

Cuzco was planned as a city by Pachacuti Inca

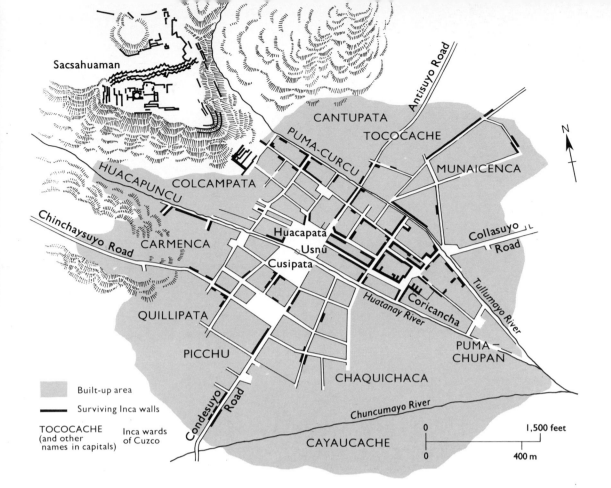

A plan of Inca Cuzco with built-up areas surrounding the central plaza. Surviving Inca walls were re-used or restored by the first generations of Spanish settlers for their own houses and buildings.

after AD 1440. Two small rivers, the Huatanay and Tullumayo, were canalized and between these the most important buildings of Cuzco were constructed, separated by an approximately orthogonal street plan. Inner Cuzco thus had an elongated shape oriented N.W–S.E and was deliberately arranged to resemble the form of a puma. The head of the puma was represented by the fortress of Sacsahuaman, which overlooked the centre of the city from the north, while the tail of the animal was located in the lower, southern section where the two rivers joined. The heart of the city was the central plaza of Huacapata, which was about 10 acres (4 ha) in extent. Adjacent to it, and across the canalized Huatanay, lay a secondary ceremonial square known as the Cusipata. Between them probably stood the Usnu or ritual throne of the ruling Inca. It was in these plazas that the great religious festivals of the empire took place.

In AD 1500 one of the most striking aspects of imperial Cuzco was the palaces of successive Inca rulers, arranged around the central plaza. Each ruling Inca received one and they were all constructed of the most finely dressed and fitted rectangular blocks of stone. The massive walls of the palaces often contained the largest stones in the lowest courses, with progressively smaller blocks as the wall rose in height. The façades were angled slightly inwards and were broken only by characteristically shaped trapezoidal doors. The walls were held in place simply by their own weight and were of such precision that a knife could not pass between the stones. The overall effect of such masonry is one of wonderful solidity and simplicity, enhanced by the narrowness of the streets separating a building from its neighbour. The roofs were made out of thatch, often quite elaborately laid, while gold and silver ornaments were frequently arranged inside the buildings, relieving the austerity of the architecture. The palaces housed the mummies of the dead Inca but also acted as administrative, educational and religious centres.

Surrounding the centre of Cuzco was a series of suburbs composed for the most part of rectangular, one-storey houses with steeply inclined, thatched roofs. The architecture was much less sophisticated, with stone used just in the lower courses and mud brick or adobe carrying the walls upwards. Wide eaves helped protect the adobe

AD 1500

Above: The circular, stone-sided depression beyond the fort of Sacsahuaman probably functioned as a reservoir. The white statue of Christ has replaced the Inca sun-god.

Below: Only the walls of the Inca temple at Coricancha remain now. A Christian church stands there now, and it takes a considerable leap of the imagination to visualize the former Inca splendour.

---

walls from the Andean rains. Some of the houses were plastered and painted red or yellow. The inhabitants of the suburbs were the officials, technicians, administrators and servants employed in the maintenance of the empire. Some were the chiefs of peoples conquered by the Incas and given what was effectively Inca citizenship. In return they had to agree to administer their formerly independent states on behalf of the Inca ruler, and reside in the suburbs of Cuzco for four months a year. These subordinate rulers were granted embassies in the suburbs of Cuzco, and their residences were positioned so that their spatial arrangement represented the geographical location of their subject peoples in the empire.

As the Spanish entered Cuzco, they were aware that the greatest prize was the Corichancha, or enclosure of gold, dedicated to the sun god. This lay south of the central plaza in the tail of the puma. Earlier in 1533 three Spanish envoys had ridden into Cuzco to secure enough gold for the ransom of the captured ruler, Atahualpa, who had been held by Pizarro in the north at Cajamarca. They were directed to the Corichancha and were amazed to see that the walls of this temple were

AD
1500

Above: The celebrated twelve-cornered stone is a magnificent testimony to the skill of Inca stonemasons. It was said that a knife could not be forced between the stones.

Below: Little now remains of textiles from the Inca period. Here a woven wool pattern is added on to a cotton base. The design is classically Peruvian from the period up to 1440.

sheathed in large plates of gold. They managed to lever off about 700 such plates, which when melted down produced some 3,080 lb (1,400 kg) of gold. Now, nothing was going to prevent the Conquistadores from looting the Coricancha. Inside the temple they found themselves in a central courtyard surrounded by rectangular chambers built of the finest Inca masonry. Many religious objects of gold were taken, including models of llamas, women, jars and other utensils. In the centre of the temple was an incredible spectacle: an artificial garden that contained delicate replicas of maize, with silver stems and ears of gold. Also in the courtyard was a polygonal basin which still survives today. Missing, however, is the golden altar and idol which stood next to the font and on which were offered sacrifices of maize and meat each day by the priestesses of the temple. A greater mystery surrounds the famous golden image of the sun, which was set with precious stones. This was never recovered by the Spanish. The roofs of the shrines were thatched with ichu grass, strands of which were interleaved with silver and gold thread so that the thatch sparkled in the sunshine. On the outside of the temple a band of gold over 6 inches

(15 cm) wide ran around the walls at roof level.

Despite such riches, the wealth of Cuzco was not confined to gold. The many storehouses contained an enormous quantity of objects and fabrics: cloaks, wool, weapons, metals, cloth, shields, leather goods, sandals and breastplates were there for the taking. Particularly impressive were the fine tunics made of feathers that were worn on important state occasions. Feathers from the humming bird, each little larger than a fingernail, were linked together on fine thread and attached to agave fibres to form extensive shawls and cloaks.

The most awe-inspiring building in Cuzco was undoubtedly the fortress of Sacsahuaman, situated on a hill to the north of the city. Three lines of zigzag fortification walls, comprising some huge stones, defended the fort from the most accessible ground to the north, while precipitous slopes on the city side obviated the need for substantial defences. The jagged profile of the walls has led some to suggest that they should be seen as representing the teeth of the puma. Certainly the regularly indented walls made it easy for the defenders to provide flanking fire along the face of the walls in the event of an attack. According to contemporary chroniclers, each of the three fortification walls was pierced by a central gate, which was closed by means of a single stone that worked like a drawbridge. Inside the fort were three tall round towers, one for the Inca ruler and his family, the other two to house the garrison. A labyrinthine complex of underground passages apparently linked the three towers. There is no doubting the military strength of Sacsahuaman. As befits the teeth of a puma, those formidable walls could have devoured many an assailant. However, there are unlikely to have been any serious attackers prior to the Spanish and Sacsahuaman was primarily an ostentatious display of strength.

The culture of the Incas was enriched by a number of highly developed skills in farming, civil engineering, architecture, mining, bronze metallurgy, astronomy, and numerous craft occupations, such as weaving, potting and gold-working. The Incas themselves did not originate these techniques but simply built on the thousands of years of Andean development and the knowledge and technology of the peoples they conquered. Most striking of all was the brilliance of the stonemasons' art. These craftsmen were supported by the government and worked on the most important buildings, in close association with the public works labour force. At Sacsahuaman as many as 20,000 non-Inca workers are thought to have laboured annually on the fortress, quarrying, transporting and building the stronghold. In the

AD
1500

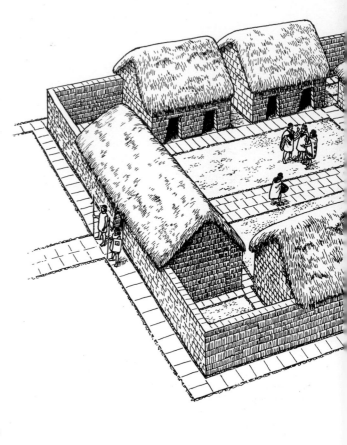

quarries huge blocks of andesite and granite were split from the bedrock by the use of wooden wedges. Water was poured on to the wedges once they were in place so that they expanded and fractured the rock. The massive slabs were transported by means of ropes and wooden rollers. At Sacsahuaman three types of stone were used. Giant blocks of diorite porphyry, some over 26 feet (8 m) high and weighing over 197 tons, were placed in the outer wall; these were located and hewn on site. Limestone from Yucay, 9 miles (15 km) away, was brought for the foundation material. Black andesite was transported from quarries further afield and used in the internal buildings. The miracle of the stonemasons' art was, of course, the way the blocks of stone were so closely fitted together, without mortar, into both courses of rectangular stone and the more incredible polygonal masonry.

The Incas believed in a pantheon of gods and goddesses. Overseeing all was the creator, a shadowy being called Viracocha, but most important was the sun, portrayed as the divine

The family compound of an Inca aristocrat. Reconstructing vanished buildings from the often slight remains found on site is always a problem for archaeologists. There will never be definitive answers to many archaeological puzzles. We can only hope that our interpretations gradually get us a little nearer the truth.

ancestor of the Inca dynasty. Temples to the sun were founded throughout the empire. The sun's movements were closely monitored by Inca astronomers, as there was a direct connection between the positions of the sun and the different operations of the agricultural year. The thunder god or god of weather was worshipped as a rain-giver. His sister, Cobo, held a jar of water and during a thunderstorm the god shot a slingstone at the jar to make it shatter and cause rainfall. The consort of the male sun god was the female mother moon, who had shrines ornamented with silver which were served by priestesses. The stars were in turn personified as the children of the sun and the moon. As well as the divine hierarchy there were thousands of holy sites or *huacas* that were associated with special powers or supernatural forces. These could include hills, fountains, wells, bridges, piles of stones in the field and portable images and amulets.

Although Cuzco in AD 1500 was a city, it was different in character from medieval London or Roman Pompeii. Cuzco was not a commercial city in which there were marketplaces where citizens could barter and exchange everyday goods and services. It was, instead, a royal city dominated by the enclosures and palaces of the Inca dynasty. The wealth of the empire flowed back to Cuzco, where it was stored by the ruling élite. The inhabitants of the city were largely nobles, servants and attendants who served in the temples or helped in the administration of the royal and religious stores. The economy of Cuzco was therefore directed by the needs of the ruling Inca, just as the whole empire was governed by the requirements of the ruling élite. The practice of conferring 'Inca by privilege' status on neighbours and provincial rulers meant that the fiction of a vast empire ruled by the single Inca tribe could be maintained.

The Spanish rode into Cuzco in 1533 in the company of an Inca ally, Manco Inca, whom they then installed as the new emperor. But in 1536 Manco Inca revolted and succeeded in amassing some 100,000 warriors in the hills around Cuzco. Inside the city were just 190 Spanish under the leadership of Francisco Pizarro. The encounter that followed was to be decisive in the future relations between the Spanish and the Incas. On Saturday, 6 May, the Incas forced their way into the city, using red-hot slingstones to set fire to the thatch roofs of the city's buildings. Despite fierce resistance, the Spanish were ultimately confined to structures around the central square and suffered relentless bombardment. Once the thatch roofs had been burnt, Inca warriors could run along the tops of the walls, out of the way of the feared Spanish cavalry, and hurl missiles at the enemy. The defenders decided on a final, bold move to try and ease their desperate situation. They realized that they could not break the siege unless they captured the fortress of Sacsahuaman. Fifty horsemen rode out from the city and, by a circuitous route, managed to storm and eventually hold the hillock opposite the fortress. On the following day they made scaling-ladders, and as night fell, applying proven European tactics of siege warfare, they clambered up the walls of the fortress and surrounded the Inca garrison in the three towers.

Use of cavalry gave the Spanish a tremendous advantage and allowed just a few of them to successfully resist a much larger Inca force fighting on foot. Once the Spanish had managed to blunt the puma's teeth, defeat for the courageous Inca defenders was only a matter of time. The fortress was taken with the loss of 1,500 Inca warriors. With Sacsahuaman in the hands of the enemy, the besieging forces around Cuzco realized the inevitability of their situation and gradually drifted back to their homelands and fields. With them disappeared the greatest empire of the Americas.

AD 1500

CONCLUSION

The most obvious physical contrasts between the five cities described in this chapter lie in their respective plans. Moscow and London follow a pattern that was well established for the growth of medieval cities in the western Europe. Both owed their street patterns and major defensive lines to their predecessors: in the case of London, the Roman walls defined the area of the medieval city; as for Moscow, it was the layout of the earlier wooden defences that largely dictated the line of the Kremlin walls and the arrangement of the surrounding defences. Both contained strongholds: the Tower of London and the Kremlin. Neither possessed a grid pattern of streets, and nor were they the product of formalized planning by a central authority. Peking and Cuzco were radically different. Both were relatively new foundations and were laid out from the start according to some rather specialized criteria: while the planners of Peking took great care to orientate the city to the cardinal directions and to protect the Forbidden City from evil, northern influences, Cuzco was designed to resemble the shape of a puma. Peking and to a lesser extent Cuzco demonstrate orthogonal street patterns. Great Zimbabwe was clearly the exception, with little hint of formal organization or defensive walls.

The use of space within the cities is interesting. The houses and taverns of London rubbed shoulders with each other and looked out over crowded streets, and so did the dwellings and shops in the suburbs of Moscow. By contrast, much of Peking was reserved for imperial palaces, audience halls and temples, often set in the centre or on the sides of vast courtyards. In Chinese architecture the area surrounding a building was just as important as the building itself. In Cuzco too a large part of the city was dedicated to palaces of successive Inca rulers. The immense areas used by imperial structures in both these cities, and the relatively restricted districts available for ordinary domestic residence suggest that in these capitals central authority was paramount. For Great Zimbabwe our evidence is limited. Presumably the stone enclosures were the remains of residences for a chief or priests.

Around and outside them were countless daga huts of the populace, although without excavation their precise extent is unknown. The location of the cities varies also. London is in a key trading position, on the banks of a navigable river. Moscow's situation is determined by the ancestral homelands of the princes of Moscow, while Great Zimbabwe's location owes much to it being beyond the range of the tsetse fly. The positions of Peking and Cuzco are eccentric. Cuzco was not best placed to control the Inca empire but was situated in the Inca heartland, high in the Andes. The move to Peking, on the other hand, was largely determined by the need to have a northern capital to monitor movements of Mongols and Manchus on the hostile frontier of the Chinese empire.

Architectural comparisons are no less significant. In London and Moscow there was a clear distinction, in form and appearance, between public and ecclesiastical architecture, and domestic buildings. In London particularly, the already crowded nature of the city made houses of two and three storeys not uncommon. By contrast, those of Peking and Cuzco were almost invariably of one storey and the public buildings, imperial palaces and temples were simply larger versions, admittedly constructed with greater care and attention to quality, of domestic buildings. The architecture of Great Zimbabwe, in its African context, is the most outstanding. The decorated walls of the compounds and their uneven thicknesses, topped by dentelle-friezes and ancestor monoliths, suggest architects working with exuberance, unrestrained by any preconceived architectural traditions.

Physical differences between the cities seem to be paralleled by variations in economic activities. In London and Moscow it is possible to talk about economic activity separate from the state. In both cities merchants could buy and sell wares in shops and marketplaces, using money as a means of exchange. The administrators of both cities could discuss the volume and importance of trade between their city and neighbouring municipalities in the same kingdom or adjacent countries. It was possible for commoners to live like kings or tsars, provided they had the necessary finances. The economies of Peking, Cuzco and perhaps Great Zimbabwe were completely different. In these

AD
1500

centres the economic activities of the individual were dictated by the demands of the state. There was no formal money in Cuzco or Great Zimbabwe and in all three the frequency and levels of exchange were rigorously controlled by officials; often any surplus was rendered to the rulers as taxes or tribute. There were no marketplaces where everyone or anyone could go and barter for a particular commodity. There was no concept of foreign trade and when, for instance, dignitaries from abroad visited the Ming court in Peking bearing gifts for the emperor, these were always assumed to be tribute from subservient states rather than presents from countries of equal standing. To that extent the economies of Peking and Cuzco were centrally planned and the circulation of certain types of goods was carefully regulated.

The differences between these five cities of the world can be largely explained by the political and religious structures of the societies in which they developed. In Moscow and London religion and politics, while constantly intertwined, were essentially separate strands in the government of the populace. Each had its own head. In London, Henry VII was the secular head but was compelled to leave religious matters to the Pope in Rome, while in Moscow Ivan III ceded sacred authority to the Metropolitanate of the Russian Orthodox Church. Churches in both cities were formally planned, following the architectural traditions established in previous centuries, whereas domestic and secular buildings, and economic life, were free to develop along more individual lines. In Cuzco and Peking there was no such separation between the sacred and secular. The emperor of China was regarded as the Son of Heaven, while the ruling Inca was the descendant of the sun god. All authority stemmed from these pre-eminent beings and the work of the humblest citizens of their empires was, in theory, performed for the well-being of the semi-divine ruler. In order to sustain the ideological background to such totalitarian government, most aspects of daily life were governed by the rulers' sacred directives, and the very organization of space and of architecture in their cities was designed to reinforce the power of the ruler, religion and the state. Great Zimbabwe, was, of course, the exception. The celebrated stone buildings may have been used by a chief, his priests and an immediate retinue who controlled a relatively small territory. Their pervasive control was exercised perhaps through regulation of an ancestor cult, represented by the stone monoliths. The importance of Great Zimbabwe was demonstrated not so much by formal planning as by an extraordinary use of stone architecture and the construction of an enormous conical tower, perhaps symbolizing a monumental grain bin. In its context it was no less an architectural achievement than the churches of the Kremlin or the palaces of the Forbidden City; its ideological role, in emphasizing the pre-eminence of a semi-divine ruler, may have been the same.

The fortunes of each of these cities varied enormously. London continued to grow, eventually becoming the capital of a hugely successful empire. The capital led the country in standing firm against the threat of invasion from Napoleon and Hitler, only to succumb to growing political and economic emasculation within the suffocating embrace of the European Community. Moscow too flourished as the tsarist state expanded its frontiers. It suffered much, however, during the Russian Revolution that gave birth to communist USSR. The Kremlin survives today, albeit as a less daunting symbol, as politicians within its walls struggle with the metamorphosis from communist empire to capitalist-driven commonwealth. Peking continued as the imperial capital of China up to 1911, when the last Emperor, Piu Yi, fled the Forbidden City and rushed into the beguiling arms of the Japanese. Communist overthrow of the imperial government transformed much of the city. Even then, the long axis of the revolutionary Tiananmen Square continues the same N–S alignment that runs through the heart of the Forbidden City, suggesting a reaffirmation rather than a rejection of some aspects of the old order. Cuzco became an important Spanish city after the conquest and church bells now ring out over the Inca rulers' square. The only site which did not continue to function was Great Zimbabwe. Here changing economic circumstances had already signalled its demise long before any European colonization. Yet it was not forgotten. Instead it was resurrected as the name of the modern state that was its eventual successor in post-colonial Africa.

AD 1500

EPILOGUE

The year AD 1500 is a convenient point at which to end this book. Western Europe stood on the margins of the civilized world, unable to rival the brilliance of Ming China, the most advanced state on earth, and outshone by the rising Ottoman and Safavid empires of the Middle East. The 100 million inhabitants of China outstripped the whole of Europe in terms of wealth and size of population. Of the world's great religions, for the time being Christianity had dissipated most of its energy through the Crusades, while Islam was still actively making converts in Central and South-east Asia and among the peoples of sub-Saharan Africa. Before AD 1500 civilization had been essentially land-centred, and contacts by sea had been largely confined to coastal trading. Around AD 1500, however, a new period of history was beginning, initiated by European voyages of discovery that were to establish direct sea contact between different continents. Such contacts began to alter the balance between Europe and the rest of the world, and were to have largely disastrous consequences for indigenous peoples in the Americas, Africa and, in subsequent centuries, Australia and the smaller islands of the Pacific.

The area that had been settled by the ancient civilizations was approximately equivalent to those regions where plough-assisted cultivation or irrigation was practised. In AD 1500 this area was still relatively small and over three-quarters of the world's surface was still inhabited by hunter-gatherers, pastoralists or societies which cultivated by hand. Nevertheless, it seems probable that between two-thirds and three-quarters of the total population were concentrated in the more productive regions where the plough and irrigation were employed. These regions of the world, where technologically simpler methods of cultivation or subsistence provided the basic food resources, were most vulnerable to the waves of colonization that followed the voyages of discovery.

The classic reconstruction of the hunting and gathering band favoured by some anthropologists is one of four or five families (around twenty-five members is the much-quoted figure) with few material possessions, moving from camp to camp on a seasonal basis to take advantage of particular wild foods. Population growth is small, given the difficulty of carrying young infants between camps, authority figures are non-existent or emerge when decisions are needed and disappear when they are not, and there is considerable emphasis on the sharing of food and an absence of private property. But this reconstruction does not square well with the three hunting and gathering societies described in Chapter 2. Only the hunters of Kalemba might have belonged to a small, quasi-egalitarian band. The two other locations, Roonka Flat and Poverty Point, were clearly favoured sites on the banks of rivers, and here it was possibly the richness of the natural environment that encouraged more than just transitory occupations for the land was capable of supporting a large number of people in a relatively small area. The productivity of these regions was manipulated by some hunters and gatherers to underline distinctions of rank and status, ideas completely foreign to our perception of hunting bands as bastions of egalitarianism. Indeed, the complex and massive earthworks at Poverty Point, and the involvement in trade by the occupants of the site, would not be out of place in a society occupying a much higher rung on the ladder of social evolution.

There was no easy way out, however, when the communities that had developed a way of life based on agriculture began to expand and impinge on lands occupied by hunters and gatherers. The latter had either to move away into less favourable habitats or to seek to preserve something of their existence by developing exchanges with the farmers and by coming to terms with them as neighbours. Most frequently they could trap game and offer meat, or perhaps supply their own labour, in return for dairy products, grain and exotic items such as metal tools. The adoption of agriculture by an ever-growing number of societies brought new concerns, however. Land, access to it and rights over it became all-important, especially when techniques of manuring and laying fallow the land had allowed the erection of permanent villages and the farming of the same fields, handed down from generation to generation. It is not surprising that many communities became divided into lineages or groups of related families, jealously protecting their rights over a defined territory, stressing their association with it by claiming inheritance of it from revered ancestors, perhaps personified by such durable phenomena as the statues on Easter Island.

The advent of agriculture also encouragd communities to think differently about the passage of time. In many traditional societies time is not counted in a linear progression, as it is in the modern world. The Hopi Indians of Arizona, for instance, make no distinction in their use of verbs between past and present; all time runs together in something like an ever-continuing present. For the early farmers their very existence depended on the rising of the sun every day and their receiving the fullest extent of its warmth during the crop-ripening season. It seems altogether reasonable that their preoccupations focused on the movements of the sun, moon and stars, often personifying them as gods and constructing both simple and elaborate devices to monitor their progress across the heavens. Stonehenge, the mounds at Poverty Point, the observatory at Monte Alban, the position of certain windows in Pueblo Bonito and the worship of the sun at Cuzco all demonstrate the ubiquity and timelessness of the association between traditional agricultural societies and concern over heavenly bodies.

The ability of individuals to manipulate the productivity of households in fertile areas eventually produced agricultural surpluses, which could be exchanged for traded items or redistributed to followers. The flow of produce towards the leaders, however, could be maintained only by continually exercising powers of persuasion since there was no public security force to coerce recalcitrant families into producing more than they needed. Bolstering the position of leadership came through the construction of large, public monuments. Stonehenge is a classic example. There was nothing like it in Britain or indeed in Europe. It was probably built in several phases, each one of which was perhaps of relatively short duration. Once constructed, and especially when its builders had died or moved back to their homes, it became part of the landscape, neither natural nor artificial, something that could be regarded with wonder and awe by future generations, its method of construction long-since forgotten, a monument that was a source of power and could be struggled over. It was also a monument that by its very permanence, in contrast to the turf-and-timber dwellings of contemporary farmers, immunized the political structure from the potentially damaging effects of political longevity. The temples of El Paraiso and the enclosures of Great Zimbabwe might have functioned in the same way.

By AD 1500 the organized use of force in the form of a regular army had long since emerged as the power behind many positions of authority. Countless city-states had developed and had by conquest evolved into territorial states. A few, by further conquest of unrelated peoples, had become the capitals of vast empires. But almost as many states had disappeared by AD 1500 too, and there does appear to be a cyclical quality to the rise, rule and fall of great states and empires. The capitals and their authority over the provinces were maintained by access to the agricultural productivity, or control over the commercial exchanges of prized goods. Once surpluses were allowed to mount in the peripheral regions, control of the centre could be challenged, leading to a devolution back to city-states after successful rebellions in the provinces.

The key challenge to many ancient states was how to prevent this oscillation of expansion and contraction. In much of the modern world we think that change means 'progress' and is something to be welcomed. In the most successful ancient empires, however, such as those of China and Egypt, change was something that was abhorred and continuity, or stasis, was the thread that bound successive generations together. The Egyptians remembered fondly the first pharaohs and followed a system of beliefs and practices that had been formulated in pre-dynastic times. Similarly, the Chinese consulted the chronicles of past dynasties and the teachings of Confucius, and used them as the guiding principles for the present. Replication of traditional architecture and enduring monuments, such as the Temple of Heaven in Peking, the ziggurat at Ur or the pyramids at Gizeh, reinforced the idea of the immutability of the political system, capable of outlasting any temporary upheavals that might occur.

The organized use of space, both at the macro and micro levels, was also another typical attribute of many developed states. In terms of domestic architecture, sometimes the same solutions were produced for similar problems. In arid or seasonally hot climates, for instance, the plans of houses often took the form of a range of rooms or buildings around a central courtyard. Such an arrangement allowed the residents of the household to go about their daily affairs with a degree of privacy and also, through the use of largely windowless walls facing the outside streets, excluded unwelcome dust from the rooms. Houses of this type were constructed at Ur, Pompeii, Siraf, Peking and at the capital of Islamic Spain, Cordoba. When we are left with just the archaeological remains of such houses, we tend to assume that the disposition of rooms and buildings was guided by functional explanations, such as those outlined above. When considering societies where both archaeological and documentary evidence have survived, however, the ideological use of space becomes apparent. In Cordoba, for instance, the blank walls of the façades were also used to protect the Islamic household from the unwelcome gazes of heathens without, while in Peking ritual reasons were paramount in the laying-out of houses. The compound usually had a N–S orientation, with all windows and doors on the south side, leaving the north wall blank. This was to protect the household from evil influences that were believed to originate in the north, but it also offered some practical shelter from northerly winds.

The use of space was also controlled at the scale of an entire city. By AD 1500, from the examples described in this book, it is possible to categorize at least four different types of spatial arrangement. The cities of Monte Alban and Cordoba, for example, with their irregular residential sectors radiating from a centre, probably developed in this way to accommodate racial or tribal differences in the make-up of the population. In the context of Cordoba, there were both tribal and racial divisions within the urban community, while at Monte Alban the different residential zones may have been occupied by contingents from the various cities ruled from the capital. Capitals like Cuzco and Peking, however, were rigorously planned throughout by a central authority, Cuzco to resemble the shape of a puma and Peking to reflect the principles of *feng-shui* and the supreme importance of the emperor in the Forbidden City. London and Moscow, by contrast, developed through a combination of organized planning for strategic places, such as strongholds, defences and marketplaces, and minimal planning in the layout and growth of residential suburbs. The last category of spatial division can be seen at Great Zimbabwe, where the curving lines of the enclosures, the circular houses and the irregular disposition of several distinct complexes give no obvious hint of any central planning.

Our word 'city', of course, stems from the Roman *civitas*, meaning any self-governing municipal unit. As such it is a wholly European concept which may have limited explanatory potential when applied to pre-AD 1500 concentrations of population beyond the confines of Europe. It is obvious from a consideration of London, Moscow, Great Zimbabwe, Peking and Cuzco in AD 1500 that only the first two are ancestral to the form of settlement that we would consider a city. The latter three were the products of societies where there was probably still a union of sacred and secular leadership in one emperor or chief, with a resultant emphasis within the complexes on ritual structures and spaces. Their economies were characteristically different too, with more development of individual enterprise and market forces in London and Moscow, while in Great Zimbabwe, Peking and Cuzco there was more state control of trade and industry.

In AD 1500 a great variety of indigenous societies, from hunting and gathering bands to complex empires, had evolved in all but the least habitable parts of the earth. Land-based empires had expanded and shrunk, alternately encompassing and then releasing their neighbours. But by AD 1500 a menacing new weapon was beginning to assist the rise and fall of empires: long-distance navigation. The European voyages of discovery meant that empires were no longer restricted to their particular continents but could export their brand of culture across the seas, with devastating consequences for the newly conquered. Between 1480 and 1780 European seaborne explorers linked together the separate areas of maritime communication and opened all seas, except in the regions of polar ice, to European ships. The tempo of the resultant change was not so rapid everywhere. Although the Aztec and Inca civilizations fell in 1521 and 1533 respectively, China and Japan remained immune, while in India, West Africa and South-east Asia the Europeans were restricted to trading stations. Chinese sailors, of course, had navigated to the Persian Gulf and the east coast of Africa earlier in the fifteenth century. Their voyages of exploration did not spawn a rash of trading-posts or subsequent colonial adventures. China was simply so large it produced from within its own borders almost everything it needed and required little from countries to the west. However, the small landmass of Europe, divided into heavily populated states, had every incentive to seek new lands across the seas. The result was the export of European culture to most areas of the world, a staggering phenomenon unrivalled in world history either before or since.

BIBLIOGRAPHY

STONEHENGE

BURL, A., *The Stonehenge People*, Barrie & Jenkins Ltd, London 1989.

CHIPPINDALE, C., *Stonehenge Complete*, Thames & Hudson, London, 1983.

CLARKE, D. V., T. G. COWIE AND A. FOXON, *Symbols of Power at the Time of Stonehenge*, HMSO, Edinburgh, 1985.

RICHARDS, J., *Stonehenge*, Batsford, London, 1991.

ROYAL COMMISSION ON ANCIENT AND HISTORICAL MONUMENTS, *Stonehenge and Its Environs*, Edinburgh University Press, Edinburgh, 1979.

UR

BAUMANN, H., *The Land of Ur*, Oxford University Press, London, 1969.

LLOYD, S., *The Archaeology of Mesopotamia*, Thames & Hudson, London 1984 (rev. edn).

MALLOWAN, M. E. L., *Early Mesopotamia and Iran*, Thames & Hudson, London, 1965.

ROUX, G., *Ancient Iraq*, World Publishing Company, Cleveland and New York, 1964.

WOOLLEY, L., *The Sumerians*, Clarendon Press, Oxford, 1928.

— *Excavations at Ur*, Ernest Benn Limited, London, 1955.

— *Ur of the Chaldees*, Book Club Associates, London, 1982 (revised and updated by P. R. S. Morley).

THEBES

ALDRED, C., *The Egyptians*, Thames & Hudson, London, 1961.

DAVID, A. R., *Ancient Egypt*, Phaidon, Oxford, 1988 (2nd edn).

KEMP, B., *Ancient Egypt: Anatomy of a Civilisation*, Routledge, London, 1989.

NAVILLE, E., *The XIth Dynasty Temple at Deir el-Bahari: Part II*, 30th Memoir of the Egypt Exploration Fund, London, 1910.

MOHENJO-DARO

ALLCHIN, B. AND R., *The Rise of Civilisation in India and Pakistan*, Cambridge University Press, Cambridge, 1982.

JACOBSON, J. (ed.), *Studies in the Archaeology of India and Pakistan*, Aris & Phillips Ltd, Warminster, in co-operation with American Institute of Indian Studies, 1987.

JANSEN, M., 'Water supply and sewage disposal at Mohenjo-Daro', *World Archaeology*, 21(2), 1989, pp.177–92.

LAL, B. B. AND S. P. GUPTA (eds.), *Frontiers of the Indus Civilisation*, Books and Books, on behalf of Indian Archaeological Society and Indian History and Culture Society, 1984.

POSSEHL, G. L. (ed.), *Ancient Cities of the Indus*, Vikas Publishing House, New Delhi, 1979.

— (ed.) *Harappan Civilisation: A Contemporary Perspective*, Aris & Phillips Ltd, Warminster, in co-operation with American Institute of Indian Studies, 1982.

WHEELER, R. E. M., *The Indus Civilisation*, Cambridge University Press, Cambridge, 1968.

EL PARAISO

CALVO, S. A., *Lima Prehispanica*, Municipalidad de Lima, Lima, 1984.

ENGEL, F. A., 'La Complexe précéramique d'el Paraiso (Pérou)', *Journal de la Société des Américanistes*, 55, 1967, pp.43–95.

KEATINGE, R. W. (ed.), *Peruvian Prehistory*, Cambrige University Press, Cambridge, 1988.

FLAG FEN

PRYOR, F., *Flag Fen*, Batsford, London, 1991.

— 'The many faces of Flag Fen', *Scottish Archaeological Forum* (in press).

PRYOR, F., C. FRENCH AND M. TAYLOR, 'Flag Fen, Fengate, Peterborough 1: discovery, reconnaissance and initial excavation (1982–5)', *Proceedings of the Prehistoric Society*, 52, 1986. pp.1–24.

TAYLOR, M. AND F. PRYOR, 'Bronze Age building techniques at Flag Fen, Peterborough, England', *World Archaeology* 21 (3), 1990, pp.425–34.

MEGIDDO

AVI-YONAH, M. AND E. STERN (eds.), *Encylopaedia of Archaeological Excavations in the Holy Land*, Vol. III, The Israel Exploration Society and Massada Press, Jerusalem, 1977.

BRIGHT, J., *A History of Israel*, SCM Press Ltd, Suffolk, 1981 (3rd edn).

DAVIES, G. I., *Cities of the Biblical World: Megiddo*, Lutterworth Press, Cambridge, 1986.

— 'Solomonic stables at Megiddo after all?' *Palestine Exploration Quarterly*, 120, 1988, pp.130–41.

KALEMBA

PHILLIPSON, D. W., *The Prehistory of Eastern Zambia*, Memoir No.6 of the British Institute in Eastern Africa, Nairobi, 1976.

— *The Later Prehistory of Eastern and Southern Africa*, Heinemann, London, 1977.

— *African Archaeology*, Cambridge University Press, Cambridge, 1988.

ROONKA FLAT

MULVANEY, D. J., *The Prehistory of Australia*, Thames & Hudson, London, 1969.

PRETTY, G. L. AND M. E. KRICUN, 'Prehistoric health status of the Roonka population', *World Archaeology*, 21(2), 1989, pp.198–224.

PRETTY, G. L. AND G. G. WARD (eds.), *Territory, Society and Ideas in Prehistoric Australia: Results of the Dating of Roonka in the Lower Murray Basin, 1977–86*, British Archaeological Reports, International Series, Oxford (in press).

WHITE, J. P. AND J. F. O'CONNELL, *A Prehistory of Australia, New Guinea and Sahul*, Academic Press, Sydney, 1982.

POVERTY POINT

GIBSON, J. L., 'Poverty Point: The First North American Chiefdom', *Archaeology*, 27, 1974, pp.96–105.

— *Poverty Point: A Culture of the Lower Mississippi Valley*, Louisiana Archeological Survey and Antiquities Commission, Baton Rouge, Archeological Study No.7, 1985.

— *Digging on the Dock of the Bay(ou): The 1988 Excavations at Poverty Point*, University of South Western Louisiana, Center for Archaeological Studies, Report No.8, 1989.

POMPEII

GRANT, M., *Cities of Vesuvius: Pompeii and Herculaneum*, Weidenfeld & Nicolson, London, 1971.

POTTER, T. W., *Roman Italy*, Guild Publishing, London, 1987.

RICHARDSON, L., *Pompeii: An Architectural History*, John Hopkins University Press, Baltimore and London, 1988.

PETRA

BROWNING, I., *Petra*, Chatto & Windus, London, 1974.

KHOURI, R. G., *Petra: A Guide to the Capital of the Nabateans*, Longman, Harlow, 1986.

MEROE

SHINNIE, P. L., *Meroe: A Civilisation of the Sudan*, Thames & Hudson, London, 1967.

— 'The Nilotic Sudan and Ethiopia c.660 BC–AD 600', in *The Cambridge History of Africa*, Vol. 2, edited by J. D. Fage, Cambridge University Press, Cambridge, 1978.

— (ed.), *The African Iron Age*, Clarendon Press, Oxford, 1972.

SHINNIE, P. L. AND R. J. BRADLEY, *The Capital of Kush I: Meroe Excavations 1965–72*, Meroitica 4, Akademie-Verlag, Berlin, 1980.

CHANG'AN

LOEWE, M., *Everyday life in Early Imperial China During the Han Period 202 BC–AD 220*, Batsford, London, 1968.

RAWSON, J., *Ancient China: Art and Archaeology*, British Museum Publications, London, 1980.

TYRWHITT, J., 'The City of Chang-an', *Town Planning Review*, 39(1), 1968, pp.21–37.

ZHONGSHU, W., *Han Civilisation*, Yale University Press, Newhaven and London, 1982.

WHEATLEY, P., 'Archaeology and the Chinese City', *World Archaeology* 2(2) 1970, pp.159–85.

MONTE ALBAN

BLANTON, R. E., *Monte Alban: Settlement Patterns at the Ancient Zapotec Capital*, Academic Press, New York, 1978.

SABLOFF, J. A., *The Cities of Ancient Mexico*, Thames & Hudson, London, 1989.

WHITECOTTON, J. W., *The Zapotecs: Princes, Priests and Peasants*, University of Oklahoma Press, Norman, 1937.

MEDINA AZAHARA

BURCKHARDT, T., *Moorish Culture in Spain*, George Allen & Unwin, London, 1972.

CASTEJON, R. AND DE ARIZALA, M., *Medina Azahara*, Editorial Everest S.A., Leon, 1985.

IMAMUBBIN, S. M., *Muslim Spain AD 711–1492*, E. J. Brill, Leiden, 1981.

WATT, W. M., *A History of Islamic Spain*, Edinburgh University Press, Edinburgh, 1965.

SIRAF

WHITEHOUSE, D., *Siraf III: The Congregational Mosque*, British Institute of Persian Studies, 1980.

— 'Maritime Trade in the Gulf: the 11th and 12th Centuries', *World Archaeology*, 14(3), 1983, pp.328–34.

— *Siraf I: Introduction*, British Institute of Persian Studies (in press).

JENNE-JENO

MCINTOSH, S. K. AND R. J., *Prehistoric Investigations in the Region of Jenne, Mali*, British Archaeological Reports, International Series, Oxford, 1980.

— 'The inland Niger delta before the empire of Mali: evidence from Jenne-Jeno', *Journal of African History*, 22, 1981, pp.1–22.

— 'Finding West Africa's oldest city', *National Geographic*, 162(3), 1982, pp.396–418.

EASTER ISLAND

ENGLERT, S., *Island at the Centre of the World*, Robert Hale & Co., London, 1972.

JENNINGS, J. D. (ed.), *The Prehistory of Polynesia*, Harvard University Press, Cambridge, Mass. and London, 1979.

KIRCH, P. V., *The Evolution of the Polynesian Chiefdoms*, Cambridge University Press, Cambridge, 1984.

METRAUX, A., *Easter island*, André Deutsch, London, 1957.

PUEBLO BONITO

CANBY, T. Y., 'The Anasazi: riddles in the ruins', *National Geographic*, 162 (5), 1982, pp.562–92.

CORDELL, L. S., *Prehistory of the Southwest*, Academic Press, New York, 1984.

JUDD, N. M., *The Architecture of Pueblo Bonito*, Smithsonian Miscellaneous Collections, Vol.147, No.1 Washington, DC, 1964.

LEKSON, S. H., T. C. WINDES, J. R. STEIN AND W. J. JUDGE, 'The Chaco Canyon community', *Scientific American*, 256(7), 1988, pp.100–109.

LISTER, R. H. AND F. C., *Chaco Canyon*, University of New Mexico Press, Albuquerque, 1987.

REYMAN, J. E. 'Astronomy, architecture and adaptation at Pueblo Bonito', *Science*, 193 (4257), 1976, pp.957–62.

SAKE, D. G., 'Architecture in prehispanic Pueblo archaeology: examples from Chaco Canyon, New Mexico, *World Archaeology*, 9(2), 1977, pp.157–73.

LONDON

PLATT, C., *The English Medieval Town*, Secker & Warburg Ltd, London, 1976

SCHOFIELD, J., *The Building of London from the Conquest to the Great Fire*, British Museum Publications, London, 1984.

SCHOFIELD, J. AND A. DYSON, *Archaeology of the City of London*, City of London Archaeological Trust, Museum of London, 1980.

MOSCOW

CRUMMEY, R. O., *The Formation of Muscovy 1304–1613*, Longman, Harlow, 1987.

KOSLOW, J., *The Kremlin, Symbol of Russia*, Macgibbon and Kee, London, 1960.

VOYCE, A., *The Moscow Kremlin*, Thames & Hudson, London, 1955.

GREAT ZIMBABWE

BEACH, D. N., *The Shona and Zimbabwe, 900–1850*, Mambo Press, Owelo, Zimbabwe, 1980.

GARLAKE, P. S., *Great Zimbabwe*, Thames & Hudson, London, 1973.

— 'Pastoralism and Zimbabwe', *Journal of African History*, 19(4), 1978, pp.479–93.

PEKING

ARLINGTON, L. C. AND W. LEWISOHN *In Search of Old Peking*, Oxford University Press, Oxford, 1987.

MOTE, F. W. AND D. TWITCHETT, 'The Ming Dynasty, Part I', In *The Cambridge History of China*, Vol.7, Cambridge University Press, Cambridge, 1988.

PALUDAN, A., *The Imperial Ming Tombs*, Hong Kong

University Press, Hong Kong and Yale University
Press, Yale, 1981.
PRATT, K., *Peking in the early Seventeenth Century*,
Oxford University Press, Oxford, 1971.
ZHONGSHU, W., *Han Civilization*, Yale University
Press, Newhaven and London, 1982.

CUZCO

HEMMING, J., *The Conquest of the Incas*, Macmillan,
London, 1979.
KENDALL, A., *Everyday Life of the Incas*, Batsford,
London, 1973.

ACKNOWLEDGEMENTS

The author wishes to record his grateful thanks to the following people who have read drafts of the text on particular sites in the book. The brief summaries that are printed in this volume are only possible to write because of their efforts, and cannot do justice to their extensive researches and publications. Any mistakes or misinterpretations remaining in this book are, of course, the author's responsibility.

Aubrey Burl (Stonehenge); **Irving Finkel** (Ur); **Rosalie David** (Thebes); **F. R. Allchin** (Mohenjo-daro); **Richard Keatinge** (El Paraiso); **Francis Pryor** (Flag Fen); **Graham Davies** (Megiddo); **David Phillipson** (Kalemba); **Graeme Pretty** (Roonka Flat); **Jon Gibson** (Poverty Point); **Roger Ling** (Pompeii); **Warwick Ball, Tim Strickland** (Petra); **Peter Shinnie** (Meroe); **An Jiayao, Carol Michaelson** (Chang'an); **Richard Blanton** (Monte Alban); **Jeremy Johns** (Medina Azahara); **David Whitehouse** (Siraf); **Susan and Rod McIntosh** (Jenne-jeno); **Joanne Van Tilburg** (Easter Island); **Linda Cordell** (Pueblo Bonito); **John Schofield** (London); **Robin Milner-Gulland** (Moscow); **Peter Garlake** (Great Zimbabwe); **An Jiayao, Carol Michaelson** (Peking); **Ann Kendall** (Cuzco).

The author and publisher wish to record their appreciation to the following institutions and individuals who have supplied photographs and colour illustrations:

Anthony Harkus 31 (inset), 32, 33 (above and below), 35 (above right and left); **British Library** 187 (right); **Chaco Centre** 170, 172 (above), 174; **Courtauld Institute of Art** 192; **David Lyons** 20–21; **David C. Ochsner/Joanne Van Tilburg** 168; **David Phillipson** 71, 72, 74, 75, 77 (above and below); **Francis Pryor** 60, 62–3 (below); **Graeme Pretty (South Australian Museum)** 79 (top), 80, 81, 82, 83; **Jason Wood** 109, 110, 111; **Jean Williamson** 18–19 (above); **John Manley** 18–19 (below left and right), 46, 47, 48, 49, 50, 58, 59 (below), 61, 114–15, 119 (above and below), 120, 122, 123, 126–7 (above and below), 143 (below), 146, 150 (below), 154 (left and right), 202, 203, 205, 206 (above), 207, 210 (above and below),

211 (above); **John Taylor** 4–5 (map); **John Waton** 130–31, 131, 134 (left above and below, and right); **Jon Gibson (Louisiana Division of Archaeology)** 86 (left), 87, 90 (left and right); **Mary Stewart** 171, 172 (below), 175; **Michael Kirtley** 11, 155, 158, 159, 161; **Museum of London** 183 (right), 186; **Nick Saunders/Werner Forman Archive** 163 (above and below), 166, 167; **Richard Blanton** 129; **Robert Donaldson** 62–3 (above); **Robert Harding Picture Library** 39, 40, 42, 43, 44, 189, 190–91 (above and below), 194; **R. & S. McIntosh** 156; **Ronald Sheridan** 183 (left); **Sonia Halliday Photographs** 6, 66, 67, 69, 70; **Spanish National Tourist Office** 143 (above), 144; **Trustees of the British Museum** 35 (below); **Victoria & Albert Museum** 103 (above), 125, 147, 187 (left), 206 (below), 211 (below); **Warwick Ball** 25, 26–7, 27, 28, 30, 106, 107, 112, 150 (above), 153 (above and below); **Werner Forman Archive** 41, 99, 102, 103, (below), 104, 104–5, 105, 116, 118 (left and right), 169, 195, 196, 198 (left), 199, 200; **Wessex Archaeology (Jane Brayne)** 23; **Wiltshire Archaeological and Natural History Society** 22.

The author and publisher also wish to thank the following institutions or individuals who have provided source material for the following line illustrations:

Arthur Voyce 190, 191, 193, reproduced in *The Moscow Kremlin*; **Jon Gibson (Louisiana Division of Archaeology)** 86 (right), 88, 89; **Iain Browning** 110, reproduced in *Petra*, published by Chatto & Windus; **Museum of London** 184, 185; **Graeme Pretty (South Australian Museum)** 79 (bottom left), 80, 81, 82, 84; **R. & S. McIntosh/R. Bonner** (after original by K. Stoher) 160; **Scientific American Inc.** 173 (below); **Trustees of the British Museum** 29; **Warwick Ball/David Whitehouse** 151.

*This release has benefited from the advice and consent of Valerie Power and Colin Cook, senior representatives of the corporation of traditional owners within the nearest adjacent descendant communities of the Ngaiawang Meru.

INDEX

Page numbers in *italics* refer to captions